# ASP.NET Core 9 Essentials

Master Razor Pages, Blazor, and MVC to build powerful,
cloud-ready web applications

**Albert S. Tanure**

# ASP.NET Core 9 Essentials

**Group Product Manager**: Kaustubh Manglurkar

**Publishing Product Manager**: Bhavya Rao

**Book Project Manager**: Arul Viveaun

**Senior Editor**: Rakhi Patel

**Technical Editor**: K Bimala Singha

**Copy Editor**: Safis Editing

**Indexer**: Tejal Soni

**Production Designer**: Jyoti Kadam

**Marketing Coordinator**: Nivedita Pandey

First published: January 2025

Production reference: 3301025

Published by Packt Publishing Ltd.
Grosvenor House
11 St Paul's Square
Birmingham
B3 1RB, UK

ISBN 978-1-83546-906-4

www.packtpub.com

*I would like to dedicate this book, first and foremost, to God for granting me the privilege of sharing knowledge, learning, and for always being by my side, empowering me. I also want to express my gratitude to my wife, Juliana, for her unwavering support throughout this journey, even when it meant spending less time together. Her encouragement and understanding of the importance of this project were invaluable. To my children, Noah and Antonela, I cannot thank you enough for your enthusiasm and encouragement. Your excitement about this book, even when it meant sacrificing a few hours of playtime, has been a constant source of motivation. To my friends, who have always believed in me and provided strength, encouragement, and inspiration, I extend my heartfelt thanks. While I cannot name everyone individually, please know that each of you is represented here. I would also like to thank the entire Packt team for their unconditional support, patience, and guidance, which made this project a reality. Finally, to you, the reader—thank you for purchasing this book. It was prepared with great care to provide you with the knowledge you need to achieve your goals.*

*– Albert S. Tanure*

# Contributors

## About the author

**Albert S. Tanure** is a cloud computing, software development, and DevOps expert with over 20 years of experience, serving as a software engineer, software architect, cloud solutions architect, and enterprise architect. He is a specialist in Microsoft technologies, having worked with .NET Framework since version 1.1. Currently, he develops cloud-native solutions, defining architectures for global companies for worldwide environments. He has been a Microsoft MVP since 2018 in the development technology category, MCT, and he actively contributes to the technical community through videos on his YouTube channel, Code FC, in addition to writing articles and giving lectures at various face-to-face and online events.

# About the reviewers

**Adnan Maqbool Khan** is a seasoned .NET full stack developer with over a decade of experience in the industry. A self-taught technology enthusiast, he continuously explores cutting-edge developments in .NET and frontend frameworks, such as React, Vue.js, and Angular, with a keen interest in web development and distributed system architectures. In his role as an engineering lead at a prominent UK-based software company, Adnan uses his extensive technical expertise to advance projects and mentor his team. A dedicated contributor to the developer community on LinkedIn, Adnan is passionate about helping others succeed with C# and .NET. He also stays current with emerging technologies through extensive reading of technology books.

*I would like to express my sincere gratitude to my parents and wife for their continued patience and support. Your contributions have been invaluable to my success.*

**Dmitry Slabko** is an accomplished software developer with over 25 years of experience. He has worked in organizations of all sizes – small shops, start-ups, and large international companies. He has developed multiple projects, from ground zero to their successful release to clients. He has extensive experience in web and cloud projects and focuses on .NET technologies. Over the past few years, he has participated as a mentor in internal mentoring programs for software developers and published a few articles. He has assisted in reviewing the second edition of *.NET Core in Action* by Dustin Metzgar. He also serves as a judge in various hackathons to help young talents grow into real professionals.

**Parthasarathy C Mandayam** is a dynamic, result-oriented IT professional with 35 years of experience in IT. He is a .NET and SQL Server expert, with 20 years of experience in .NET and 25 years of experience in SQL Server. He has developed several cutting-edge ASP.NET websites for top US Fortune 500 companies such as Progressive Insurance, Eddie Bauer, Providence Health System, and Blue Cross Blue Shield.

## Join us on Discord!

Read this book alongside other users, experts, and the author himself. Ask questions, provide solutions to other readers, chat with the author via Ask Me Anything sessions, and much more. Scan the QR code or visit the link to join the community.

`https://packt.link/aspdotnet9essentials`

# Table of Contents

Preface                 **xv**

Free Benefits with Your Book    xxii

## Part 1: ASP.NET Core 9 Fundamentals

1

### Introducing ASP.NET Core 9 Concepts    **3**

| | | | |
|---|---|---|---|
| Technical requirements | 4 | Windows installation | 8 |
| Why ASP.NET Core 9? | 4 | macOS installation | 10 |
| Comparing .NET | | Linux installation | 11 |
| and .NET Framework | 6 | Visual Studio Code | 11 |
| Preparing our development | | Testing the development environment | 12 |
| environment | 7 | **What is new in ASP.NET Core 9?** | **16** |
| The development tool | 7 | **Summary** | **16** |
| SDK and runtime | 8 | Get This Book's PDF Version | |
| CLI (Command-Line Interface) | 8 | and Exclusive Extras | 17 |

2

### Building Dynamic UIs with Razor Pages, MVC, and Blazor    **19**

| | | | |
|---|---|---|---|
| Technical requirements | 19 | ASP.NET Core Razor Pages | 21 |
| Learning about the ASP.NET Core UI | 20 | ASP.NET Core MVC | 37 |
| Rendering the UI | 20 | **Exploring UI client rendering with** | |
| **Implementing a UI server render** | | **Blazor and JavaScript frameworks** | **44** |
| **model with Razor Pages and ASP.** | | Rich UIs with Blazor | 44 |
| **NET MVC** | **21** | ASP.NET Core 9 and JavaScript frameworks | 48 |

Working with hybrid solutions          50
Summary                                53

Get This Book's PDF Version
and Exclusive Extras                   53

# 3

## Crafting Web APIs for Service Delivery                              55

Technical requirements                 55
Delivering business as a service       56
HTTP verbs and conventions             57
REST                                   57
HTTP status codes                      58
Exploring minimal APIs                 59

Implementing APIs using the
controller-based approach              66
Creating a controller-based API        67

Understanding the product controller   68
ControllerBase utilities               70
Working with binding                   72
Performing validations                 75

Working with documentation             76
Documenting APIs with Swagger          77

Summary                                87
Get This Book's PDF Version
and Exclusive Extras                   87

# 4

## Real-Time Interactions with SignalR                                89

Technical requirements                 89
What is SignalR?                       90
Understanding the concepts of
Servers and Clients                    92
Working with a task management application  92
Creating the Hub                       95
Preparing the server application       97
Preparing the client application       98
Understanding the client and server
communication flow                     101

Working with streaming                 103
Implementing basic streaming           104

Hosting the ASP.NET Core SignalR
application                            109
The basics of hosting a SignalR application  109

Summary                                110
Get This Book's PDF Version
and Exclusive Extras                   111

# Part 2: Data and Security

## 5

## Working with Data and Persistence                    115

| | | | |
|---|---|---|---|
| Technical requirements | 115 | SQL versus NoSQL | 123 |
| Docker installation | 116 | ORM and Micro ORM | 126 |
| Azure Data Studio | 116 | **Working with EF Core and Dapper** | **131** |
| **Connecting to a SQL database** | **116** | EF Core | 131 |
| Preparing SQL Server | 117 | Dapper | 140 |
| Using the SQL client | 120 | **Summary** | **142** |
| **Understanding SQL, NoSQL, ORM, and Micro ORM** | **123** | Get This Book's PDF Version and Exclusive Extras | 143 |

## 6

## Enhancing Security and Quality                       145

| | | | |
|---|---|---|---|
| Technical requirements | 146 | Configuring the database context | 157 |
| **Understanding the security principles of web-based applications** | **146** | Updating the database | 158 |
| | | Adding ASP.NET Core Identity services and routes | 160 |
| Security topics in web applications | 147 | Securing APIs with ASP.NET Core Identity | 166 |
| **Comparing authorization and authentication** | **149** | Securing application routes | 168 |
| | | Requesting an API with the access token | 173 |
| Authentication | 150 | **Strengthening application security** | **176** |
| Authorization | 151 | Managing secrets properly | 177 |
| Understanding OAuth 2.0 and OIDC | 152 | Enforcing HTTPS and working with CORS | 180 |
| **Working with the ASP.NET Core Identity framework** | **154** | Preventing common vulnerabilities | 182 |
| Understanding the ASP.NET Core Identity architecture | 154 | **Summary** | **184** |
| Getting started with integrating ASP.NET Core Identity | 155 | Get This Book's PDF Version and Exclusive Extras | 185 |

# Part 3: Applying Best Practices

## 7

## Adding Capabilities to Applications                                189

Technical requirements                    189
Working with ASP.NET Core 9 best
practices                                 190
HTTP request best practices               190
Asynchronous requests and I/O optimization  195

Improving performance with a cache
strategy and making the application
resilient                                 197
Caching strategies                        198
Integrating Redis in our application      199

Working with cache in the controller class  200
Configuring Redis Insight                 205
Resilience mechanisms                     207

Understanding and implementing
logging and monitoring                    210
Introduction to logging and monitoring    211
Get This Book's PDF Version
and Exclusive Extras                      216

Summary                                   216

## 8

## Enhancing Applications with Middleware in ASP.NET Core 9    217

Technical requirements                    217
Knowing the middleware pipeline           218
Understanding middleware flow             220
Benefits of middleware and best practices 222

Implementing custom middleware            224
Working with factory-based
middleware                                227
Adding capabilities to applications
using middleware                          229

Global error handling                     230
Adding request logging                    233
Rate limiting                             235

Creating an extension method for
middleware registration                   239
Get This Book's PDF Version
and Exclusive Extras                      242

Summary                                   242

## 9

## Managing Application Settings                             243

Technical requirements                    243
Understanding IConfiguration
concepts and abstractions                 244

IConfiguration interface                  244

Working with configuration providers 246
Adding configuration providers            246

Creating a custom configuration provider    248

**Learning the Options pattern    250**

What is the Options pattern?    250

Implementing the Options pattern    252

**Working with dynamic configurations and behaviors    257**

Working with dynamic settings    257

Connecting an ASP.NET Core 9 application to Azure App Configuration    269

**Summary    276**

Get This Book's PDF Version and Exclusive Extras    277

# Part 4: Hosting, Deploying, and Preparing to the Cloud

## 10

## Deploying and Hosting Applications    281

**Technical requirements    281**

**Preparing to publish your application and host locally    282**

The importance of the publishing process    282

Generating a publishing package    283

**Publishing the solution in a cloud environment    286**

Creating Azure app services and database resources    287

Configuring Azure SQL Server    292

Publishing an application with Visual Studio Code    295

**Understanding the Docker principles and how to package the application in a container    298**

Understanding what a container is    298

Understanding Docker fundamentals    300

Packing the UrlShortener application    302

Generating a container image    305

Running a Docker container    306

**Understanding the DevOps approach with CI/CD    308**

CI    309

CD    310

Automating with GitHub Actions    312

**Summary    321**

Get This Book's PDF Version and Exclusive Extras    322

# 11

## Cloud-Native Development with ASP.NET Core 9     323

| | | | |
|---|---|---|---|
| **Technical requirements** | **323** | Port binding | 341 |
| **Creating a cloud-native mindset** | **324** | Concurrency | 343 |
| | | Disposability | 344 |
| Understanding the service layers in a cloud environment | 324 | Dev/prod parity | 346 |
| Cloud-native development best practices | 326 | Logs | 347 |
| Going beyond code development | 328 | Admin process | 349 |
| | | The importance of the twelve-factor app methodology | 350 |
| **Working with cloud-native tools** | **328** | | |
| Getting to know CNCF | 331 | **Understanding cloud architecture principles** | **350** |
| Working with CNCF | 331 | Working with modern design architecture | 351 |
| **The twelve-factor app principles** | **333** | Event-driven architectures | 351 |
| Code base | 334 | Understanding microservices | 355 |
| Dependencies | 335 | Considering deployment strategies | 357 |
| Config | 335 | | |
| Backing services | 337 | **Summary** | **358** |
| Build, release, run | 338 | Get This Book's PDF Version and Exclusive Extras | 359 |
| Processes | 340 | | |

# 12

## Unlock Your Exclusive Benefits     361

| | |
|---|---|
| Unlock this Book's Free Benefits in 3 Easy Steps | 361 |

## Index     365

## Other Books You May Enjoy     376

# Preface

Have you ever stopped to think about the number of technologies, languages, and frameworks that currently exist for developing software solutions? It is certainly almost impossible to list them since, with technological advancement, new frameworks, and technologies emerge every day. Associated with the collaboration model proposed by the open source movement, access to information and source code of technologies from major players allows people to develop their own technologies, which end up becoming a path for developing solutions.

In the context of web applications, there have been several developments and, with these, different approaches and tools have emerged that allow the development of increasingly rich and complex applications. Often, the traditional client-server development model is no longer sufficient for certain contexts, and with the evolution of technologies, the use of other approaches to improve the user experience of web applications has made JavaScript frameworks popular, giving rise to other development models such as the use of **Single-Page Applications** (**SPAs**), which, combined with a powerful server-side processing model, make web applications more interactive and richer than ever. When we look back at the development model from a few years ago, we needed a few JavaScript files, an interpreted language such as PHP, Perl, or Classic ASP to process requests on the server side, and a database to persist information.

However, the market has become more dynamic and demanding, making technological advances increasingly faster. The web solution development model has gone from a stack of three or four technologies to a multitude of resources, packages, frameworks, standards, design patterns, and, no less important, interaction with cloud environments. While we have a modern development scenario, we are also involved in a great complexity of available resources so that we can create rich solutions that have the capacity to support the diverse needs of the market and dynamically follow the constant evolution and changes in the needs of organizations to deliver solutions that are increasingly more adherent to the market, remaining competitive.

Dealing with different technologies is also a challenge for several teams that must learn different languages and standards, and also use different tools to combine these technologies and maintain a sustainable distributed development model. This book aims to provide tools, standards, and possibilities to software engineers who need to deliver web solutions in a dynamic manner, delivering constant value, while benefiting from best practices and staying up to date in a scenario of constant technological evolution. To achieve these goals, we will learn about the ASP.NET Core 9 platform, which is a powerful open-source solution from Microsoft that allows us to develop high-quality applications, prepared to deal with the standards and requirements of cloud-native applications and, best of all, centralized in a single platform.

ASP.NET Core 9 is a technology that is constantly evolving and has modern features, allowing software engineers to have the ability to extend and customize while using high-level approaches for solutions that must be prepared to run in different types of environments, whether local, on-premises or especially in cloud environments. With ASP.NET Core 9, software engineers benefit from the use of practices such as interaction with CLI tools. It is independent of the operating system, has great support from the technical community that provides several packages and providers, and the framework is constantly evolving through the open-source community. It is a technology that has extensive documentation and support and is prepared for the most diverse types of solutions, in addition to adapting to the cloud-native model and, of course, has the capacity to integrate with other technologies, in addition to JavaScript frameworks.

ASP.NET Core 9 is a powerful web development platform, with several tools available for development on different operating systems. However, it is important to understand concepts that go beyond the coding process.

During the course of this book, we will learn about the concepts and fundamentals of the ASP.NET Core 9 platform, in addition to understanding development approaches and cloud architectures, learning about the best resources for designing web solutions, using mechanisms for delivering constant value in an automated manner such as **Continuous Integration (CI)** and **Continuous Delivery (CD)**, among other patterns and best practices of the cloud-native solution development model, and much more.

## Who this book is for

This book provides a broad perspective on the use of ASP.NET Core 9 technology for developing web-based solutions. It goes beyond the traditional aspect and brings an innovative perspective based on the needs of the technology market. It addresses fundamental issues ranging from platform knowledge, updates, environment preparation, implementation and use of best security and development practices, and constant delivery through automated solutions such as CI and CD, cloud-native development practices, containerization, and several other aspects of the ASP.NET Core platform.

This book is intended for developers involved in the development of both backend and frontend solutions, familiar with basic or intermediate object-oriented programming, using high-level languages such as C# and Java, and having some experience with HTML and CSS.

## What this book covers

*Chapter 1*, *Introducing ASP.NET Core 9 Concepts*, starts with the fundamentals of ASP.NET Core 9, understanding the evolution of the .NET platform, which went from a development model exclusively for Windows to becoming an open source platform, supported and constantly updated by Microsoft together with the technical community. We will also learn how to prepare the development environment by installing development tools and the **Software Development Kit (SDK)** necessary for creating applications.

*Chapter 2, Building Dynamic UIs with Razor Pages, MVC, and Blazor*, covers the aspects involving the development of web applications such as client-server and server-side models, in addition to knowing and implementing applications using the ASP.NET Core 9 UI Framework such as Razor Pages, ASP. NET MVC, Blazor, and integration with JavaScript frameworks.

*Chapter 3, Crafting Web APIs for Service Delivery*, addresses concepts and best practices in the development of API technologies, widely used in web-based applications. We will learn about the business delivery model as a service through HTTP, and understand the fundamentals and standards available in the ASP.NET Core 9 platform such as minimal APIs, filters, documentation, and other standards associated with the REST-based service development model.

*Chapter 4, Real-Time Interactions with SignalR*, presents a rich user interaction solution through the concept of real-time applications using SignalR, where we will learn the fundamentals of real-time programming with ASP.NET Core 9, supported technologies, work with streams, and understand how to host a real-time solution.

*Chapter 5, Working with Data and Persistence*, explores a very important and necessary aspect in most applications, which is the ability to connect to data sources for information persistence. We will understand how ASP.NET Core 9 allows us to connect to a database using a high-level persistence model through the use of frameworks such as Entity Framework Core and Dapper, in addition to understanding the main persistence models and existing technologies.

*Chapter 6, Enhancing Security and Quality*, covers one of the most sensitive and important aspects of modern web-based applications, which is security. We will understand the principles for protecting applications, demystify the concepts of authorization and authentication, and implement an access management model through ASP.NET Core Identity.

*Chapter 7, Adding Capabilities to Applications*, aims to expand the context of application source code and add fundamentals and best practices, in addition to the interaction with other resources necessary in modern applications, such as the use of cache strategies to keep applications more resilient. We will also explore the logging, tracing, and monitoring solution model, which is extremely important in applications that are capable not only of supporting users but also of allowing teams to have the ability to optimize, solve problems, and take proactive actions.

*Chapter 8, Enhancing Applications with Middleware in ASP.NET Core 9*, explores a powerful feature available in ASP.NET Core, which is the control of the request and response flow of applications through middleware. Through middleware, we have the ability to expand the functionalities available in the request flow of web applications using the best implementation practices. We will understand how the pipeline works, how to add middleware, and how to create custom middleware.

*Chapter 9, Managing Application Settings*, expands in greater detail on some aspects related to the security of sensitive information in an application. All solutions depend on a type of parameterization, and these, as a good practice, are generally managed through configuration files. Through the model proposed by ASP.NET Core 9, prepared for cloud environments, we will understand how to connect different configuration management providers in a secure way and use the best development practices with the support of the `IConfiguration` configuration abstraction interface. We will also learn how to add the ability to change application configurations and behaviors in real time, through the use of feature toggles and the Options pattern.

*Chapter 10, Deploying and Hosting Applications*, aims to introduce you to other aspects involving the development flow and continuous value delivery. Modern applications need to be dynamic and constantly changing and must be delivered at any time, even while users are using them. With this, we will learn about the use of automated processes such as CI and CD, associated with the principles of DevOps culture. We will understand the process of packaging and publishing applications in a web environment using pipelines connected to Azure.

*Chapter 11, Cloud-Native Development with ASP.NET Core 9*, teaches you about the best practices, tools, and principles to take applications developed in ASP.NET Core 9 to another level, adapting to the dynamic and modern model of developing web-based solutions. In this chapter, we will learn about the importance of going beyond the code and creating a cloud-native mindset. We will also learn about best practices and principles such as the Twelve-Factor App, containers, and deployment strategies, as well as resources that support software engineers in designing robust solutions for the cloud.

## To get the most out of this book

This book has a theoretical/practical approach, and to be able to take advantage of the available knowledge, it is important to have prior knowledge of the following:

- Software development in any technology
- Object-oriented programming, at the basic or intermediate level
- High-level languages such as C# and Java
- HTML and CSS at the basic level

Furthermore, some tools that will be used in the book are summarized in the following table:

| Software/hardware covered in the book | Operating system requirements |
| --- | --- |
| Visual Studio Code/Visual Studio | Windows, macOS, or Linux |
| Docker | Windows, macOS, or Linux |
| GitHub (account needed) | SaaS platform (`https://github.com`) |
| Git | Windows, macOS, or Linux |
| Postman | Windows, macOS, or Linux |
| Azure | Microsoft cloud platform (`https://azure.microsoft.com`) |

During the chapters, we will work with each of the technologies and tools mentioned in the preceding table, providing details on usage and configurations in a simple way.

**If you are using the digital version of this book, we advise you to type the code yourself or access the code from the book's GitHub repository (a link is available in the next section). Doing so will help you avoid any potential errors related to the copying and pasting of code.**

# Download the example code files

You can download the example code files for this book from GitHub at `https://github.com/PacktPublishing/ASP.NET-Core-9.0-Essentials`. If there's an update to the code, it will be updated in the GitHub repository.

We also have other code bundles from our rich catalog of books and videos available at `https://github.com/PacktPublishing/`. Check them out!

# Conventions used

There are a number of text conventions used throughout this book.

`Code in text`: Indicates code words in text, database table names, folder names, filenames, file extensions, pathnames, dummy URLs, user input, and Twitter handles. Here is an example: "Request delegates are configured using the `Run`, `Map`, and `Use` extension methods, typically configured in the `Program.cs` file."

A block of code is set as follows:

```
string key1 = _configuration.GetValue<string>
  ("MyCustomSetting:Key1");
string key2 = _configuration.GetValue<string>
  ("MyCustomSetting:Key2");
```

When we wish to draw your attention to a particular part of a code block, the relevant lines or items are set in bold:

```
var builder = WebApplication.CreateBuilder(args);
 // Add configuration from environment variables
builder.Configuration.AddEnvironmentVariables();

// Add configuration from command-line arguments
builder.Configuration.AddCommandLine(args);
var app = builder.Build();
app.Run();
```

Any command-line input or output is written as follows:

```
dotnet add package Microsoft.Azure.AppConfiguration.AspNetCore
```

**Bold**: Indicates a new term, an important word, or words that you see onscreen. For instance, words in menus or dialog boxes appear in **bold**. Here is an example: "On the next screen, click on the **+Create** option to add the new resource."

> **Tips or important notes**
> Appear like this.

# Get in touch

Feedback from our readers is always welcome.

**General feedback**: If you have questions about any aspect of this book, email us at customercare@ packtpub.com and mention the book title in the subject of your message.

**Errata**: Although we have taken every care to ensure the accuracy of our content, mistakes do happen. If you have found a mistake in this book, we would be grateful if you would report this to us. Please visit www.packtpub.com/support/errata and fill in the form.

**Piracy**: If you come across any illegal copies of our works in any form on the internet, we would be grateful if you would provide us with the location address or website name. Please contact us at copyright@packt.com with a link to the material.

**If you are interested in becoming an author**: If there is a topic that you have expertise in and you are interested in either writing or contributing to a book, please visit authors.packtpub.com.

## Share Your Thoughts

Once you've read *ASP.NET Core 9 Essentials*, we'd love to hear your thoughts! Scan the QR code below to go straight to the Amazon review page for this book and share your feedback.

https://packt.link/r/183546906X

Your review is important to us and the tech community and will help us make sure we're delivering excellent quality content.

# Free Benefits with Your Book

This book comes with free benefits to support your learning. Activate them now for instant access (see the "*How to Unlock*" section for instructions).

Here's a quick overview of what you can instantly unlock with your purchase:

| PDF and ePub Copies | Next-Gen Web-Based Reader |
|---|---|
| 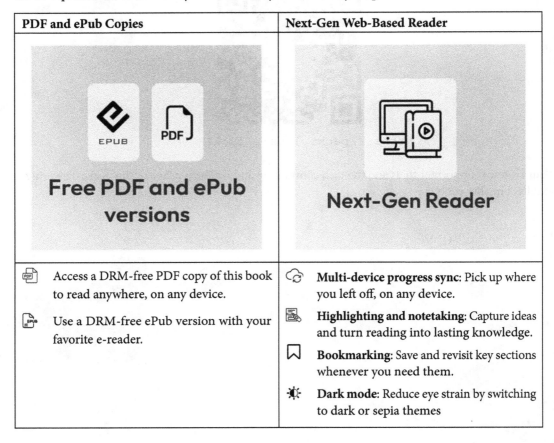 | |
| Access a DRM-free PDF copy of this book to read anywhere, on any device.<br><br>Use a DRM-free ePub version with your favorite e-reader. | **Multi-device progress sync**: Pick up where you left off, on any device.<br><br>**Highlighting and notetaking**: Capture ideas and turn reading into lasting knowledge.<br><br>**Bookmarking**: Save and revisit key sections whenever you need them.<br><br>**Dark mode**: Reduce eye strain by switching to dark or sepia themes |

## How to Unlock

Scan the QR code (or go to `packtpub.com/unlock`). Search for this book by name, confirm the edition, and then follow the steps on the page.

*Note: Keep your invoice handly. Purchase made directly from packt don't require one.*

# Part 1:
# ASP.NET Core 9 Fundamentals

In this first part, we will focus on the fundamentals of the ASP.NET Core 9 platform, learning about the principles of the platform and the new features in the version. We will also be preparing the development environment using development tools such as Visual Studio Code and Visual Studio, in addition to the **Software Development Kit (SDK)** that contains packages and CLI tools for implementing solutions. All the knowledge acquired in this first part is essential for the reader to be able to learn more clearly the other topics covered in the rest of the book.

This part contains the following chapters:

- *Chapter 1, Introducing ASP.NET Core 9 Concepts*
- *Chapter 2, Building Dynamic UIs with Razor Pages, MVC, and Blazor*
- *Chapter 3, Crafting Web APIs for Service Delivery*
- *Chapter 4, Real-Time Interactions with SignalR*

# 1

# Introducing ASP.NET Core 9 Concepts

Before starting to develop solutions using the ASP.NET Core 9 platform, we must learn the fundamentals and how to prepare the environment, as well as become accustomed to the main concepts that will be used during the development process.

In this chapter, we'll learn about how to prepare our development environment, understand the differences between .NET and .NET Framework, and see what's new in ASP.NET Core 9.

We'll cover the following topics in this chapter:

- Why ASP.NET Core 9?
- Comparing .NET and .NET Framework
- Preparing our development environment
- What's new in ASP.NET Core 9?

My purpose is to introduce you to the main concepts of ASP.NET Core 9 and how to use this powerful platform to deliver web-based applications. I will explain the fundamentals of the platform, giving you context about the difference between .NET and .NET Framework and how to prepare your own Windows, Mac, or Linux environment, which you are going to work on until the end of this book. Furthermore, we'll learn the most important improvements on this platform that have seen an increase in new features over the years. Let's start to learn the basics of ASP.NET Core 9.

> **Free Benefits with Your Book**
> Your purchase includes a free PDF copy of this book along with other exclusive benefits. Check the *Free Benefits with Your Book* section in the Preface to unlock them instantly and maximize your learning experience.

## Technical requirements

To take advantage of all the knowledge that will be shared in this book, it is important that you have access to a computer, with administrative privileges, and also access to the internet.

Other necessary software will be shared in this chapter and the rest of the book where necessary.

You can find all code examples and other materials used in this book in the following repository: `https://github.com/PacktPublishing/ASP.NET-Core-9.0-Essentials`.

## Why ASP.NET Core 9?

ASP.NET core is a platform that has existed since 2016 and has been constantly improved, allowing the development of high-performance, modern, and cloud-ready solutions.

A few years ago, it was only possible to develop solutions on the .NET platform using the Windows operating system. However, with the great market demand and the rapid evolution of technologies, Microsoft began a one-way process of restructuring and redesigning the platform, adopting the open source model, which gave the developer community the opportunity to adopt a robust development model, independent of the operating system.

The last major version of ASP.NET to run exclusively on the Windows operating system was 4.x, and after the redesign, the platform was renamed *ASP.NET Core*, which is currently in version 9 STS(Standard Term Support).

Recently, ASP.NET Core 9 has become an extremely rich platform, enabling the delivery of solutions for different types of purposes and, what's more, with the full support and focus of the open source community.

Using ASP.NET Core 9 provides us with a rich tool with the following benefits:

- The ability to develop web UI solutions
- The ability to develop web APIs
- Interoperability of operating systems
- Cloud-readiness
- High performance
- Integrations with modern client-side frameworks
- The use of best practices and design standards

It is a complete platform that unifies everything necessary for the development of rich solutions using the best practices, technologies, and other aspects, which you will learn about throughout the chapters of this book.

## Performance improvements

ASP.NET Core 9 features several important performance improvements over ASP.NET Core 7, making it the best-performing version to date. Some important improvement points are as follows:

- **Faster execution and startup**: ASP.NET Core 9 is faster than the previous version. Every version have been receiving many contributions from the technical community. The et runtime, responsible for the application execution, has some improvements like loop optimizations, many other code generation and Garbage Collector improvements.

- **Minimal API Performance**: According to benchmarks, the new version of the Minimal API is 15% faster than the previous version and consumes 93% less memory.

- **Native AOT (Ahead-of-Time) compilation**: Expanded support for native AOT in ASP.NET Core 9 allows applications to be compiled to native code, reducing disk footprint, improving startup times, and decreasing memory consumption, which is ideal for cloud-native environments.

- **ML.NET** important improvements enabling integrations with machine-learning models with the version ML.NET 4.0, with additional tokenizer support, necessary for modern IA models.

- **.NET Aspire** The .Net Aspire was introduced on the previous version .Net 9 adding an improved cloud-ready stack for building observable, production ready, distributed applications in ASP. NET Core 9. Many concerns related to the cloud-native approach during the development phase was abstracted with .NET Aspire, combining a couple of Nuget Packages and projects templates.

- **.NET MAUI**: The .Net MAUI (Multi-platform Application UI) which provides an unified way to develop applications for platforms like Web and Mobile, including IOS and Android. .NET MAUI has quality improvements like test coverage, end to end scenario test, and bug fixes. Now, as part of the project templates of ASP.NET Core 9 there is a hybrid project including MAUI integrated with Blazor. With this project software engineers are able to delivery applications not only for web, but also for mobile and windows.

- **Entity Framework Core**: Entity Framework Core is one of the most powerful feature of .Net, providing a way to abstract the communication between applications and database, using an approach called ORM(Object Relational Model). In the new version some more features and improvements was added like a Azure Cosmos DB for NoSQL provider and capabilities to work with AOT.

- **ASP.NET Core**: The entire ASP.NET Core platform has many improvements on Blazor, SignalR, minimal APIs, authentication and authorization and better support to the OpenAPI.

- **Swagger:** One of the most famous libraries for generating API documentation, Swagger, from the **Nuget** package **Swashbuckle.AspNetCore** will no longer be part of the default API template of ASP.NET Core 9. This is due to the fact of reducing the dependence on this library in .NET projects and improving support for Open API, a language-agnostic and platform-neutral of web based APIs.

For more details, check out the following link: `https://devblogs.microsoft.com/dotnet/performance-improvements-in-net-9/`.

However, before starting to prepare our environment and use the ASP.NET Core 9, in the next section, let's understand how the platform has been evolving with collaboration between Microsoft and the open source community, by comparing the .NET platform and the .NET Framework.

## Comparing .NET and .NET Framework

Both .NET and .NET Framework (usually called *Full Framework*) have similarities – that is, they are platforms that allow us to deliver great solutions.

In general, the platform is a framework with a set of features that allows us to develop different types of applications. In February 2002, .NET Framework brought a new development model using a centralized platform, allowing us to develop applications for Windows and the web through technologies such as Windows Forms, ASP.NET Web Forms, ASP.NET MVC, as well as console applications, among some other extensions.

Since the first versions, it was already possible to develop applications in different languages such as C#, Visual Basic, and any other languages that implemented the .NET Framework specifications. However, it depended on the Windows operating system and its system APIs.

The evolution and redesign of the .NET Core platform has brought many benefits to the Microsoft ecosystem, while maintaining the main idea of being a unified platform for the development of robust solutions. It is possible to develop in languages such as C#, F#, or even Visual Basic.

The structuring and redesign meant that the .NET core platform, now called just .NET, was developed in a modularized manner and independent of the operating system, with the support of the open source community.

Today, the entire .NET platform ecosystem is maintained by the .NET Foundation (`https://dotnetfoundation.org/`), a non-profit, independent organization that supports the entire open source platform ecosystem. With that, new possibilities were created for the .NET community, including the reduction in the lead time for delivery of new versions of the framework with new features and bug fixes.

The new releases of the .NET platform are made available annually, every November, in STS(**Standard Term Support**) versions, launched in even years and receiving support for 18 months, or LTS(**Long Term Support**), launched in odd years and receiving support for three years. There are also monthly patch updates, which speed up the agile correction of problems and vulnerabilities, maintaining compatibility between each patch and eliminating the greater risk of updates.

Understanding the platform update process brings great benefits to development times, as updates can cause non-conformities in applications, generating several problems.

Microsoft provides a complete roadmap of features that are added to the platform, as well as the implementation of improvements and, most importantly, fixes of bugs and vulnerabilities. Keep the roadmap link as a favorite in your browser: `https://github.com/MoienTajik/AspNetCore-Developer-Roadmap`.

Now that we understand some of the platform's basics, let's prepare our development environment on different operating systems.

# Preparing our development environment

The .NET platform has a set of tools available to offer the best experience to developers, regardless of the operating system used.

ASP.NET Core 9 applications can be developed and run on Windows, Linux, and macOS operating systems.

Code snippets will be presented throughout the book in order to demonstrate the concepts of ASP.NET Core 9 through practical examples. All supporting material for the book can be found in the GitHub repository, the link to which can be found in the *Technical requirements* section.

In this section, we will configure our environment on the three operating systems and create our first ASP.NET Core 9 project, but first, let's see what things we will require to get started.

## The development tool

We can develop ASP.NET Core 9 applications using any text editor and then compile the developed code using the SDK(**Software Development Kit**), which will be discussed in the next section.

Microsoft offers two code-editing tools, Visual Studio and Visual Studio Code.

Visual Studio Code is a rich, extensible, and lightweight code editor that makes it possible to develop any type of application. It is a free tool, has several extensions, is widely used by the community, and can run on any operating system.

Conversely, Visual Studio is a more robust version of the IDE, having several visual functionalities that support development, in addition to several tools such as application profiling and a rich debug tool. Visual Studio only runs on the Windows operating system and a license must be purchased. However, Microsoft offers a version of Visual Studio called Community that is free and, despite some limitations, offers an excellent development experience. For the remainder of this book, we use Visual Studio Code as the main code editor, because it is extensible and, most importantly, free.

> **Visual Studio for Mac**
> Visual Studio for Mac will not be continued by Microsoft, and its support will end on August 31, 2024.

## SDK and runtime

When proceeding with the installation of the .NET platform on your machine, some questions may arise regarding the SDK and the runtime.

The SDK allows us to develop and run ASP.NET Core 9 applications, while the runtime only has the necessary dependencies to run the applications.

In general, we always choose to use the SDK on development machines; however, when hosting environments, only the runtime is required. We'll discuss hosting applications in more detail in *Chapter 10*.

## CLI (Command-Line Interface)

Along with .NET and/or Visual Studio Code, a **CLI** will also be installed that will be used extensively throughout this book.

The CLI is nothing more than software executed through the command line, allowing to you to execute tasks for different purposes, such as the following command:

```
dotnet new webapp --name hello-world
```

The CLI command here is called dotnet. This command has some parameters, responsible for determining the type of task that will be executed.

In a nutshell, the previous command creates a new project (new) of type webapp with the name (--name) hello-world.

CLI tools bring great flexibility, avoid UI dependencies, are extensible, and allow us to use automation strategies through scripts.

Throughout the book, we will use some CLI commands to support solution development and learning.

In the next sections, we will look at installing the ASP.NET Core 9 SDKs for all three operating systems.

## Windows installation

Windows offers some options for installing the SDK for the .NET platform:

- Installation together with Visual Studio.
- Using the Windows package manager, **Winget**. The SDK can be installed by running the following command:

```
winget install -e --id Microsoft.DotNet.SDK.9
```

- Via PowerShell.

However, we will proceed with the installation through Visual Studio, but if you prefer to use other installation options, check out this link: `https://learn.microsoft.com/en-us/dotnet/core/install/windows`.

Installation through Visual Studio is very simple and involves just a few steps:

1.  Go to `https://visualstudio.microsoft.com/`.

2.  Download Visual Studio for Windows and save it. After downloading it, run the following file: `VisualStudioSetup.exe`.

3.  After installation, locate the `VisualStudioSetup.exe` file, run it, and then click on **Continue**.

Figure 1.1 – The Visual Studio Installer message

4.  On the **Workloads** tab, select the **ASP.NET and web development** option:

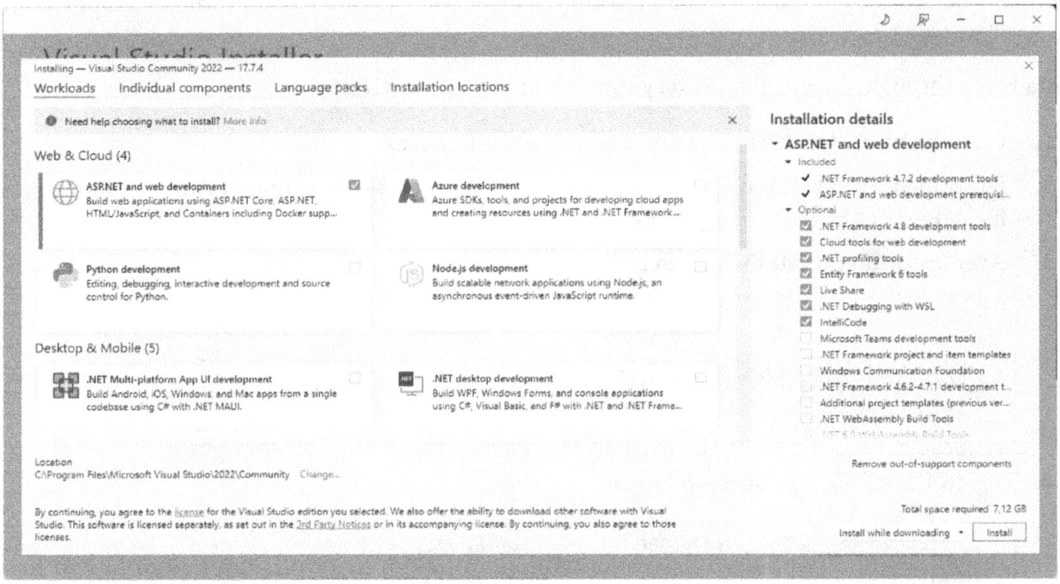

Figure 1.2 – Visual Studio installation options

5.  Then, click on the install button and proceed with the installation.

## macOS installation

macOS offers an executable that allows you to follow a simple installation process:

1.  Download the .NET platform from https://dotnet.microsoft.com/download/dotnet.

2.  Select the version best suited to your processor (ARM64 or x64)

3.  After downloading, run the installer and complete the steps to complete the installation.

> **Supported versions**
>
> Microsoft does not support .NET in versions before 6. From version 6 (LTS) onwards, current Apple processors are supported.

For more details on installing on macOS, refer to this link: https://learn.microsoft.com/en-us/dotnet/core/install/macos.

## Linux installation

.NET supports several versions of Linux. For the next steps, we will focus on the Ubuntu 22.04 version, and we will run the process based on the script provided by Microsoft:

1. Access the command terminal, and create a folder called `dotnet-install` in your home directory.

2. Download the `sh` script, provided by Microsoft with the following command:

   ```
   wget https://dot.net/v1/dotnet-install.sh -O dotnet-install.sh
   ```

3. You will need to add permission to the script before running it with the command:

   ```
   chmod +x ./dotnet-install.sh
   ```

4. Now, run the installation command:

   ```
   ./dotnet-install.sh --version latest
   ```

5. This command will install the latest SDK version.

> **Dependencies**
>
> The .NET platform depends on some libraries that are specific to each version of Linux. For more details, see the following link: `https://learn.microsoft.com/en-us/dotnet/core/install/linux-ubuntu#dependencies`.

Next, let's install Visual Studio Code.

## Visual Studio Code

Visual Studio Code is a great editor, and its installation is very simple.

Just go to `https://code.visualstudio.com/download`, download the version specific to your operating system, run the installer, and complete the steps.

### Code command

When installed, Visual Studio Code also installs its CLI. On Windows and Linux systems, the CLI is usually automatically added to the system *PATH environment variable*. On macOS, additional configuration will be required. To do this, follow these steps:

1. Press the *CMD + Shift + P* keys.

2. Type in the following command:

```
Install 'code' command in PATH
```

3. Press *Enter*, and the CLI will be added to the *Path environment variable*.

The time has come to validate the functioning of the environment, and to do so, we will create our first project.

## Testing the development environment

After installing the editor, code, and SDK, it's time to create our first application and ensure that the environment is functional for the rest of the book.

In this step, we will use the Terminal or Bash, the dotnet CLI, and also Visual Studio Code as the IDE. We will create a simple web application using the command line.

To do so, open a command terminal or bash and follow these instructions:

1. In your preferred directory, create a folder called `Projects`:

```
mkdir Projects
```

2. Access the created folder with the following command:

```
cd projects
```

3. Now, run the following command:

```
dotnet new
```

The `dotnet new` command needs some instructions for us to proceed with creating a project. When running it, the following instructions are displayed:

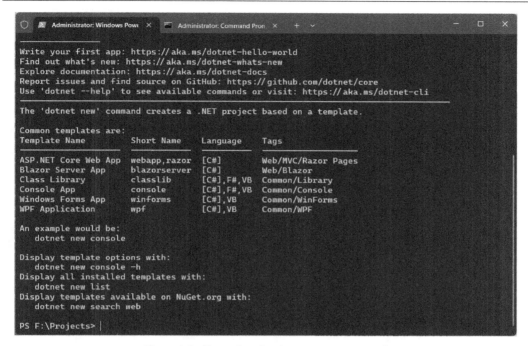

Figure 1.3 – Executing the dotnet new command

4.  As in Visual Studio, the .NET CLI has some templates that are used when creating projects. You will be able to see the templates installed on your machine by typing the highlighted command:

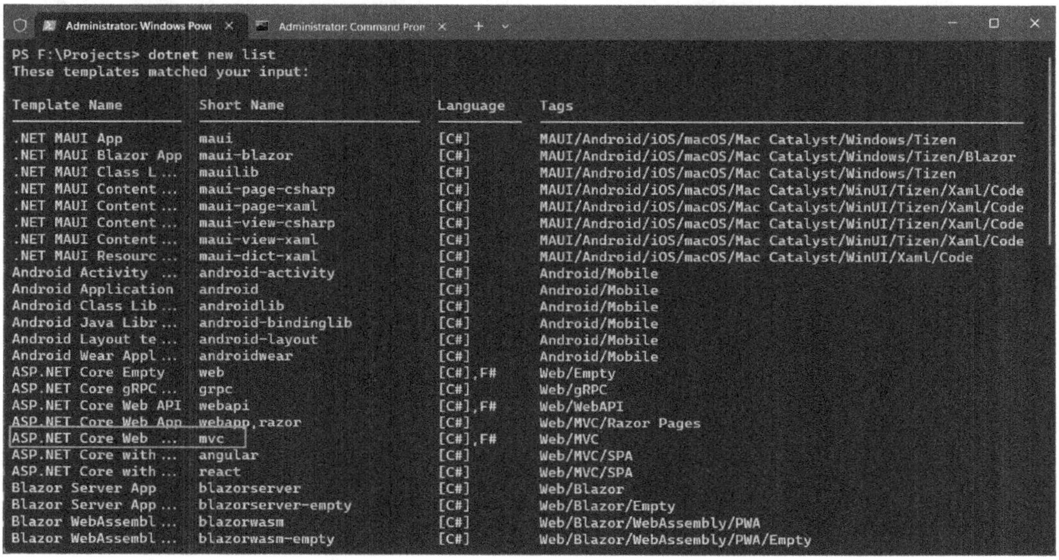

Figure 1.4 – The available dotnet templates

5.  We will continue with the creation of a web application in the MVC template. To do this, run the following command:

```
dotnet new mvc --name my-first-app
```

The previous command is basically a template for the type of project that will be created. In this case, we will use the MVC model, which is a project that uses the **Model-View-Controller** (**MVC**) architectural pattern. Don't worry about these details at this point. We will learn more about the .NET CLI tool, project models, and the MVC model throughout the book.

6.  Now, access the directory of the created application with the following command:

```
cd my-first-app
```

7.  Next, let's open Visual Studio Code to make some changes to the application's source code with the following command:

```
code .
```

8.  The previous command will open a new instance of Visual Studio Code in the previously created application directory.

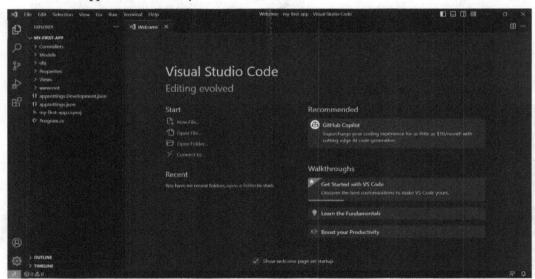

Figure 1.5 – My first app, opened on Visual Studio Code

9.  In Visual Studio Code, locate the index.cshtml file in **Views** | the Home folder.

10. Replace line 6 of the index.cshtml file with the following code, and then select **File |ZSave**, or just press *Ctrl + S*:

```
<h1 class="display-4">
  Welcome to the ASP.NET Core 9!
</h1>
```

11. Return to the terminal or bash and run the following command:

```
dotnet run
```

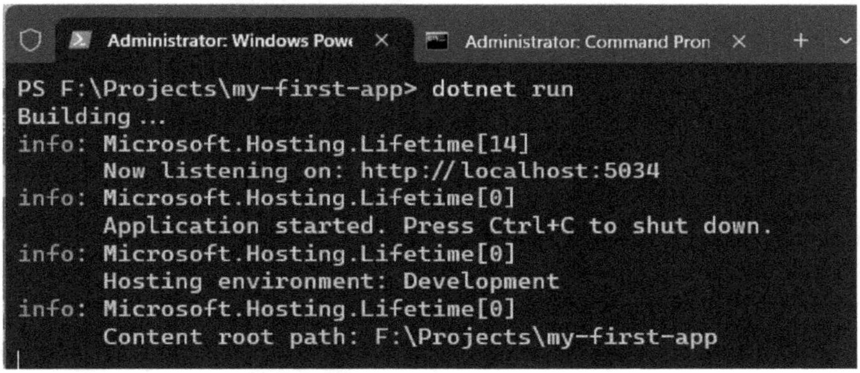

Figure 1.6 – Running the dotnet run command

If you can see a message like the one shown in *Figure 1.6*, then your environment is working correctly.

12. Now, access the browser and type the address presented, as in the http://localhost:5034 example.

Note the address on your terminal, as the application execution port number may be different.

Figure 1.7 – The application running

If all the previous steps were executed successfully, it means that your code editor was correctly configured, as well as the .NET SDK.

If there is any problem, review the installation steps according to your operating system.

With our environment configured, we are ready to continue learning the platform and implementing the examples set out in the book.

## What is new in ASP.NET Core 9?

As it is open source and independent of any operating system, the .NET platform has received several improvements in recent years, further improving the experience of developers and bringing several new features constantly requested by the community and, in addition, several improvements in performance and bug fixes.

Some improvements are as follows:

- **Native AOT**: This option was introduced in version 7.0 of the framework to create a self-contained application, in a single file, adding support for the x64 processors and ARM64 architectures of macOS and greatly reducing the size of the file, reaching up to 50% reduction in Linux environments.

- **Improvements in serialization libraries**: Applications constantly interact with data in JSON and the **System.Text.Json** API, native to .NET, has been constantly revised and improved, avoiding dependence on third-party libraries and considerably improving its performance and support.

- **Performance**: There has been a performance improvement of approximately 15%. You can check this link for more performance improvement details: `https://learn.microsoft.com/en-us/aspnet/core/release-notes/aspnetcore-8.0?view=aspnetcore-8.0`.

These and many other features can be consulted directly from the platform roadmap at the following link: `https://github.com/dotnet/aspnetcore/issues/44984`.

The .NET roadmap is very well maintained and updated by the community, together with Microsoft and the .NET Foundation. It is exactly this great support from the community, as well as the other companies and organizations involved, that has turned .NET into a powerful development platform for different purposes. By following the other need of the market, it has considerably improved the options for the development of web-based solutions, using different approaches to meet different needs.

## Summary

In this chapter, we learned about the .NET platform and ASP.NET Core 9, available in the main operating systems. We learned the differences between the .NET and .NET Framework, in addition to learning about the process of updating the framework versions and the difference between the STS and LTS versions. We also configured our development environment on different operating systems and developed an ASP.NET MVC application, validating the entire working environment .

In *Chapter 2*, we'll use our already configured environment to learn the different approaches and options available to develop UIs in ASP.NET Core 9.

## Get This Book's PDF Version and Exclusive Extras

**UNLOCK NOW**

Scan the QR code (or go to packtpub.com/unlock). Search for this book by name, confirm the edition, and then follow the steps on the page.

*Note: Keep your invoice handly. Purchase made directly from packt don't require one.*

# 2

# Building Dynamic UIs with Razor Pages, MVC, and Blazor

ASP.NET Core 9 has a complete UI framework to suit different types of approaches and applications that allow the use of page rendering strategies on both the client side and server side. In this chapter, we will learn about the options available in the ASP.NET Core UI framework, in addition to understanding how to define the best option for each scenario.

Initially, we will understand some important concepts and then continue with a practical approach so that we are able to exercise the concepts learned.

In this approach, we will initially understand what the ASP.NET Core UI framework is, learning about the different approaches to rendering applications both on the server, using Razor Pages and ASP. NET MVC, and rendering on the client, using JavaScript frameworks. Finally, we will understand the power of merging different technologies into a hybrid solution that uses the best of both the client and the server.

In this chapter, we're going to cover the following main topics:

- Learning about the ASP.NET Core UI
- Implementing a UI server render model with Razor Pages and ASP.NET MVC
- Exploring UI client rendering with Blazor and JavaScript frameworks
- Working with hybrid solutions

## Technical requirements

You can find all code examples and other materials used in this chapter in the following repository: https://github.com/PacktPublishing/ASP.NET-Core-9.0-Essentials

# Learning about the ASP.NET Core UI

Dynamic web-based applications have a flow that basically involves two distinct "worlds" the frontend and the backend. In general, the frontend deals with the mechanisms that are visualized and allow interaction between users and the various functionalities proposed by the solution. Therefore, a frontend is made up of buttons, texts, lists, menus, images, and other aspects that together form the UI. The backend is the representation of the mechanisms used to allow dynamism to the frontend, according to user interaction. We will discuss more about backend-related aspects in *Chapter 3*.

Each of the terms expressed in the previous paragraph works in different contexts. The *frontend* usually runs on the client, which translates into the user's browser. *Client* is a generic term that can express other types of user interaction. But in this case, we will talk about the client as the browser of your choice. The *backend* runs on the server, whether in a data center or even a cloud provider such as Azure.

Through user interactions in the UI, the user must communicate with the backend and subsequently be able to adapt to the server's responses to deliver some type of response and interaction, again , to the user.

The browser basically uses three technologies: HTML, CSS, and JavaScript. HTML is static; that is, it is interpreted by the browser and then rendered in the form of a UI. CSS is responsible for making visual elements more attractive, defining colors, shadows, and formatting, among other design aspects. JavaScript is used to make static elements dynamic, and this includes, for example, making a call to a server, and depending on the result, modifying the user's UI to adapt to the response of the processing carried out. JavaScript is responsible for increasing the ability of web-based applications to become dynamic and interactive. However, it can be complex to create and manipulate elements through JavaScript code and, in addition, to manage calls on the server. There are several excellent JavaScript frameworks available, such as Angular or React that allow you to develop richly dynamic UI solutions.

It is essential to have knowledge of UI technologies; however, in addition, we can benefit from an integrated development model that allows us to work on both the UI and the backend in a rich way.

ASP.NET Core 9 has a complete UI framework to meet any UI requirement for web applications and is fully integrated with the .NET platform, using best practices for separation of responsibilities, management, and maintenance, among other important aspects. Despite this, ASP.NET Core is not restricted to the use of the UI renderers proposed by the platform; it also integrates well with JavaScript frameworks and even allows you to use the best of the available options by adopting a hybrid approach.

However, before we move on to a more specific understanding of the options available in ASP.NET Core 9, let's learn about important aspects related to web systems architecture.

## Rendering the UI

There are different approaches to developing web-based solutions when it comes to the UI layer, even before talking about technologies.

There are basically two models, client-side and server-side, with their respective pros and cons. There is also a third possibility, which would be to use a hybrid approach.

In the client-side model, processing is done locally in the browser. In this way, all the HTML, CSS, JavaScript, and other assets are processed by the browser, responding to user stimuli. Interactions with users are handled locally through scripts containing UI-related logic without the need to request the server.

However, this approach depends on server resources, such as access to data, among other things, and so it is necessary to make frequent calls to the server in order to obtain information based on the user's needs, which is then processed and presented in the UI.

In the server-side approach, all the processing is delegated to the server, which returns a customized HTML page ready to be rendered in the browser. The server processes all the necessary information, allows access to data, manages business logic, has the ability to abstract sensitive information using secrets, and delegates minimal processing to the client. However, if the server is not available, it will not be possible to use the system.

In the hybrid approach, there is a combination of the best of "both worlds."

There are many JavaScript frameworks prepared to make web-based systems dynamic, providing a great user experience by processing resources on the client and, likewise, having the ability to interact with the server, delegating the processing of only relevant information to the UI rather than the entire processing of a page.

Fortunately, ASP.NET Core 9 is prepared for the development of web-based solutions in the different approaches mentioned. We'll start to understand the first UI development model, using Razor Pages, in the next section.

# Implementing a UI server render model with Razor Pages and ASP.NET MVC

ASP.NET Core 9 offers two powerful server-render models: Razor Pages and MVC. They are similar models, but MVC is more elaborate and implements the Model-View-Controller architectural design pattern—we'll talk more about this in the *ASP.NET Core MVC* section. For now, let's start learning about Razor Pages.

## ASP.NET Core Razor Pages

Razor Pages is a server-rendered framework that implements a page-based model. The page-based model basically contextualizes the implementation of a specific page, taking into account the UI and business logic, but correctly segregating responsibilities.

Razor is a markup language that acts similarly to a template engine and combines its use with HTML and C# code.

> **Razor's origins**
>
> Razor's development began in June 2010, but it was only released in January 2011 with MVC 3, as part of Microsoft Visual Studio 2010. Razor is a simple-syntax visualization engine.

This page-based development model brings great advantages, such as ease of creating and updating the UI; it's testable, keeps UI and business logic separate, and although it has similarities to ASP.NET Core MVC, it's simpler. Taking all these advantages into consideration, let's create our first project using Razor Pages.

### Creating our first project with Razor Pages

To create a Razor Pages project, you can use Visual Studio or the `dotnet` CLI tool.

Creation using Visual Studio is very simple; just open the IDE, select **Create a new project**, and then select the **ASP.NET Core Web App** template, as shown in *Figure 2.1*:

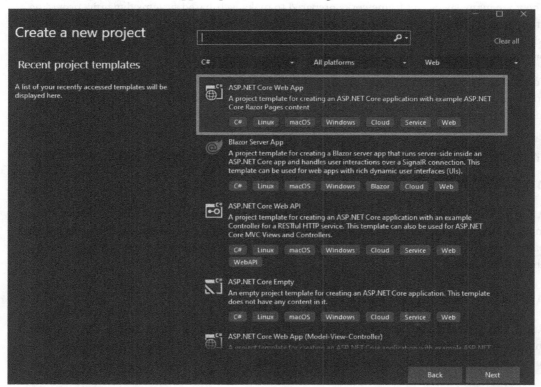

Figure 2.1 – Selecting a project template

Both Visual Studio and the CLI tool work with the concept of templates. With the .NET platform, it is possible to develop different types of projects, whether for web, Windows, or mobile. Each template creates a basic project structure.

Throughout the rest of the book, we will use the CLI tool to create projects, as well as other needs that we will discuss later. From now on, we will use the .NET CLI tool to create a Razor Pages project, as this tool offers us several benefits that we will discuss in the rest of the book.

When you install the .NET 9 SDK, a number of tools are available. The main tool we will use in this book is `dotnet`.

The `dotnet` CLI tool also has a concept of templates. To test this functionality, open your operating system's Command Prompt and run the following command:

```
dotnet --version
```

After running the preceding command, the current version of the tool will be displayed. This time, still at the prompt, run the following command:

```
dotnet new
```

After running the preceding command, you will see the following:

Figure 2.2 – dotnet CLI tool templates

As can be seen in *Figure 2.2*, some templates and examples of use were listed. Each model has a set of parameters that are used to customize project creation. If you want to know more about the parameters of each template, just type the following command; for example, for the `webapp` template, you'd type this command:

```
dotnet new webapp -h
```

The `-h` (help) parameter will provide a list of parameters and documentation for the desired template.

Depending on the installation on your machine, there may be other templates. Run the following command:

```
dotnet new list
```

You will see a list containing many types of project templates; we will focus on the projects highlighted in *Figure 2.3*:

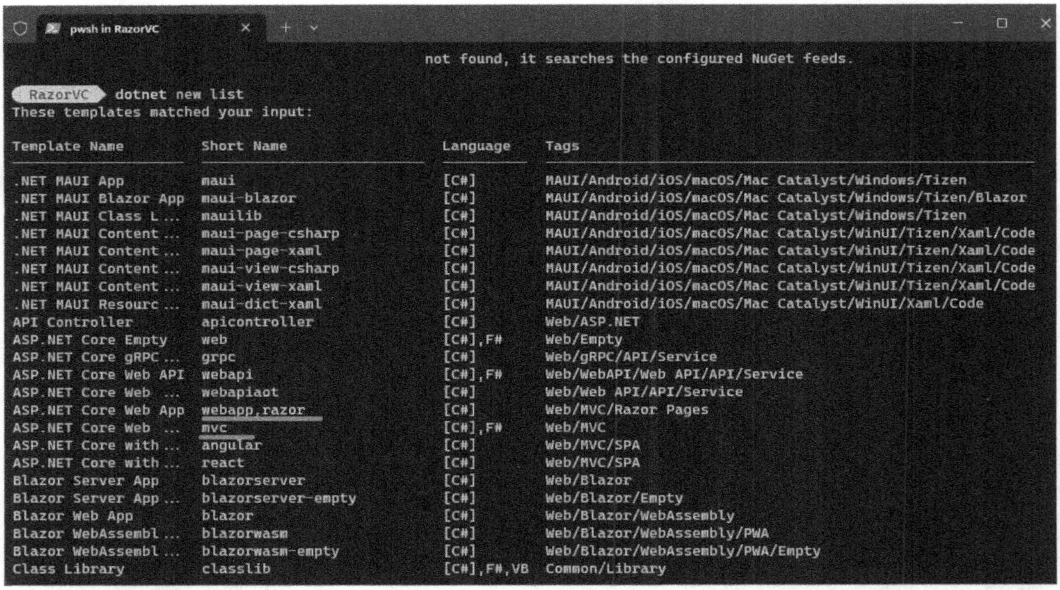

Figure 2.3 – All available project templates

Now that we've understood templates, let's finally create a new Razor Pages project via the command line. To do this, open Command Prompt, create a new folder called `NewRazorPages`, and run the following command on this folder:

```
dotnet new razor -n MySecondWebRazor
```

The previous command is composed of the new command, to create a new project, then `razor`, representing the short name of the desired template, and finally the `-n` parameter, which defines the name of the project.

After executing the command, a new folder containing the project will be created.

> **Command details**
>
> Each of the commands available in the CLI tool can have a set of parameters. To find out more about these parameters, simply add the `-h` option after a command; for example, `dotnet new -h`.
>
> You can also consult the tool's documentation at the following link: `https://learn.microsoft.com/en-us/dotnet/core/tools/dotnet`

For the rest of the book, we will consider creating projects via the command line. Now, let's go into more detail about the Razor Pages project we've created.

## Understanding the Razor Pages project

The Razor Pages project has a very simple directory structure and configurations compared to ASP.NET Core MVC. However, many of the concepts used in this project serve as a basis for the MVC project, so we'll take advantage of all the content.

*Figure 2.4* shows the structure of the project created in the previous section and has been expanded to express each important item that we will discuss in more detail:

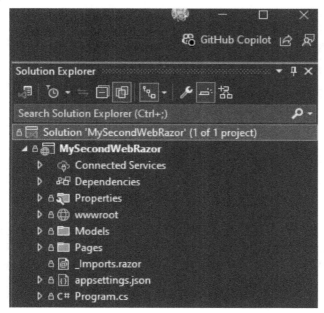

Figure 2.4 – Razor Pages project structure

Razor Pages has a simple structure that can basically be divided into four important items:

- **wwwroot folder:** This folder contains the application's static files, such as JavaScript, CSS, libraries, and images. By default, three subdirectories are configured, such as `css`, `js`, and `lib`, used to contain JavaScript files from external libraries, such as jQuery, among others. You can also create other directories to contain files such as images, fonts, and so on.

- **Pages folder:** This folder contains the application's pages, subdivided into a pair of files with the `cshtml` extension that contain the HTML code and C# code using Razor syntax, and `cshtml.cs`, which contains the C# code responsible for handling page events.

- `appsettings.json`: This is a file in **JSON** format that is used to maintain application settings centrally, as well as database connection strings, API keys, and other parameters. We'll talk more about settings in *Chapter 9*.

- `Program.cs`: This is the most important file in the Razor Pages project, written in C# and containing all the execution settings for the entire application flow.

Some other details and configurations related to the project will be seen in the other chapters of the book as we add more features and concepts to the learning process. For now, it's very important to understand some of the project's premises.

Let's look at the `Program.cs` file to understand some details:

```
var builder = WebApplication.CreateBuilder(args);
builder.Services.AddRazorPages();
var app = builder.Build();
if (!app.Environment.IsDevelopment())
{
    app.UseExceptionHandler("/Error");
    app.UseHsts();
}
app.UseHttpsRedirection();
app.UseStaticFiles();
app.UseRouting();
app.UseAuthorization();
app.MapRazorPages();
app.Run();
```

The following points explain the preceding code:

- The first line of the file creates an instance of an ASP.NET Core web application, using some standard configurations, such as adding middleware, between *lines 9* and *13*, that acts on the application flow and convention configurations for generating routes, among other aspects provided by the framework itself.

- Next, we have the execution of the `builder.services.AddRazorPages` line, which is responsible for configuring the web application with the characteristics of the Razor Pages project. This project has dependencies on certain classes that are used by the platform when running the application.

- Between *lines 4* and *8*, there is a check related to the environment in which the application is running. This block ensures that if there are any errors not dealt with by the application, the user will be redirected to a generic error page, preventing details of the application from being exposed. The `app.UseHsts()` code aims to force communication via the **HTTP Strict Transport Security** (**HSTS**) protocol to add security and the use of HTTPS.

- On *line 9*, we guarantee the use of the HTTPS protocol.

- *Line 10* is necessary for the Razor Pages application to take into account static files, localization, and the use of HTTPS.

It is important to consider, at this point, that the code described in the `Program.cs` file will affect how the application will behave at runtime. We must also consider the order of each of the methods located in the file.

Further details and configuration variations will be discussed later in the book. We are already familiar with the Razor Pages project structure, so let's learn more about the syntax used in HTML pages and how to interact with C# code.

## Working with pages

Razor acts as a powerful templating engine, allowing you to create pages using HTML, CSS, JavaScript, and C# code in the same file. This approach brings great flexibility in generating dynamic pages.

Let's look at an example of the `Index.html` page:

```
@page
@model IndexModel
@{
    ViewData["Title"] = "Home page";
}
<div class="text-center">
    <h1 class="display-4">Welcome</h1>
    <p>Learn about <a
      href="https://learn.microsoft.com/aspnet/core">
      building Web apps with ASP.NET Core</a>.</p>
</div>
```

The first lines of code refer to page-related settings, and then we have the pure HTML code.

Let's understand the main components described in the file:

- The @page directive must be the first directive in a Razor page view. It indicates that the page will function as an action handler.

- The @model directive indicates which type of model will be passed to the page. Razor Pages has a set of two files that make up a page, .cshtml and .cshtml.cs.

The ViewData["Title"] code is a dictionary, which represents another way of passing data to pages. In general, ViewData is used to pass small amounts of data. In the case of the preceding code, ViewData is being used to pass information from the page title to the HTML template.

The first concerns HTML; as with the previous example, .cshtml.cs refers to the C# code of the page handler, which contains the model or information that will be used on the page. Thus, the Index.cshtml file has an association with the index.cshtml.cs file.

In the following code, we have the IndexModel class that represents the model that will be used on the page:

```
public class IndexModel : PageModel
  {
      private readonly ILogger<IndexModel> _logger;

      public IndexModel(ILogger<IndexModel> logger)
      {
          _logger = logger;
      }
      public void OnGet()
      {


      }
  }
```

As we noted in the example, the Index.cshtml page does not have the entire structure of an HTML page. This is because Razor Pages allows the concept of Layout. That is, pages can often share a similar structure. This way, we can reuse the code to both generate common Layouts and create shared View blocks.

In the project structure, Layouts are kept within the Pages/Shared folder. By convention, shared views start with an underscore. The _Layout.cshtml file has a common HTML structure and, in addition, a special directive, @RenderBody():

```
<html lang="en">
<head>
    <!-- The rest of the code has been omitted for
      readability. -->
```

```
    <title>@ViewData["Title"] - MyFirstRazorWebApp</title>
    <!-- The rest of the code has been omitted for
      readability. -->
<div class="container">
    <main role="main" class="pb-3">
        @RenderBody()
    </main>
</div>
```

The RenderBody() method specifies the location where views will be rendered after server processing. In the case of the index.cshtml page, all HTML will be rendered between the main tags, in the _Layout.cshtml file. Also, note the use of ViewData["Title"], which will display the value set on a page, as done in the index.cshtml file.

There are two other special files that, by convention, should be located in the Pages folder:

- _ViewStart.cshtml: This is a file that allows us to define code that must be executed before displaying each Views. In this case, this file has a code where it defines which Layout file will be used for Views.

- _ViewImports.cshtml: This file is used to define the namespace and import features into the page, in a common way. This way, there is no need to declare namespaces and other features on each page.

Now that we understand the entire project structure and how Razor pages are managed in the project, let's add some customizations to the Index page and the IndexModel model and learn how to use Razor syntax and interact with C# code.

### Interacting with the Razor syntax and C# model

As explained previously, Razor pages have two files, one responsible for rendering the UI and the other responsible for containing the page's business logic. Furthermore, there is the possibility of using C# code together with HTML, meaning that the page can be generated during processing time on the server, according to user interactions.

We will make some changes to the index.cshtml file, adding some controls as shown in *Figure 2.5*:

MySecondWebRazor   Home   Privacy

# Welcome

Learn about building Web apps with ASP.NET Core.

## I'm using the Razor Syntax.

### It's funny

Red Green

Total: [_____] [ Load Products ]

| Id | Nome | Preço |
|----|------|-------|
| 1 | Product 1 | $62.05 |
| 2 | Product 2 | $71.96 |
| 3 | Product 3 | $4.06 |
| 4 | Product 4 | $74.13 |
| 5 | Product 5 | $18.80 |
| 6 | Product 6 | $20.34 |
| 7 | Product 7 | $91.10 |
| 8 | Product 8 | $70.85 |
| 9 | Product 9 | $10.45 |
| 10 | Product 10 | $37.88 |

# Load Technologies

 Load

Figure 2.5 – Customizing the index.cshtml file using Razor syntax

Open the index.cshtml file in Visual Studio or Visual Studio Code to make the changes and follow these steps:

1. Between the @{ } instance, add the following code:

```
string subtitle = "It's funny";
```

2. Now, change all the content between the div tags, which contain the page content, to the following code:

```
<h1 class="display-4">Welcome</h1>
    <p>Learn about <a
```

```
        href="https://learn.microsoft.com/aspnet/core">
        building Web apps with ASP.NET Core</a>.</p>
<h2>@Model.Message</h2><br />
<h3>@subtitle</h3>
    <a asp-page-handler="DefineColor"
      asp-route-id="1">Red</a>
    <a asp-page-handler="DefineColor"
      asp-route-id="2">Green</a>
    <div style="width: 200px;height:200px;
      background-color:@Model.Color"></div>
    <form method="post">
      <label>Total:</label><input type="text"
        name="quantity"/>
      <input type="submit" value="Load Products"
        name="btn" />
    </form>
    <table class="table">
      <thead>
          <tr>
              <th>Id</th>
              <th>Nome</th>
              <th>Preço</th>
          </tr>
      </thead>
      <tbody>
          @foreach (var product in Model.Products)
          {
              <tr>
                  <td>@product.Id</td>
                  <td>@product.Name</td>
                  <td>@product.Price.ToString("C")</td>
              </tr>
          }
      </tbody>
    </table>
```

The preceding code creates formatting for the Price property so that it is displayed in currency format. This formatting will take into account your browser's regional settings. In the case of the example run in this book, the formatting will display the price in en-US culture format.

3.  To ensure that the property is displayed in a specific format, a new property can be created:

```
public string FormattedPrice
    {
        get { return price.ToString("C",
            CultureInfo.GetCultureInfo("en-US")); }
    }
```

4.  This way, we can update the existing code for price display to the following:

```
<td>@product.FormattedPrice</td>
```

5.  However, we can define the application culture globally, avoiding the need to create a new property. To make this change, add the following code to the `Program.cs` file below the `var app = builder.Build()` line:

```
app.UseRequestLocalization(new
    RequestLocalizationOptions
{
    DefaultRequestCulture = new RequestCulture("en-US"),
    SupportedCultures = new List<CultureInfo>
    {
        new CultureInfo("en-US")
    }
});
```

> **Important note**
>
> For more information about managing cultures in ASP.NET Core 9, see the following link: https://learn.microsoft.com/en-us/aspnet/core/fundamentals/localization?view=aspnetcore-9-0

Some elements that use inline C# code have been added, in addition to some calls to the server code. At the moment, it is important to understand how Razor syntax can be used together with HTML. Let's understand all the elements added to the UI and how they interact with C#.

The first snippet added on *line 5*, `string subtitle = "It's funny"`, is C# code, declaring a variable of type `string`.

Note that all the code is enclosed between `@{` and `}` symbols, as per the example between *lines 3* and *6* of the `index.cshtml` file. This syntax allows the addition of a block of code capable of containing C# and HTML instructions.

**Combining C# and HTML code and a block**

Within a C# code block, it is also possible to add HTML tags. Using this strategy brings great advantages, such as determining what type of HTML tag will be rendered, according to an `if` statement, as in the following example:

```
@{
    if (total > 0)
    {
        <h1>The available amount is: @total</h1>
    }
    else
    {
        <h2>There is no amount available</h2>
    }
}
```

In addition to the code block, the use of the @ symbol allows the addition of C# code in one line, as in the example of the preceding code, which will display the value of the `Message` property of the `Model` object and display the value of the `subtitle` variable, previously defined:

```
<h2>@Model.Message</h2><br />
<h3>@subtitle</h3>
```

Razor Pages provides directives, which are features added to HTML tags. The following code adds two anchors to the page:

```
<a asp-page-handler="DefineColor" asp-route-id="1">Red</a>
<a asp-page-handler="DefineColor"
   asp-route-id="2">Green</a>
    <div style="width: 200px;height:200px;
      background-color:@Model.Color"></div>
```

Note that there are two attributes, `asp-page-handler` and `asp-route-id`. These are directive Razor pages, which determine, respectively, the name of the event handler when the link is clicked and the value that will be sent as a parameter to the handler.

Also, note that the `div` style has the `@Model.Color` code, inserted as the value of the `background-color` property. The color of the `div` tag will be set dynamically, according to the link.

For the rest of the controls created on the page, we have a purely HTML form and a table that lists randomly generated products. The form does not have the `action` attribute, used to determine the page or script that will process the posting of data. This attribute was omitted because Razor Pages follows a convention, which in this case is to infer the action to the form page itself.

The following code generates the rows and columns of the product table:

```
@foreach (var product in Model.Products)
{
    <tr>
        <td>@product.Id</td>
        <td>@product.Name</td>
        <td>@product.Price.ToString("C")</td>
    </tr>
}
```

The preceding code is a mix of HTML and C# code. After executing the `foreach` statement, the columns and rows of the product table are defined. Products are generated in the `Products` property of the `Model` object.

---

**Remember to separate responsibilities**

As we can see, it is possible to add any C# code to an HTML page using Razor Pages. However, use this approach to manipulate UI elements, but it is important to separate responsibilities correctly, avoiding multiple implementations of business rules together with UI manipulation rules.

---

All the elements we need at this point have been added, and we now know how to add C# code to manipulate our UI. Let's finalize the `Index` page, adding the necessary code for its operation in the `index.cshtml.cs` file.

### Working with the page model

For the previously created UI to work correctly, we must add some properties and methods to the page model. Open the `index.cshtml.cs` file so that we can add the necessary functionality.

The `Index` page model is, in fact, a C# class that has an inheritance from the `PageModel` class, which is an abstraction of several properties and methods used by models in Razor Pages.

Let's make changes to the `IndexModel` class and understand each piece of code added:

1.  Add a `Message` property to the `Index.cshtml.cs` file. It will be used to define a message that will be displayed in the UI:

    ```
    public string Message { get; set; }
    ```

2.  In the project root, create a folder named `Models` and then add a class called `Product.cs`. This class must have the following code:

```
public class Product
{
    public int Id { get; set; }
    public string Name { get; set; }
    public decimal Price { get; set; }
}
```

3.  Go back to the `Index.cshtml.cs` file and add a `Products` property that will contain a list of objects that will be listed in the table created in the UI previously:

```
public List<Product> Products { get; set; }
```

4.  Also, add a `Color` property:

```
public string Color { get; set; }
```

5.  The basic properties have been created. Now, let's create a method that randomly generates a list of products. Add the `GenerateProduct` method as per the following code:

```
private List<Product> GenerateProduct(int quantity)
{
    var random = new Random();

    var products = Enumerable.Range(1,
      quantity).Select(i => new Product
    {
        Id = i,
        Name = $"Product {i}",
        Price = (decimal)(random.NextDouble() * 100.0)
    });

    return products;
}
```

6.  We will change the class constructor and add default values for the `Products` and `Message` properties. This way, as soon as the page is displayed, we will have a randomly generated list of products and an **I'm using the Razor Syntax** message:

```
public IndexModel(ILogger<IndexModel> logger)
{
    _logger = logger;
    Products = GenerateProduct(10);
    Message = "I'm using the Razor Syntax.";
}
```

7. The method that generates the products is being used in the constructor to generate an initial listing. However, we want to interact through the UI and generate a list based on a value that will be entered in the form. To do this, we will create an `OnPost` method. This method generates a new list, based on the quantity entered in the UI form:

```
public void OnPost(int quantity)
{
    Products = GenerateProduct(quantity);
}
```

8. Finally, let's define a last method that will be responsible for setting the value of the `Color` property:

```
public void OnGetDefineColor(int id)
{
    Color = id == 1 ? "#FF0000" : "green";
}
```

Our model is ready to interact with the UI. But before running the application, let's understand a simple concept of Razor Pages convention.

The `OnPost` method has this name, following a convention, and is related to the GET, POST, DELETE, and PUT HTTP verbs. This way, by defining methods such as `OnGet`, `OnPost`, `OnDelete`, and `OnPut`, they will be able to handle page events, according to the HTTP verb. The `Index` page UI has a form with the POST method. Therefore, when clicking on the **Load Products** button, Razor Pages will automatically call the `OnPost` method on the `IndexModel` model.

The `OnGetDefineColor` method has this name to follow the convention, but there is no obligation to use the `OnGet` prefix in the method name. In HTML, we do not define the link handler as `OnGetDefineColor`; this is because, by convention, Razor Pages will infer the prefix from the method name, and also because a GET request is performed. But if you wish to provide your full name, there will be no problem. The `OnGetDefineColor` method has another important characteristic: its `id` parameter. The `id` parameter receives the value defined in the directive added in the HTML link, as shown in the following code example:

```
<a asp-page-handler="DefineColor" asp-route-id="1">Red</a>
```

This action is called binding, which means that when passing the `id` parameter, Razor Pages sets the values of the method arguments according to the name of each parameter.

---

**Directive tip**

Passing parameters in the previously defined HTML link is done using the `asp-route` directive together with the name of the parameter expected in the method—in this case, `id`. This way, the complete directive is defined by `asp-route-id`. If there were another argument called `name`, for example, the directive would be `asp-route-name`.

Now that you know the entire implementation of the Index page, run the application and interact with the controls created previously.

So far, we have learned how to use Razor Pages to create dynamic pages using the server-side approach. With each interaction with the controls created on the Index page, a call will be made to the server, which will manipulate the information, interpret the Razor page code implemented in the UI, and later return an HTML output with the result.

This approach is quite similar to ASP.NET Core MVC, which we will learn about in the next section.

## ASP.NET Core MVC

ASP.NET Core MVC is also a very powerful server-side framework that implements the MVC design pattern. Let's understand how the MVC design pattern works and then learn how to benefit from this approach by creating a new project.

### MVC pattern

MVC is an architectural design pattern that works on the separation of responsibilities or context:

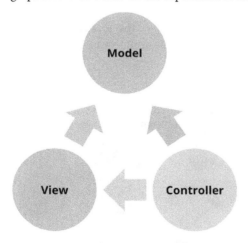

Figure 2.6 – MVC pattern

As you can see in *Figure 2.6*, the **Controller** acts as an orchestrator, responding to user interactions through the **View**, and delegating actions to the **Model**, which represents the application state and business rules. Subsequently, the Controller returns the result, defining which View will be responsible for displaying the UI to the end user.

The View and the Controller have a dependency on the Model, but the Model is agnostic, allowing the separation of responsibilities and the use of good code practices, such as the use of unit tests, as there is independence from the visual presentation.

ASP.NET Core MVC is based on the MVC pattern, adapting the project model and conventions. Let's understand how this pattern is implemented in this type of project.

### The ASP.NET Core MVC project structure

Creating the ASP.NET Core MVC project is very simple, and we use the CLI tool, in addition to Visual Studio Code as an editor.

Follow the next instructions:

1. Open your operating system's Command Prompt and access a directory of your choice where the project will be created.

2. Enter the following command to create the project:

```
dotnet new mvc --name MyFirstMVCApp
```

The preceding command uses the dotnet CLI tool, where we specify the action of creating a new project through the new command. Then, we define which type of project will be created. In this case, we inform that the template will be mvc, and a --name parameter has been added, whereby we inform the name of the project.

3. A folder will be created with the name of the application. Access this folder and then open Visual Studio Code by running the following command:

```
cd MyFirstMVCApp
code.
```

The preceding command will open up the following:

Figure 2.7 – ASP.NET MVC project structure

When looking at the structure of the MVC project created, we will notice a similarity with Razor Pages.

There are three main project folders:

- Views: It has the same characteristics as the Pages folder in Razor Pages; that is, it is the application's UI. It has .cshtml files, and these are organized into subfolders that represent a page and contain all the UIs that can be used as responses to actions. However, there are no .cshtml.cs files.

- Controller: The controller has a similar role to the class defined in the Razor Pages .cshtml.cs file. As mentioned, it is an orchestrator that has methods to manipulate events executed in Views. In MVC, each controller method is called actions and can return Views, redirections, or even data.

- Models: This folder is used to manage the business classes and models that will be used to exchange information between Views and HTML.

This structure follows a convention, which, in a way, facilitates development in this approach. However, the platform allows us to make customizations if necessary.

The MVC project also presents a small difference in the settings defined in the program.cs file in relation to Razor Pages. Before executing the app.Run() line, there is a call to the app.MapControllerRoute method. This method is responsible for configuring all of the application.

Routes define what will be accessed and how it should be accessed through application requests.

As shown in the following code, a default route is configured, called default, which has the controller/action/parameter pattern. Furthermore, the controller and action have a default value, Home and Index, respectively, while the parameter is optional:

```
app.MapControllerRoute(
    name: "default",
    pattern: "{controller=Home}/{action=Index}/{id?}");
```

This is a standard MVC convention and can be easily changed. In this model, if access to the application does not have a definition of the controller and which action should be executed, then the default controller, Home, and the Index action will be defined as the response to the request.

It is interesting to note that we are referring to Controllers and not pages. This is because the MVC pattern allows the Controller to orchestrate the request, according to the desired action, and then return a result or a View.

As we progress through the chapters of the book, we will have other examples of using routes.

## Understanding patterns and conventions

The MVC project follows a convention that benefits the file structure presented previously.

As we learned, the Controller acts as an orchestrator between the Model and the View. This way, instead of using a concept of pages, there is the idea of actions.

Given the user's intention or interaction, it triggers an action. This action is captured by a Controller, which then performs the processing and returns either a value or a View, as shown in *Figure 2.8*:

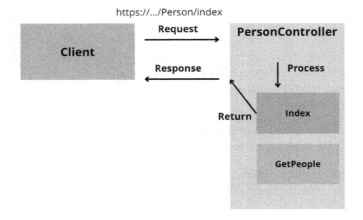

Figure 2.8 – MVC request flow

The `Controller` class is a C# class, which has attributes and methods. The `Controller` class's public methods are called actions.

Imagine a registry of people. We would then have the following class:

```csharp
public class PersonController : Controller
{
    public IActionResult Index()
    {
        return View();
    }
    public JsonResult GetPeople()
    {
        var model = new List<PersonModel>() {
            new PersonModel("Person 1",
              new DateTime(1980, 12, 11)),
            new PersonModel("Person 2",
              new DateTime(1983, 12, 15))
        };
        return Json(model);
    }
    public IActionResult Register(PersonModel personModel)
    {
        return RedirectToAction("Result",
```

```
                new { message =  $"The {personModel.Name}
                was registered successfully." });
        }

        public IActionResult Result(string message)
        {
            ViewData["Message"] = message;
            return View();
        }
    }
}
```

The `PersonController` class follows the name convention, adopting the `Controller` suffix at the end of the class name. Furthermore, this class has an inheritance from the `Controller` class, which is a base class that already has some utility methods responsible for processing and returning data and information through the controller.

Next, we have a method called `Index`, which just returns a View, executing the `return View()` command.

---

**Which View is returned?**

The `View()` method takes into account the Asp.NET Core MVC convention. So, when executed, the view that is instantiated considers the following path: `/Views/<ControllerName>/Action.cshtml`. This means that in the case of the `PersonController` class, calling the `Index` method will return a View: `Views/Person/Index.cshtml`.

The `View()` method has other overloads, making it possible to pass an object that will be used as a Model into the View or even define a Controller View that should be displayed.

---

The `GetPeople()` method just returns a list of people in JSON format, as shown in *Figure 2.9*:

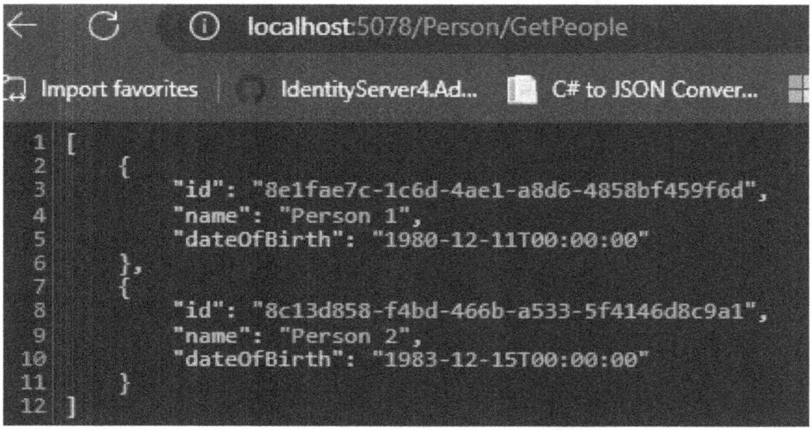

Figure 2.9 – JSON with a list of people

The `Register()` method processes the form request and returns an object to the `Result` View. However, in this case, it is making the call to an action from the `PersonController` controller, executing the `RedirectToAction` method, called `Result`, which expects a string as a parameter. *Figure 2.10* demonstrates the display of the action result after registering a person:

Figure 2.10 – Register Person view

> **Base Controller class**
>
> The abstract `Controller` class has some utility methods that allow you to work on the communication flow between the Controller and the View.
>
> The `Json()`, `View()`, and `RedirectToAction()` methods are some of the resources that are commonly used in a controller class.

The MVC model and Razor Pages have similarities, but a big difference is the use of actions instead of pages. In this way, the controller has the ability to decide what type of View or information should be returned, in relation to some user interaction, orchestrating the processing flow.

The Controller responds to user events, and the View is an important aspect of this type of project. Based on the `PersonController` example, we will understand how the View was created and learn how the interaction with the Controller's actions works in the next section.

### Working with Views on ASP.NET MVC

The concept of Views in ASP.NET MVC is the same as that used in Razor Pages, using the Razor syntax. As we can see in the following code, there is a form tag, using Razor directives, defining which Controller and action will process the registration:

```
@model MyFirstMVCApp.Models.PersonModel
@{
    ViewData["Title"] = "Home Page";
}


<div class="text-center">
    <h1 class="display-4">Person View</h1>
</div>

<div>
```

```
        <form method="post" asp-controller="Person"
          asp-action="Register">
            @Html.LabelFor(p => p.Name)
            @Html.TextBoxFor(p => p.Name)
            <br/>
            @Html.LabelFor(p => p.DateOfBirth)
            @Html.TextBoxFor(p => p.DateOfBirth)

            <input type="submit" value="Register" />
        </form>
</div>
```

The preceding file was created in the `Views/Person/Index.cshtml` directory structure. Following the convention, for the `PersonController` controller, there must be a `Person` folder, a subfolder of Views, which will contain all the Views that will be displayed through the `PersonController` controller.

---

**The view index is a good practice**

It is good practice to have an `Index.cshtml` file and an `Index()` action in each controller. Following the route pattern, defined in the `Program.cs` file, by default, when an action is not specified, an `Index()` action will be executed. In this case, having a View and Action Index will avoid usability problems in your application.

---

To create the labels and inputs used in the form, **tag helpers** were used. Tag helpers are Razor Pages methods that basically render HTML. The difference, in the preceding code presented, is that there is a connection with the Model.

In the first line of the `Index.csthml` page, a Model was defined, using the `@model MyFirstMVCApp.Models.PersonModel` code. This makes the Model strongly typed. By using a tag helper, together with a Lambda expression, we are implementing good practice in relation to the MVC binding model.

As a result, the HTML generated by tag helpers for the form will have the correct names in relation to the model properties, following the flow outlined next:

1. The data is the name and date of birth informed in the inputs.

2. The user clicks the **Register** button.

3. The ASP.NET framework makes a request to the `Result` action.

4. The ASP.NET framework identifies that the `Result` action has a `PersonModel` object as a parameter and then creates an instance.

5. The ASP.NET framework binds the data posted by the form and sets the values in the corresponding properties of the instantiated object.

6. The ASP.NET framework executes the `Result` action.

As the bind is done through property names, if any name is typed incorrectly, some properties will not have a value.

The use of the tag helpers approach also helps in other aspects such as attributes added to the `Model` class that allow validations, among other aspects. We will discuss more about attributes and bind during *Chapters 3* and *5*.

The MVC pattern provides us with several benefits, especially in more complex projects where there is a need to control different business flows and return dynamic Views according to the need.

There are other approaches to working with UIs in ASP.NET Core 9. Let's learn a little more about other options, such as using Blazor and integrations with JavaScript frameworks, in the next section.

# Exploring UI client rendering with Blazor and JavaScript frameworks

ASP.NET Core 9 has several frameworks that provide the creation of UIs with high quality and good user experience, using client-side and server-side approaches.

We will talk about the newest technology that uses the **WebAssembly** standard, called Blazor, which is a powerful and flexible UI framework. However, if you are used to JavaScript frameworks, you can also benefit from the .NET platform.

## Rich UIs with Blazor

Just as with Razor Pages and MVC, Blazor offers a **single-page application** (**SPA**) framework on the .NET platform, running both client-side and server-side, using all the power of C#.

### Blazor WebAssembly

The client-server version of Blazor runs on the WebAssembly platform, which is a compact bytecode with an optimized format, fast to download, and provides great performance when running on the client side, creating rich UI experiences.

As we can see in *Figure 2.11*, Blazor is an abstraction of ASP.NET Core for WebAssembly. This way, the Blazor code will generate application assemblies, which require the .NET runtime for execution, also allowing interaction between WebAssembly and the HTML document.

> **WebAssembly**
>
> WebAssembly is a web standard, and you can learn more about it at the official website: `https://webassembly.org/`

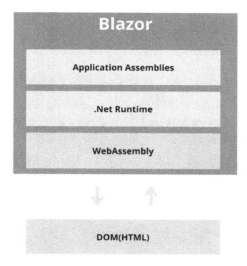

Figure 2.11 – WebAssembly and Blazor

The WebAssembly platform uses an interoperability model, which allows it to interact with all browser APIs, running in a sandbox, providing security against malicious actions, and also allowing the execution of .NET code.

All page code developed is compiled into .NET assemblies. Thus, when accessing the page through the browser, both the assemblies and the .NET runtime are downloaded. Then, with the support of WebAssembly, the application runs and uses JavaScript interop to handle **DOM (Document Object Model)** manipulation and browser API calls.

Blazor is a flexible framework that also allows you to create projects with the benefits of server-side processing, offering an excellent client-side experience.

### Blazor Server

Blazor also allows for a server-side UI rendering approach. However, unlike what happens with Razor Pages and MVC, instead of rendering the entire HTML for each client request and returning a complete document as a response, Blazor creates a graph, which represents the page components, considering properties and state.

Then, with each interaction, Blazor performs an evaluation of the graph and produces a binary representation, which is sent back to the client.

Blazor's server-side approach uses **SignalR** technology, which allows you to update the UI through a direct connection to the server, bringing better usability and a rich user experience. We will cover SignalR in *Chapter 4*.

Blazor Server brings great benefits in the development of web-based solutions, with C# as a common language, bringing security, reliability, and performance.

Let's understand the development approach using Blazor.

### *Blazor components and structure*

Just as with some JavaScript frameworks, such as Angular, Blazor works with a component structure.

A component is one or more UI elements developed with a specific objective, according to the needs of the application. This component can be reused throughout the application, enabling separation of responsibilities, reusability, and flexibility.

All Blazor components have the `.razor` extension and use both the Razor syntax and all the benefits of C#.

To create a Blazor project, simply use the `dotnet` CLI, with the following command:

```
dotnet new blazor --name MyFirstBlazorApp
```

**Interactivity Render Mode**

ASP.NET Core 9 introduces the render interactive mode on Blazor Apps. The interactive render mode feature enhances the way Blazor apps handle rendering, introducing a mode where the server-rendered static HTML is progressively enhanced into a fully interactive client-side application.

The goals of this feature are:

Progressive Enhancement: When a Blazor app is initially loaded, the server pre-renders the HTML, providing a fully functional page for users to interact with immediately. This allows the app to seamlessly transition from this static HTML to a fully interactive Blazor app once the Blazor framework is loaded on the client side.

Seamless Transition: ensures the app appears interactive even while the client-side Blazor runtime is being initialized and users can start interacting with the app before the complete Blazor runtime is ready, making the user experience smoother.

Improved Performance: optimizes the time-to-interactivity by reducing the noticeable delay that users might experience in traditional Blazor Server or Blazor WebAssembly apps.

Enhanced User Experience: minimizes interruptions or loading indicators during transitions, giving users a better perception of speed.

If you create a Blazor app using the command:

**dotnet new blazor --name MyFirstBlazorApp**

The default interactive mode is Server. In case you want to leverage the new feature, use the following command:

**dotnet new blazor --name MyFirstBlazorApp --interactivity Auto**

To learn more about this new feature, access the following URL: `https://learn.microsoft.com/en-us/aspnet/core/blazor/components/render-modes?view=aspnetcore-9.0`

After creating the project, just open the `Pages` folder, and you will then find some components as shown in *Figure 2.12*:

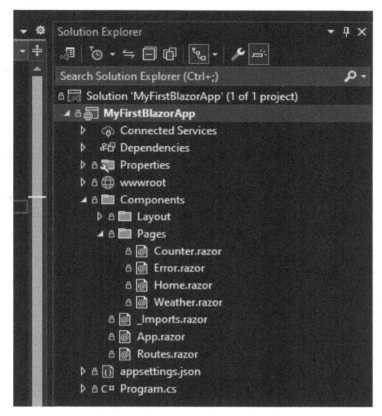

Figure 2.12 – The Blazor project structure

There are components that are defined as pages and therefore have the @pages directive, where a route to access the page is defined. There are also components that are added to pages.

The `Counter.razor` file is a page component and has the following content:

```
@page "/counter"
@attribute [RenderModeServer]
<PageTitle>Counter</PageTitle>
<h1>Counter</h1>
<p role="status">Current count: @currentCount</p>
<button class="btn btn-primary"
  @onclick="IncrementCount">Click me</button>
@code {
    private int currentCount = 0;
```

```
private void IncrementCount()
{
    currentCount++;
}
}
```

Note that there is use of Razor and HTML syntax, as we learned in the Razor Pages and MVC approaches. There is also C# code between the @code { } tags.

The C# code defined in the preceding file has the functionality to increment a counter when the user clicks on the **Click me** button.

The HTML button tag has the @onclick attribute, which is defined with the name defined in the C# code block.

For simple components, the approach of using HTML and C# code in the same file may be valid. However, it is good practice to separate business rules from the UI. Therefore, Blazor allows a file to be created containing the component's C# code.

In the preceding code example, there would be two files: Counter.razor and Counter.razor.cs. All C# code could be moved to the new file generating the following class:

```
namespace MyFirstBlazorApp.Pages;
public partial class CounterPartialClass
{
    private int currentCount = 0;
    private void IncrementCount()
    {
        currentCount++;
    }
}
```

Blazor is very flexible and offers a huge range of possibilities for developing rich web-based applications, integrated with HTML, CSS, and JavaScript and using the most modern technologies. It would take an exclusive book to talk about Blazor, however; this book will focus on approaches based on Razor Pages and MVC.

ASP.NET Core 9 is very flexible when it comes to developing UIs, featuring different frameworks. But if you are familiar with Angular, React, or Vue.js, you can benefit from the power of the .NET platform.

## ASP.NET Core 9 and JavaScript frameworks

As we learned during the other topics in this chapter, ASP.NET Core 9 offers several approaches to building a UI, interacting with C# code. There are several related benefits, including the use of a common development model, using the Razor syntax, and all the benefits of the .NET platform.

However, if you are used to using a framework for building SPAs, such as Angular, Vue.js, and React, the .NET platform has some templates available for this purpose:

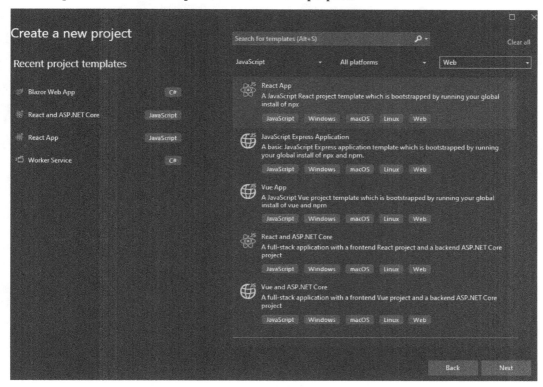

Figure 2.13 – ASP.NET Core 9 JavaScript frameworks template

The **React and ASP.NET Core** template creates two projects, one for the frontend and the other for the application's backend.

SPAs use the approach where the UI is developed independently of the backend, which is generally an external service or application.

When using the model offered by ASP.NET Core, there is also a clear separation between the UI and the backend. The project is already configured for integration with the web API developed in .NET. One of the great benefits of this is the convenience of publishing the UI and backend project in a single simple unit, facilitating publication:

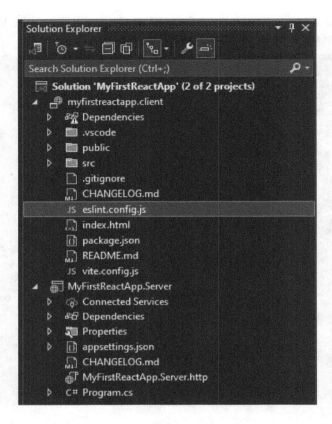

Figure 2.14 – ASP.NET Core React standalone project structure

Using project templates for frameworks such as Angular, Vue.js, or React is completely optional. Even if the UI project is created independently, we can benefit from ASP.NET Core by developing web APIs to serve the UI. We'll talk about creating web APIs in *Chapter 3*.

As we can see, the platform offers several approaches for developing high-quality web-based systems. Each ASP.NET Core UI framework has several benefits that can be combined to generate even more powerful solutions, and we will look at these solutions in the next section.

## Working with hybrid solutions

One of the great benefits of working on a powerful platform such as ASP.NET Core is having the ability to integrate between technologies. Therefore, we can combine all the power of Razor Pages, MVC, and Blazor in the same project.

In the case of integration with Blazor, there is the benefit of using `.razor` components, providing reusability.

Blazor integration into Razor Pages or MVC projects must be configured according to the following steps:

1.  In the project root, add a file named `_Imports.razor`. This file will be responsible for importing the namespaces necessary for the project:

```
@using System.Net.Http
@using Microsoft.AspNetCore.Authorization
@using Microsoft.AspNetCore.Components.Authorization
@using Microsoft.AspNetCore.Components.Forms
@using Microsoft.AspNetCore.Components.Routing
@using Microsoft.AspNetCore.Components.Web
@using Microsoft.AspNetCore.Components.Web
   .Virtualization
@using Microsoft.JSInterop
@using {CHANGE_FOR_THE_NAMESPACE_OF_YOUR_PROJECT}
```

    Note that at the end of the file, there is a `{CHANGE_FOR_THE_NAMESPACE_OF_YOUR_PROJECT}` tag. Change this value to your project namespace.

2.  Now, it will be necessary to change the `_Layout.cshtml` file, located in `Pages/Shared` directory in the case of the Razor Pages project or in the `Views/Shared` directory for MVC projects. Add the following code in the head element:

```
<base href="~/" />
<component type="typeof(Microsoft.AspNetCore
  .Components.Web.HeadOutlet)"
    render-mode="ServerPrerendered" />
```

    The purpose of defining `<base href="~/" />` is to define the base path of the application, while the `component` tag is used to render the contents of the Razor components in the HTML head element.

3.  Add the following script before the `@await RenderSection(...)` render section:

```
<script src="_framework/blazor.server.js"></script>
```

    Don't worry about the script path, much less creating it. This will be done automatically by the framework.

4.  Now, open the `Program.cs` file to make some modifications. First, we must register the Blazor services so that they are available while the application is running. Add the following code:

```
builder.Services.AddServerSideBlazor();
```

5.  You also need to add the Blazor route mapping control. Add the following line below the `MapRazorPages` call (in the case of a Razor Pages project) or the `MapControllerRoute` call (in the case of an MVC project):

```
app.MapBlazorHub();
```

Now that the project is integrated with Blazor, let's create a component with the following steps:

1.  Create a file called `technology.razor` in the `Pages/Shared` (Razor Pages) or `Views/Shared` (MVC) folder and add the following code:

```
<h1>Load Technologies</h1>
<button class="btn btn-primary"
  @onclick="LoadTechnologies">Load</button>
@if (technologies != null)
{
    <ul>
        @foreach(var tech in technologies)
        {
            <li>@tech</li>
        }
    </ul>
}
@code {
    private int currentCount = 0;

    private string[]? technologies;


    private void LoadTechnologies()
    {
        technologies = new[] { "Razor Pages",
            "MVC", "Blazor"};
    }
}
```

The preceding code creates a **Load** button with a click event that will load a list of technologies. This list of technologies was created in the `@code{ }` session, using an array of strings. When running the application, the screen will be similar to *Figure 2.15*:

# Load Technologies

Load

Figure 2.15 – Page/View using the Blazor component

2.  To use this component, add the following code to any MVC Razor page or View:

```
<component type="typeof(Counter)"
  render-mode="ServerPrerendered" />
```

When running the application, simply use the component to obtain the expected result, as shown in *Figure 2.16*. This component is reusable and can be added to any page or view, bringing greater flexibility and power to UI development:

# Load Technologies

- Razor Pages
- MVC
- Blazor

Figure 2.16 – Using a Blazor component with Razor Pages and MVC

Combining ASP.NET Core UI frameworks can bring benefits during the web-based application development process, using the best of each approach.

## Summary

In this chapter, you've delved into the rich world of the ASP.NET Core UI, gaining valuable insights into the available tools for crafting dynamic and engaging UIs. You've not only understood the key concepts and tools required for implementing a server-side UI, but you've also discovered the remarkable benefits of WebAssembly through Blazor, enabling you to create powerful SPAs in conjunction with ASP.NET Core. As you wrap up this chapter, you've learned how to seamlessly combine ASP.NET Core UI solutions. Now, with a solid foundation in place, I invite you to embark on the next exciting journey in *Chapter 3*, where we'll explore the world of web APIs and their pivotal role in delivering outstanding services. Get ready to take your skills to the next level!

# 3

# Crafting Web APIs for Service Delivery

As part of ASP.NET Core 9, web APIs can be used to build HTTP services, which can be made available for both web page consumption and mobile applications. The structure provided by the .NET Core platform enables the development of APIs with high quality and performance. In this chapter, we will learn more about web APIs and the standards, conventions, and best practices for delivering solutions using them.

In this chapter, we're going to cover the following main topics:

- Delivering business as a service
- Exploring minimal APIs
- Implementing APIs using the controller-based approach
- Working with documentation

## Technical requirements

This chapter uses the Postman tool, which will be used as a client for consuming APIs. This tool will also be used in other chapters of the book and its installation and use are free.

You can download Postman on your operating system through the following link: https://www.postman.com/downloads/.

The code examples used in this chapter can be found in the book's GitHub repository: https://github.com/PacktPublishing/ASP.NET-Core-9.0-Essentials/.

## Delivering business as a service

As we have learned in the last chapters, ASP.NET Core 9 offers different frameworks for the development of rich web-based applications. Regardless of the chosen model, whether client-side or server-side, we must implement negotiation flows that are responsible for the operation of the applications.

Imagine a system for a digital bank where users can perform different types of operations in their checking account, such as transfers, analyzing extracts, checking the account balance, and even purchasing a new service package. Each of these operations has business requirements and rules. For example, it should not be possible to transfer 200 euros if the user's account balance is 100 euros.

This negotiation flow can be implemented perfectly using Razor Pages, MVC, or a hybrid model, as we have learned. We can easily have a web-based application being performed on a server.

However, imagine that users have requested a mobile application. It should offer the same features as the web version.

In this case, any technologies could be used for this purpose, either for native or hybrid development. But how would the business logic of the application be developed? What if there was a change to an application rule? Would it be necessary to update two distinct types of code to make the applications run correctly?

The best practice, in this case, is to centrally manage all the code that concerns the business rules. This would allow different types of application interfaces, whether browsers, mobile applications, or even other applications, to interact with a business context.

This centralized application is made available in web API format, which is actually an application that is distributed through the internet. The **Representational State Transfer** (**REST**) protocol, which is based on the HTTP protocol commonly used in web application interactions, allows clients (browsers, mobile apps, and other applications) to consume resources independently in a controlled and centralized way.

The model for providing business contexts over the internet is called **business as a service** (**BaaS**), allowing organizations to offer specific features or resources such as services that can be consumed by other companies or applications.

Figure 3.1 – BaaS

Fortunately, ASP.NET Core 9 offers us a powerful model for creating web APIs; however, we must understand some foundations before learning how to create BaaS resources. In the rest of this section, we look at some of the important foundational concepts.

## HTTP verbs and conventions

Communication with an API is done through the **HTTP** protocol, which has some operations called **HTTP verbs.**

These verbs determine the type of intention in a given resource. The most common HTTP verbs are these:

- **GET**: This method is used to request data in a feature, such as a read-only operation; when we type a URL in the browser, as a response, we receive an HTML page. GET can also be used to determine the intention to obtain a list of registered users, for example.

- **POST**: When you send a POST request, you are usually creating a new feature on the server. This method includes data in the body of the request.

- **PUT**: PUT requests are used to update a feature. In this case, any changes made to a resource's attributes must be sent in the request body, and the server replaces the resource with the sent data.

- **DELETE**: DELETE requests are used to request the removal of a specified feature.

- **PATCH**: PATCH requests are used to apply partial modifications to a feature. Unlike the PUT verb, which replaces the entire feature, PATCH updates only the specified parts of the feature.

- **HEAD**: This is often used to verify the availability and metadata of a feature without downloading its content.

- **OPTIONS**: An OPTION requirement is used to describe communication options for the destination feature. It can be used to consult the server about the supported methods and other information about the feature.

Verbs are very important to determine which type of operation will be performed by an API. As we can see from the preceding list, there are some verbs that are similar to each other, such as POST and PUT. Both can be used to create and update resources. However, using the right verb means the integration process can always be easily understood. There is no strict rule for the use of certain verbs, but it is a good practice to use the right ones.

## REST

REST is an architectural style, a set of constraints and principles that encourage stateless, scalable, and easily maintainable web service design.

One of the characteristics of REST services is stateless communication, where each request from a client to a server must contain all the information necessary to understand and process the request. The server must not store any information about the client's state between requests. This ensures that requests can be handled independently, making the system scalable and easy to maintain.

There is also the concept of resources, be it a physical object, a conceptual entity, or a piece of data. Each resource is identified by a unique URL.

REST services use standard HTTP methods to perform **Create, Read, Update, Delete** (**CRUD**) operations on resources. Each HTTP method corresponds to a specific action on the resource. For example, GET is used to retrieve data, POST to create a new resource, PUT to update a resource, and DELETE to remove a resource. This approach provides a uniform and consistent interface for interacting with resources. This means that the same HTTP verbs and methods are used consistently across different resources.

HTTP codes are important and enable easy integrations and use of APIs. HTTP status codes, in the same way, make API responses standardized and allow applications to handle different scenarios appropriately.

## HTTP status codes

HTTP status codes indicate the result of an HTTP request and help clients understand the result of their actions. These status codes are essential for effective communication between clients and servers.

HTTP status codes are grouped into five classes:

- Information responses (100-199)
- Successful responses (200-299)
- Redirection responses (300-399)
- Client error responses (400-499)
- Server error responses (500-599)

> **HTTP status code references**
> You can learn more about status codes here: `https://httpwg.org/specs/rfc9110.html#overview.of.status.codes`.

Each status code has a return type that can be used by the client application or even the browser. When making an HTTP request, the response has a header, where the HTTP status code is located, and there may even be a body providing further details about the request response.

In general, the main HTTP status codes used are these:

- **200 OK**: Indicates a successful request
- **201 Created**: Indicates that a resource was created successfully
- **400 Bad Request**: Indicates an error in the client request
- **401 Unauthorized**: Indicates that the client does not have proper authentication
- **404 Not Found**: Indicates that the requested resource does not exist
- **500 Internal Server Error**: Indicates a server-side problem

The following code represents an example of a successful response to an API request:

```
HTTP/1.1 200 OK
Content-Type: application/json
{
    "status": "success",
    "message": "Data retrieved successfully",
    "data": {
        "id": 123,
        "name": "Example Resource",
        "description": "This is an example resource
          for the API.",
        "created_at": "2023-10-26T10:00:00Z"
    }
}
```

In this example, the status code (in the first line of code) is 200, indicating that the request was successful. Furthermore, there is a body in the response containing more information.

Using HTTP status codes appropriately allows APIs to be easily integrated into different types of systems. As we create our APIs using them, this will become clearer.

BaaS delivery offers several benefits for teams to segregate the responsibilities of each context into applications that can be easily integrated into different scenarios. We've learned enough about the fundamentals of APIs; it's time to start creating APIs using the ASP.NET Core 9 minimal APIs.

## Exploring minimal APIs

One of the ways to create web services in ASP.NET Core 9 is to use the minimal APIs approach, which offers a simple way to make APIs available and add features and configurations as needed.

The simple structure of minimal APIs allows developers and teams to provide REST-based functionalities in an agile manner.

There are many applicable scenarios for using this approach, and the one you choose will depend on the size of the project and the teams involved. The fact is that minimal APIs offer, in general, the same functionalities as the controller-based model, which we will discuss in the next section.

To create a minimal API project, we will base ourselves on a product management model. To do this, we will provide an API according to the following table:

| Route | Description | Request Body | Response Body |
|-------|-------------|--------------|---------------|
| GET /Product | Get all products | None | Array of products |
| GET /Product/{id} | Get a product by ID | None | A product object |
| POST /Product | Add a new product | Product object | A product object |
| PUT /Product/{id} | Update an existing product | Product Item | None |
| DELETE /Product/{id} | Delete an existing product by ID | None | None |

*Table 3.1 - Product management actions*

The Table 3.1 basically maps the routes that will be used in the product API, mapping the corresponding HTTP verbs.

We can also see in the table that some routes are similar, differing only by the HTTP verbs used. This is a convention used by the REST model, where HTTP verbs indicate the intention for a given resource.

In this case, the resource is the product, defined by the /Product route. In some cases, the /Product/{id} route indicates that there will be a parameter added to the resource route. This parameter will be part of the resource URL and will be mapped as a parameter of the method to be executed in the API.

Now let's create a minimal API project and implement product registration:

1. Open your operating system's command prompt, in a directory of your choice, and run the following line of code:

    ```
    dotnet new web --name ProductAPI
    ```

2. The web project template is a shortcut for creating an empty ASP.NET Core project, which will be used as the minimal API.

    A folder called ProductAPI will be created containing all the files needed for the project. The main file is Program.cs.

3. Navigate to the ProductAPI directory and then type the following command and press *Enter*:

    ```
    Code.
    ```

The Visual Studio Code editor will appear.

4.  Then, open the `Program.cs` file, which will have the following structure:

```
var builder = WebApplication.CreateBuilder(args);
var app = builder.Build();
app.MapGet("/", () => "Hello World!");
app.Run();
```

As we can see, there is no definition of a class. This is the main application file, the entry point that will be used to execute the API.

In the first two lines of the file, we have the app definition, through the web application builder class. This definition was presented in *Chapter 2*, where we discussed the structure of a project in ASP.NET Core 9. However, it is important to note that the app will be created with some basic configurations, abstracted by the framework, such as filters and settings, among other aspects.

Another important aspect of this file is the `MapGet` method of the `app` variable. This is a method that extends the previously created app, allowing the creation of a route that will be accessed via URL using the HTTP GET verb.

This method has a parameter that defines the route pattern; in this case, / is used, which means the root of the application. The second parameter is an action, which uses one of C#'s features. This action will be executed when this route is requested.

---

**Actions and methods**

Actions can be seen as methods defined inline and are composed of two main parts, just like methods:

- **Setting parameters**: Setting parameters if necessary

- **Action body**: The code that will be executed

Actions can be replaced by methods, instead of being defined inline.

---

5.  To perform a test, just run the application by typing the following command at the prompt:

```
dotnet run
```

6.  Logs containing the API URL will be displayed. Now, open **Postman**, select **File | New Tab**, enter the application address, and then click **Send**:

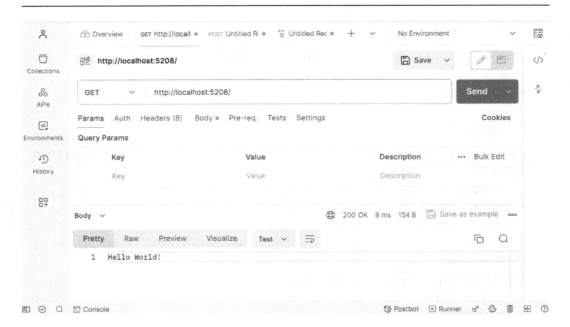

Figure 3.2 – Getting an API resource using a minimal API

As we can see, in just a few lines of code, it was possible to execute an API, even returning a simple `Hello World` string.

The minimal API offers the ability to quickly make APIs available in a simple way and allow other features and configurations to be added according to a project's needs. This brings great agility to teams.

Let's add some features to the `ProductAPI` project. To do this, create a class called `Product.cs` in the root of the project. The class will be defined according to the following code:

```
public class Product
{
    public int Id {get; set;}
    public string Name { get; set; }
    public decimal Price { get; set; }
}
```

We are just defining an object that will represent a product. Now you will need to change the `Program.cs` file; we will include the methods listed in the preceding table, mapping the API routes and adding functionality to the API methods.

The `Program.cs` file will contain some methods as shown in the following example:

```
var builder = WebApplication.CreateBuilder(args);
var app = builder.Build();
```

```
List<Product> products = new List<Product>();

app.MapGet("/Product", () => Results.Ok(products));

app.MapGet("/Product/{id}", (int id) => {
    var product = products.FirstOrDefault(p => p.Id == id);

    return Results.Ok(product);
});

app.MapPost("/Product", (Product product) => {

    if (product != null)
    {
        product.Id = products.Count() + 1;
        products.Add(product);
    }

    return Results.Ok(product);
});

app.MapPut("/Product/{id}", (int id,
  Product updatedProduct) => {

    if (updatedProduct != null)
    {
        var oldProduct = products.FirstOrDefault
          (p => p.Id == id);

        if (oldProduct == null) return Results.NotFound();

        oldProduct.Name = updatedProduct.Name;
        oldProduct.Price = updatedProduct.Price;

    }
    return Results.NoContent();
});

app.MapDelete("/Product/{id}", (int id) => {

    var product = products.FirstOrDefault(p => p.Id == id);
```

```
    if (product == null) return Results.NotFound();

    products.Remove(product);

    return Results.NoContent();
});

app.Run();
```

As we can see, the APIs were created similarly to the previously defined route table, respecting the HTTP verbs defined through the `MapGet`, `MapPost`, `MapPut`, and `MapDelete` methods.

The code in question is very simple, creating a simulation of a product register. To do this, a variable was defined using the code `List<Product> products = new List<Product>()`, which will contain the products available in the API at runtime.

Another important functionality described in the preceding code is the use of the utility class called `Results`. This class is used in all methods, encapsulating important functionalities for returning the request, such as defining the status code related to the request in the response header.

Let's look at the API for the POST verb in more detail.

The `MapPost` method defines the `/Products` string as a route and as an action; it expects a product as a parameter, adds it to the list, and returns OK (status code 200).

But how do we submit a product to the API? ASP.NET Core 9 has the concept of a **bind**, which processes the request and creates and maps an object according to the request's needs. In this case, an object in JSON format must be sent, which will be mapped to a product object when the POST method is executed.

This is an excellent feature of ASP.NET Core 9, which abstracts all the complexity and, during the execution of a route, resolves the parameters expected by the action.

Let's add a product using the API with the following commands:

1.  Run the application with the following command:

    ```
    dotnet run
    ```

2.  Then open Postman and go to **File | New Tab**.

3.  Set the method to POST and add the API address with the `/Product` suffix.

4.  Then select the **Body** tab, as shown in *Figure 3.3*.

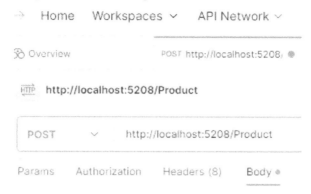

Figure 3.3 – Configuring a POST request

5.  Select the **raw** option and then set the type to **JSON**, as shown in *Figure 3.4*.

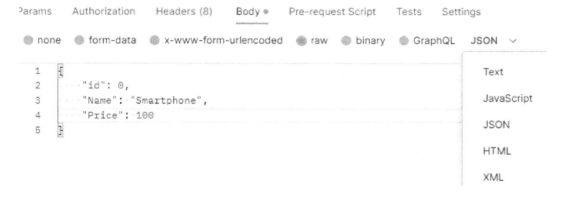

Figure 3.4 – Defining the request body

6.  Add the following JSON:

```
{
    "id": 0,
    "Name": "Smartphone",
    "Price": 100
}
```

The preceding code just represents a JSON object that has the properties of a product. These properties were defined in the `Product.cs` class that was added to the project. You can see the full code through the book's source code link, provided in the *Technical requirements* section.

7.    Click on the **Send** button.

Figure 3.5 – POST request result

As a result, the registered product object was returned. Note the HTTP status code highlighted in *Figure 3.5*, with the value 200 and the description OK.

When executing a POST call to the API, ASP.NET Core identified a route mapped to the HTTP verb. Then, it binds the JSON object, sent as the request body, to the product object, defined as the POST request parameter. After that, the action request is made, which finally registers a product in the memory list and returns it, again serialized in JSON.

As we learned, it is very simple to create an API using a minimal API. With just a few lines of code, it was possible to create a complete product register. Of course, as it is a .NET platform project, it is possible to define different classes to better structure your projects, since as the complexity increases, along with the number of APIs, it will become very difficult to manage all the routes in just one file.

However, even though a minimal API supports most ASP.NET Core 9 functionality for creating web APIs, using a more structured and prepared approach for large projects can be a great option, and this is the case for controller-based projects, which we will discuss in the next section.

## Implementing APIs using the controller-based approach

Controller-based projects are another way to deliver APIs using ASP.NET Core 9. This project type also implements the **Model-View-Controller** (**MVC**) pattern, which we learned about in *Chapter 2*.

The controller-based approach has a more complete and robust structure to deliver any type of API, so it supports different business contexts. In the same way as minimal APIs, it is possible to extend API functionalities by adding different types of configurations and customizations.

## Creating a controller-based API

To create a controller-based API, you just need to type the following code in the terminal, in a directory of your choice:

```
dotnet new webapi -n ProductMVC -controllers true
```

This command uses the `webapi` template, which by default creates a minimal API project. In this case, we are adding a `-controllers` argument to state that a web API should be created using the controller-based approach.

As we can see in *Figure 3.6*, the structure of the controller-based API project is very similar to MVC, which we learned about in *Chapter 2*.

Figure 3.6 – Controller-based project structure

The difference between this project and minimal APIs is the segregation of responsibilities and organization of the project. Since each controller is related to a specific resource, there is no need to implement all the API code in the `Program.cs` file, in addition to bringing greater possibilities, especially in larger projects.

However, the approach to configurations and extensions is similar to what we learned about in regard to minimal APIs; it is all done through the `Program.cs` file.

The default project has some settings already defined, which can be easily modified. The following code is from the `Program.cs` file, which is created automatically:

```
var builder = WebApplication.CreateBuilder(args);
builder.Services.AddControllers();
builder.Services.AddEndpointsApiExplorer();
builder.Services.AddSwaggerGen();

var app = builder.Build();
```

```
if (app.Environment.IsDevelopment())
{
    app.UseSwagger();
    app.UseSwaggerUI();
}

app.UseHttpsRedirection();

app.UseAuthorization();

app.MapControllers();

app.Run();
```

At this point, we will focus on two main configurations added in the file, which concern the `AddEndpointsApiExplorer` and `MapControllers` methods. The rest of the methods will be discussed later:

- `AddEndpointsApiExplorer`: This is an extension method that aims to register services that are used to expose information about the application's endpoints. This information is used by API documentation generation services, such as **Swagger**, which we will discuss in the next section.

- `MapControllers`: This is an application configuration responsible for mapping added attributes into controller classes and, therefore, automatically defining APIs and routes.

These methods allow the application to adapt more easily to the need to expose services as APIs and enable the implementation of good practices, making any additions and modifications more dynamic.

Using the same example of a product service previously created in the minimal API approach, let's understand this implementation adapted for the controller model.

## Understanding the product controller

The implementation of the product API using the controller-based approach follows the class definition model. Therefore, each API must have a controller, which will be responsible for processing requests for each resource.

Based on the previous example, the product API will have the following definition:

```
[ApiController]
[Route("[controller]")]
public class ProductController : ControllerBase
```

```
{
    [HttpGet]
    public IActionResult Get()
    {
        // ..
    }


    [HttpGet("{id}")]
    public IActionResult Get(int id)
    {
        // ..
    }

    [HttpPost]
    public IActionResult Post(Product product)
    {
        //..
    }

    [HttpPut]
    public IActionResult Put(int id,
        Product updatedProduct)
    {

//..
    }

    [HttpDelete]
    public IActionResult Delete(int id)
    {
        //..
    }
}
```

Some code blocks have been omitted to make it easier to read and understand the most important points in this class definition.

The class represents a controller that will handle requests to the product API.

Let's analyze some details of the code:

- ApiController: This is an attribute that is added to a class, causing it to be mapped as an API controller. This way, when adding the MapController configuration to the Program. cs file, all classes marked as attributes will be responsible for processing requests from the respective APIs.

- `Route`: This attribute can be used either in a controller, represented by a class, or in an action, represented by a method. Its function is to define a URL pattern for the route. The `[controller]` parameter is a token that is automatically replaced, at runtime, by the class name, without the `controller` suffix. For the route to take the method name into account, in the case of annotating an action with the route attribute, the `[action]` token must be used.

- `ProductController`: This is the name of the class following the MVC convention. There is no obligation to use this suffix, but it is a good practice, as controllers do not need to be in the `Controllers` folder, making it easier for other members of a development team to read.

- `ControllerBase`: All controller classes should inherit from the `ControllerBase` class, which is appropriate for APIs. This class provides many properties and methods that are useful for handling HTTP requests.

- `HttpGet`: This attribute determines the HTTP verb that an action should respond to processing. For each verb, there is a different attribute. In the preceding example, there are two GET methods, but one is an overload, with one parameter. For the controller to know which GET method should be requested, a different route must be defined for methods with the same name. In this case, the second GET method has an `{id}` parameter, which will be included in the route, differentiating the actions. The ASP.NET Core 9 framework will take care of binding the method's `id` parameter.

As we can see, a big difference in relation to the innovative approach of the minimal API is the ability to segregate responsibility into different controllers. Furthermore, the controller-based approach brings other features that are important in large projects, such as various types of utilities, both through the framework and other resources available in `ControllerBase`, such as bind resources and model validations.

## ControllerBase utilities

As mentioned previously, the `ControllerBase` class has several properties and methods that are useful for handling HTTP requests, making the APIs capable of handling requests using REST API best practices and conventions.

The standard for communication between applications through HTTP is extensive, and a book entirely dedicated to this subject would be needed in order to cover it properly. However, let's address some patterns used in the `ProductController` class.

As we learned at the beginning of the chapter, requests in APIs are made to a specific resource, and for each request, there is an intention associated with a verb. Each request has a set of information that is sent to the API, such as a body and headers. Likewise, after being processed, this request returns headers and, in addition, may contain a body. An HTTP status code is also defined in the response.

This entire pattern is abstracted by the methods available in `ControllerBase`, which takes care of the return definitions for each request.

Let's analyze the GET method for retrieving a product by id:

```
public IActionResult Get(int id)
    {
        var product = ProductService.Get(id);

        if (product is null) return NotFound();

        return Ok(product);
    }
```

The purpose of this method is to return a product according to the ID, passed as a parameter to the method. This API could be used, for example, in a frontend, where the user clicks on a product link to see its details. Since the API consumer does not have access to the implementation details, the API needs to be consistent in returning appropriate responses.

In the case of the preceding method, if the product is not found, a NotFound response is returned, using the HTTP status code 404. This is the same approach as when trying to access a non-existent URL through the browser, which generally displays a 404 message, stating that a resource was not found.

On the other hand, if the product is found, an Ok response is returned, using the HTTP status code 200. Note that the Ok method has one parameter, which is exactly the product found. In this case, this object will be serialized in JSON format and returned to the client. The Ok method is responsible for serializing the object and creating the response taking into account the body, the serialized product object, and the headers, including stating that Content-Type is application/json. This way, the client can process the message return correctly.

The ControllerBase class has several other methods that abstract the complexity of interacting with the HTTP protocol in addition to implementing REST standards and conventions.

It is important to note that APIs serve different types of clients, whether they are web-ready frontends, operating systems, or mobile applications, and they even allow integration between systems. Each of these consumers does not have any details about the API implementations, having access only to the signatures of the required methods and parameters, as well as the possible returns.

Therefore, it is necessary to use standards and conventions correctly, making the API consistent and interoperable between consumers.

---

**More details**

If you want to know more about the ControllerBase class, see the documentation at the following link: https://learn.microsoft.com/en-us/dotnet/api/microsoft.aspnetcore.mvc.controllerbase?view=aspnetcore-9.0.

The ASP.NET Core 9 abstracts most of the complexity involved in this service delivery model by using APIs, in addition to providing other types of functionality such as a consistent validation model and object binding.

## Working with binding

Binds are important features available in ASP.NET Core. Their main function is to translate or adapt the API request model to the actions that are performed in the controller.

As we observed in our examples of the `ProductController` call, the methods receive as parameters these primitive types, such as `int`, or even complex types, such as objects of type `product`.

Each method or action has a signature or interface, which describes the attributes required, if any, for the method or action to be processed. When you make a request for action and enter the attributes according to the action signature, these will be mapped by the ASP.NET Core pipeline execution flow, which will bind the information for each attribute entered, taking into account its type, attribute name, and value.

For example, the `product` object has the following attributes:

```
public int Id {get; set;}
public string Name { get; set; }
public decimal Price { get; set; }
```

This object represented in JSON format would be defined as follows:

```
{
  "id": 1,
  "name": "Smartphone",
  "price": 1000.0
}
```

As we can see, the objects are identical but represented differently. ASP.NET Core does the work of transforming the JSON `product` object into a C# `product` object, mapping the properties according to the name.

This is a standard behavior of the framework, but there is the possibility of customizing and even binding different aspects of a request.

As we know, a request has a body, URL, query string parameters, and also parameters that are sent through forms. A request has an abstraction in a C# object called `HttpRequest`. You can easily access all the properties of a request through the `Request` property of the previously mentioned `ControllerBase` class.

If it is necessary, for example, to obtain a value in a query string, the following code can be used:

```
string fullname1 = Request.QueryString["fullname"];
string fullname2 = Request["fullname"];
```

However, this same value could be obtained from the query string, using the bind model provided by the FromQuery attribute:

```
[HttpGet]
public IActionResult GetTasks([FromQuery]bool
   isCompleted = false)
    {

// ..
   }
```

As we can see in the preceding code, isCompleted was annotated with the FromQuery attribute. This way, ASP.NET will be responsible for binding the query string to the action parameter. In this case, it is expected that the query string has the same name as the method parameter. But if this is not the case, just use an attribute overload and define the parameter name, as follows:

```
public IActionResult GetTasks([FromQuery("completed")]bool
   isCompleted = false) { /**/ }
```

There are other types of attributes that can be used to perform binding:

| Attribute | HTTP verb | When to use | Data format | Example of use |
|---|---|---|---|---|
| FromBody | POST, PUT, PATH | Use to bind parameter data from the request body. It can only be used once per action method, as it assumes the entire request body is used to bind to the action's parameter. | JSON, XML | `[HttpPost]`<br><br>`public IActionResult Create([FromBody] Product product) { ... }` |
| FromForm | POST | Use to bind parameter data from form fields. | Form data (key-value pairs) | `[HttpPost]`<br><br>`public IActionResult Update([FromForm] ProductUpdateDto dto) { ... }` |

| Attribute | HTTP verb | When to use | Data format | Example of use |
|---|---|---|---|---|
| `FromService` | Any | Use to inject services directly into action methods. This is useful for obtaining services without using constructor injection. | Depends on the service being injected | ```public IActionResult Get([FromServices] IProductService productService) { ... }``` |
| `FromHeader` | Any | Use when you need to retrieve data from HTTP headers. Useful for tokens or API versioning. | Simple string or comma-separated values in a single header | ```public IActionResult Get([FromHeader(Name = "X-Custom-Header")] string value) { ... }``` |
| `FromQuery` | GET | Use to bind parameters from the query string of the URL. Ideal for filtering or pagination parameters in a RESTful API. | Simple types such as strings, integers, or custom string-convertible types | ```public IActionResult Search([FromQuery] string keyword) { ... }``` |
| `FromRoute` | Any | Use when parameter values are embedded in the URL path. Typically used with REST URLs that include resource IDs. | Simple types compatible with URL segments | ```[HttpGet("{id}")] public IActionResult GetById([FromRoute] int id) { ... }``` |

Each of these parameters can be used as a means of customizing the bind model in each action of a controller.

> **Custom binds**
>
> In some cases, the default bind model available in ASP.NET Core may be limited in relation to the needs of an application, which can often have other, more complex types. With this, it is possible to implement customized binds. This implementation is outside the scope of this book, but you can learn more here: `https://learn.microsoft.com/en-us/aspnet/core/mvc/advanced/custom-model-binding?view=aspnetcore-9.0`.

The binds model available in ASP.NET Core abstracts much of the implementation complexity by taking care of filling in the values that each action requires. However, there is no guarantee that the parameters were filled in correctly in accordance with the application's business rules. To do this, you need to perform validations, and ASP.NET Core offers a powerful validation model.

## Performing validations

When it comes to creating robust APIs, model validation is one of the fundamental pillars. ASP.NET Core 9 makes this process easier and more powerful than ever, thanks to **ModelState**. Think of it as a border guard that checks and validates data before it enters the core of your application.

ModelState is a framework in ASP.NET Core that acts to verify that data complies with the rules defined in your models. If a piece of data does not meet the validation criteria, ModelState marks it as invalid.

Let's take a look at the product registration API:

```
[HttpPost]
    public IActionResult Post(Product product)
    {
        if (product == null) return BadRequest();

        if (!ModelState.IsValid)
          return BadRequest(ModelState);

        // ..
    }
```

As we can see, there is a condition that evaluates the ModelState.IsValid property. If false, then an HTTP status code of 400 (for a bad request) is returned, containing a body that will represent the ModelState object:

```
{
    "Name": [
        "The field Name is required"
    ]
}
```

ModelState is actually a dictionary, which, when serialized in JSON format, is represented by an object. Each object property represents a validated property. The value of each object property is represented by an array of strings that contains the validation results.

In order for ModelState to consider the model valid or not, it is necessary to annotate the properties of the objects with validation attributes; otherwise, the validations will be disregarded.

The product class was changed by adding validation to the Name attribute, as in the following code:

```
public class Product
{
    public int Id {get; set;}
    [Required(ErrorMessage ="The field Name is required")]
```

```
[MinLength(3, ErrorMessage = "The Name field must have

at least 3 characters.")]
    public string Name { get; set; }
    public decimal Price { get; set; }
}
```

As we can see, the Name property is considered mandatory and, in addition, must have at least three characters. This way, it is possible to combine validation attributes in the same property, and this is managed by ModelState through the execution flow of an action, provided by ASP.NET Core 9.

Validations are part of an API, whether through attributes added to models or even manually, in the body of an action, using the ModelState.AddModelError method, as shown in the following example:

```
if (product.Price < 0) ModelState.AddModelError("Price",
  "The Price field cannot have a value less than zero.");

      if (!ModelState.IsValid)
        return BadRequest(ModelState);
```

> **Other attributes**
>
> ASP.NET Core also offers several other attributes that can be used as model validation: https://learn.microsoft.com/en-us/aspnet/core/mvc/models/validation?view=aspnetcore-9.0#built-in-attributes.

As we can see, ASP.NET Core 9 provides a great feature for managing the states of models used by APIs, with parameters or even objects, allowing us to have the ability to carry out validations in a rich way on the application's endpoints, in addition to giving us a simple way to maintain the integrity of information.

These features become even more powerful with the use of approaches such as documentation, response formatting, and error management. Therefore, in the next section, we will see how to make APIs even more consistent for consumers.

# Working with documentation

APIs are a powerful resource for delivering an application's business model through services, and for an API project to be made available properly, it is important to add features that standardize the interaction model with customers.

To achieve this, every API must be documented, allowing customers to know which resources are available and how this documentation is done.

So, let's learn how we can benefit from API feature documentation automatically using Swagger's NuGet package, which implements the OpenAPI specification.

## Documenting APIs with Swagger

APIs are consumed by clients and other applications through the HTTP protocol, where there is a request and a response. For this communication to happen, it is necessary to have knowledge about what is provided by the API, in this case, which methods are available and which contracts are used to establish connections.

To do this, we have to establish a source of knowledge about the resources made available by APIs, such as methods, HTTP verbs, parameters, and bodies. To achieve this objective, it is necessary to have documentation.

However, this documentation needs to be dynamic, since, especially during the development process, APIs can constantly change, adding functionalities or new features. It would be laborious to make changes to each bit of documentation and send it to all API consumers.

ASP.NET Core 9 still supports Swagger for providing API documentation. However, Swagger is no longer part of the project template by default as it was in previous releases. New projects can now support OpenAPI document generation in controller-based and minimal API applications. The OpenAI specification provides a programming language-agnostic approach to API documentation. As such, ASP.NET Core 9 provides built-in support for generating endpoint information in an application through the **Microsoft.AspNetCore.OpenAI** package, avoiding dependencies on external libraries.

Therefore, in order to have documentation, as well as an experience of using a UI to test the APIs, we will integrate the API project with Swagger, which is easy-to-use suite of API developer tools, in addition to implementing the OpenAPI specification standards.

---

**OpenAPI Specification**

The OpenAPI Specification is part of the Linux Foundation and aims to specify RESTFul interfaces to provide ease in the development and consumption of APIs. You can learn more about OpenAPI at `https://spec.openapis.org/oas/latest.html`.

To learn more about ASP.NET Core 9 OpenAPI, visit the following URL: `https://learn.microsoft.com/en-us/aspnet/core/fundamentals/openapi/overview?view=aspnetcore-9.0`

When integrating it into your API solution, Swagger acts as a specification generator in the OpenAPI format, which is based on a JSON file, where all the APIs available in your application are described:

```json
{
  "openapi": "3.0.1",
  "info": {
    "title": "API V1",
    "version": "v1"
  },
  "paths": {
    "/api/Todo": {
      "get": {
        "tags": [
          "Todo"
        ],
        "operationId": "ApiTodoGet",
        "responses": {
          "200": {
            "description": "Success",
            "content": {
              "text/plain": {
                "schema": {
                  "type": "array",
                  "items": {
                    "$ref": "#/components/schemas/ToDoItem"
                  }
                }
              },
              "application/json": {
                "schema": {
                  "type": "array",
                  "items": {
                    "$ref": "#/components/schemas/ToDoItem"
                  }
                }
              },
              "text/json": {
                "schema": {
                  "type": "array",
                  "items": {
                    "$ref": "#/components/schemas/ToDoItem"
                  }
                }
              }
            }
          }
```

```
                    }
                  }
                }
              },
              "post": {
                ...
              }
            },
            "/api/Todo/{id}": {
              "get": {
                ...
              },
              "put": {
                ...
              },
              "delete": {
                ...
              }
            }
          },
          "components": {
            "schemas": {
              "ToDoItem": {
                "type": "object",
                "properties": {
                  "id": {
                    "type": "integer",
                    "format": "int32"
                  },
                  "name": {
                    "type": "string",
                    "nullable": true
                  },
                  "isCompleted": {
                    "type": "boolean"
                  }
                },
                "additionalProperties": false
              }
            }
          }
        }
```

The preceding JSON describes the resources available for an API, the response schema, and the available verbs, in addition to the prediction of objects used in the API.

To integrate Swagger into a project, we must add the Nuget package by running the following command on the command line, in the project directory:

```
dotnet add package Swashbuckle.AspNetCore
```

Next, we must change the Program.cs file. We will perform this configuration for the Product MVC project, and you can analyze the changed code, adding Swagger, in the code below:

```
var builder = WebApplication.CreateBuilder(args);
builder.Services.AddControllers();
builder.Services.AddEndpointsApiExplorer();
builder.Services.AddSwaggerGen();
var app = builder.Build();
if (app.Environment.IsDevelopment())
{
    app.UseSwagger();
    app.UseSwaggerUI();
}
app.UseHttpsRedirection();
app.UseAuthorization();
app.MapControllers();
app.Run();
```

The implementation consists of the following:

- Line 4 adds the Swagger generation services through the `builder.Services.AddSwaggerGen()` method.

- Between lines 6 and 10, we have the addition of Swagger to the ASP.NET execution pipeline, through the `app.UseSwagger()` method, and also the provision of the UI through the `app.UseSwaggerUI()` method. These methods are only executed if the application is running in development mode, `if (app.Environment.IsDevelopment)`.

When running the application, simply access the API link with the swagger suffix, as shown in *Figure 3.7*:

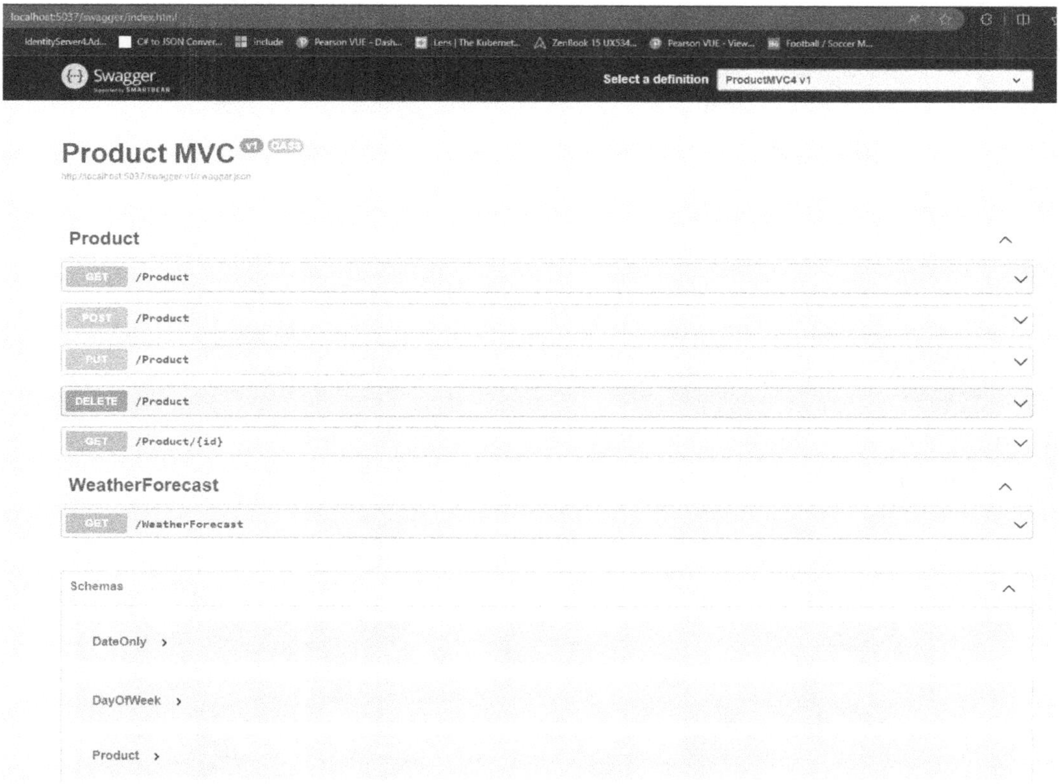

Figure 3.7 – Swagger UI for the Product MVC API

Looking at *Figure 3.7*, we can see that the methods available in the product API were listed in the UI, in addition to the specification of the objects worked on the API. No changes were required to the source code.

Swagger identifies the controllers and actions available in the source code, generates the specification, and consequently generates the UI. However, more details can be added to the documentation in order to enrich the API usage model. Let's take a closer look at how to improve documentation using the features available in the Swagger package.

## Improving the documentation

As we learned previously, Swagger is added by default in ASP.NET Core 9 API projects and automatically generates a UI containing a minimum version of the usage details of the API, inferring the data by reading the controllers and actions.

As we can see in *Figure 3.8*, to add a product, it is necessary to provide JSON as the body of the request; in addition, we have a description of the response, containing the HTTP status code 200, which represents the success.

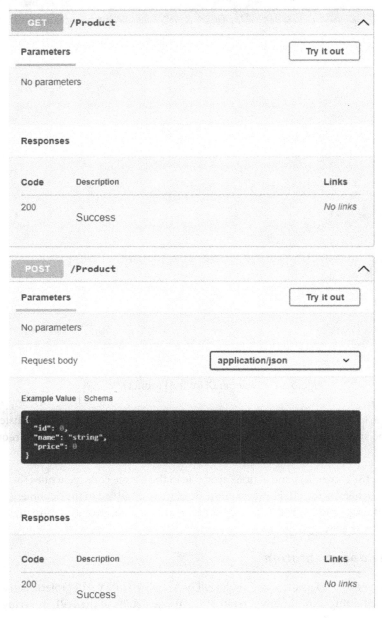

Figure 3.8 – Documentation details for an API

However, if we look at the POST method code (made available through the `ProductController` class available in the book repository mentioned in the *Technical requirements* section), which registers a product, there is no explicit definition of the HTTP status code 200:

```
[HttpPost]
    public IActionResult Post(Product product)
    {
        if (product == null) return BadRequest();

        if (product.Price < 0)
          ModelState.AddModelError("Price",
          "The Price field cannot have a value less
          than zero.");

        if (!ModelState.IsValid)
          return BadRequest(ModelState);

        product.Id = ProductService.Products.Count() + 1;
        ProductService.Add(product);

        return CreatedAtAction(nameof(Get),
            new {id = product.Id}, product);
    }
```

The method returns two possible HTTP status codes, which are 400, represented by calling the `BadRequest` method, and 201, which is represented by the `CreatedAtAction` method.

As we can see in *Figure 3.8*, there is a button labeled **Try it out**. Upon clicking this button, the UI will be prepared so that it is possible to add the request body, which in this case will be some JSON that represents a product and its respective properties. Modify the JSON to add a new product, defining the properties as in the example proposed in *Figure 3.9*.

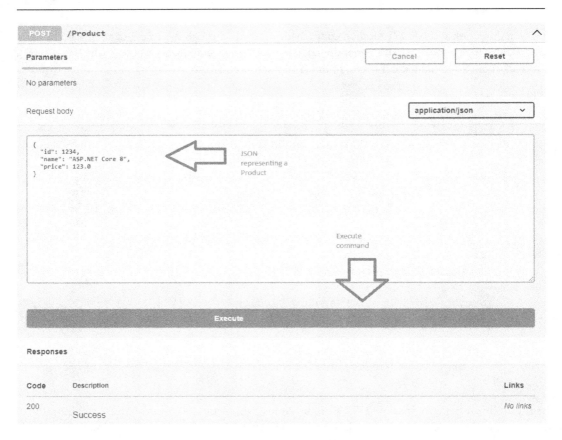

Figure 3.9 – Running an API request from the Swagger UI

After defining the body of the request, click the **Execute** button. Just make sure your application is running.

At the end of the execution, the Swagger UI displays the API response, and as we can clearly see in *Figure 3.10*, we have an HTTP status code of 201, in addition to the JSON of the newly registered product and some information in the header.

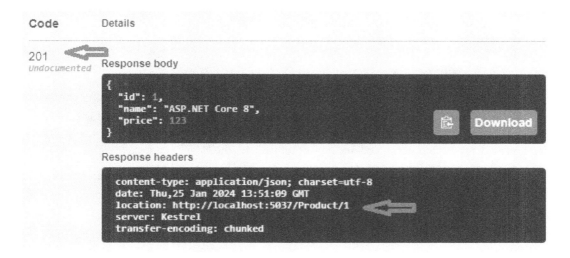

Figure 3.10 – Swagger API Response screen

The `CreatedAtAction` method creates a response with HTTP status code 201 and adds a link to the header to access the resource created using the GET method, as highlighted in the preceding figure using the address `http://localhost:5037/Product/1`. This address may vary depending on the execution address in your environment.

This type of return is good practice and follows the standards defined in the REST protocol. However, although it is not a major problem in the context in which we are presenting the examples, API consumers must be clear about how to consume and what to expect in return to properly deal with each response. In the case of the product registration method, there being no information means that this method would also return an error status, which could cause some non-compliance for the API consumer.

To adjust this behavior, we must add more information to the API methods using attributes provided by ASP.NET Core 9 such as `ProducesResponseType` and `Consumes`.

The `ProducesResponseType` attribute is used to determine the type of HTTP status code that will be returned as a response and also the type of content that will be returned. This attribute can also be used in the generic version, typing the return.

The `Consumes` attribute determines the type of content expected by the API. The content is defined as a media type and the complete list can be obtained through the `MediaTypeNames` class available in the `System.Net.Mime` namespace.

Let's analyze the new implementation of the POST method with the addition of attributes:

```
[HttpPost]
[Consumes(MediaTypeNames.Application.Json)]
[ProducesResponseType<Product>(StatusCodes
  .Status201Created)]
```

```
[ProducesResponseType(StatusCodes.Status400BadRequest)]
    public IActionResult Post(Product product)
    {
        // code omitted for readability
    }
```

As we can see in the preceding code, the `ProducesResponseType` attribute can be added as many times as necessary to represent different return types. In this example, the HTTP status code 201 is being reported, for created items, and one type of return with the HTTP status code 400.

When running the application again, we can observe the changes made to the code and automatically generated in the Swagger UI, according to *Figure 3.11*:

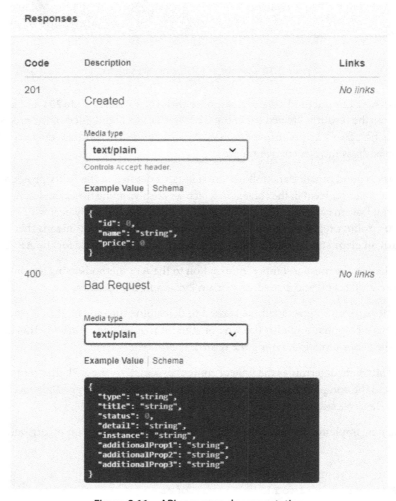

Figure 3.11 – API response documentation

We now have the correct documentation on the aspects involved in the product controller's POST method, which enables the API to be consumed appropriately by taking into account alternative response flows.

---

**XML comments**

In addition to the attributes added to the API methods, it is also possible to use XML comments for each method as part of the Swagger UI documentation. To do this, it will be necessary to configure the project so that the documentation XML is generated during the compilation process and is obtained from the Swagger UI. You can find a complete explanation of this configuration at the following address: `https://learn.microsoft.com/en-us/aspnet/core/tutorials/getting-started-with-swashbuckle?view=aspnetcore-9.0&tabs=visual-studio#xml-comments`.

---

In addition to having the ability to create quality APIs with ASP.NET Core 9, we also have the support of a rich API documentation interface, in addition to the option to execute requests and get more details about the request parameters and response.

Understanding this documentation approach will greatly help you to generate quality services that can be integrated into different systems and contexts. As we progress through the next few chapters, we will further study the use of APIs, documentation, and other technologies such as database connections.

## Summary

In this chapter, we dove deep into the world of HTTP-delivered APIs, discovering the power they have to provide services to a variety of clients. With the robust support of ASP.NET Core, we learned how to make the most of this potential, learning about approaches such as using minimal APIs to create HTTP APIs quickly and efficiently. We also explored the creation of robust APIs using controller-based projects. We looked at other aspects that involve APIs, such as documentation. In the next chapter, we will continue to explore the characteristics of ASP.NET Core 9, understanding how to develop real-time applications using SignalR.

# 4
# Real-Time Interactions with SignalR

As part of ASP.NET Core 9, the web API is a framework for building HTTP services, which can be made available for both web page consumption and mobile applications. The structure provided by the .Net Core platform provides the development of APIs with high quality and performance. In this chapter, we will learn more about WebAPI, including the standards, conventions, and best practices for delivering solutions via a service.

We will work on creating a real-time task management application where we will use various techniques available on the .NET platform and SignalR to learn about the concepts and implement an example of applications that use the Stream concept. We will also explore the premises for hosting SignalR applications on a server.

In this chapter, we're going to cover the following main topics:

- What is SignalR?
- Understanding the concepts of server and clients
- Working with streaming
- Hosting the ASP.NET Core SignalR applications

## Technical requirements

The code examples used in this chapter can be found in the book's GitHub repository:

https://github.com/PacktPublishing/ASP.NET-Core-9.0-Essentials/tree/main/Chapter04

# What is SignalR?

As we learned in previous chapters, web-based applications have two parts: the client and the Server.

A **browser** generally represents the client, where the user interacts with the application. Applications have actions executed on a server to process information and return a response.

This process is based on two phases, which are **request** and **response**. These phases happen in sequence. With each interaction between the client and the server, a new communication process is created.

Most web applications have these features that are sufficient for most business contexts. However, there are scenarios where there is a need for a **real-time communication model**, where the information processed by an application is constantly updated. This provides an immediate response to users, enriching usability and certain functional requirements.

A good example of real-time applications would be, for example, a map application where users have traffic information on a given route, and are notified about any aspects that affect navigation. Furthermore, other types of applications such as games, social networks, or even collaborative web text editors depend on constant updates to users.

To develop applications that contain real-time features, it would be necessary for the server and client to be able to communicate constantly on an active channel.

The .NET platform has SignalR. This is a library that adds the ability to build real-time solutions in a simplified way, instantly allowing constant communication between client and server.

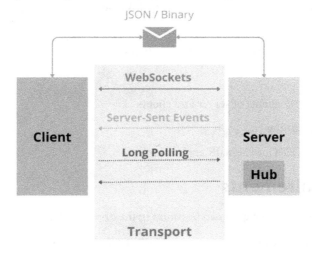

Figure 4.1 – SignalR components

As you can see, *Figure 4.1* demonstrates most of the SignalR components that abstract the communication model between the client and the server. Communication between the client and the server occurs over an active connection, using a transport technique that transports JSON or binary messages. WebSockets is the standard communication technique used by SignalR. The other two options are used as fallback. In other words, if WebSockets is not supported, Server-sent events or long polling will be used immediately. The order of precedence for transport is the same as that established in the following list:

1. **WebSockets**: It provides the ability to establish a *full-duplex connection*, that is, allowing constant communication between client and server.

2. **Server-sent events**: It establishes a *one-way connection* from the Server to the client. The client does not have the ability to send messages to the server over the same connection, requiring a separate HTTP request.

3. **Long polling**: It is a more basic technique whereby the client sends a message to the server. Instead of sending an immediate message, the server then processes the information and only returns the response after finishing.

SignalR abstracts the choice of transport, making it possible to define the use of just WebSocket, if necessary.

The connection between the client and the server depends on an important component called the Hub. The Hub is a special object. It's a part of the SignalR API that acts as a proxy, allowing server-client communication, where the server can execute functions or methods on the client, remotely, through the use of **RPC (Remote Procedure Call)**.

---

RPC

RPC is a communication protocol that has existed since 1970 and serves as the basis for several innovations that currently exist, such as gRPC, a high-performance communication model developed by Google. You can find more information about RPC at `https://en.wikipedia.org/wiki/Remote_procedure_call`.

---

SignalR abstracts all the complexity of connection and communication management, in addition to bringing other capabilities, such as sending notifications to all connected clients, specific clients, or a group of clients. Additionally, APIs can be used in conjunction with .NET applications, even console, Java, and JavaScript.

It is possible, for example, to have a server that communicates with a console application developed on the .NET or even Java platform.

It may seem complex at first, but as we learn about the main concepts and good practices, we will come to understand how powerful the SignalR library is. Let's explore some concepts, patterns, and good practices that involve SignalR and how to develop a real-time application using this library.

# Understanding the concepts of Servers and Clients

As we learned earlier, SignalR is a powerful library that abstracts much of the complexity of creating real-time applications.

However, it is important to know the concepts and standards related to using the SignalR library to benefit from its features.

As we know, web applications basically have two main components, the Client and the Server. Likewise, real-time applications using SignalR require both client and server components. We will learn how these components interact with each other through a task management application.

## Working with a task management application

The task management application will be created using **Razor Pages** technology and have the following functionalities:

- Implement concepts in real time
- Create tasks
- Complete tasks
- View created tasks
- View completed tasks

All functionalities will be resolved using Visual Studio Code. JavaScript will be used to work with the functionalities on the Client side and C# will be used on the Server side.

We can see an outline of the main components used in the application in *Figure 4.2*:

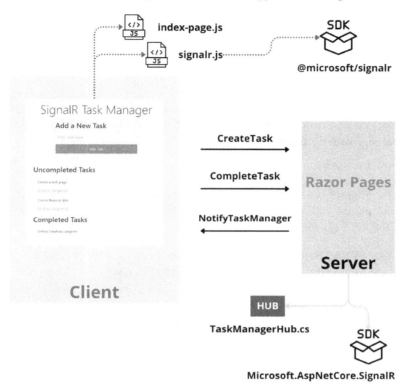

Figure 4.2 – TaskManager application components

As we can see in *Figure 4.2*, we have some important components that will be used in the application.

The Client will be implemented using Razor Pages, which will aim to allow user interaction in relation to the application's functionalities:

- The index-page.js file will be responsible for managing interactions between the server and the application's main page.
- The signalr.js file is part of the SignalR JavaScript SDK.
- The server is the Razor Page application that will act as an orchestrator server.
- The Hub implementation will be responsible for managing real-time communication between the server and the client.

As we create the project, we will explain how each component works and implementation details. For now, let's start with creating the project.

We will focus on the main activities for creating a task manager project. However, you can check the entire implementation of the solution in the book GitHub repository, mentioned in the *Technical requirements* section. Here are the steps we will be following:

1. To create the project, open the terminal in a directory of your choice and run the following command:

```
dotnet new webapp -o TaskManager
```

2. A new folder called `TaskManager` will be created containing the entire project structure. Access this page with the following command:

```
cd TaskManager
```

3. Now that the project has been created, we need to add the SignalR JavaScript SDK. It will not be necessary to add the SDK to the server, as it is automatically added when creating the project, as part of the .NET platform.

As we are using Razor Pages, we will have the client and server in the same project. However, we can create a **Single-Page Application (SPA)** solution and a WebAPI in Asp.NET Core 9 and perform the same procedures.

We will continue with the Razor pages and go to the installation of the SignalR JavaScript SDK. We will use a tool called **LibMan**, which is a **Command Line Interface (CLI)** from Microsoft, responsible for managing client libraries. Its operation is similar to **Node Package Management (NPM)**.

To use it, it is advisable to uninstall any previous version existing on your operating system. Therefore, we'll follow these steps:

1. Run the following commands in sequence to install the tool:

```
dotnet to LibraryManager.Cli ol uninstall -g Microsoft.Web.
dotnet tool install -g Microsoft.Web.LibraryManager.Cli
```

2. Next, we will run the command to install the SignalR SDK. Run the following command and check in the application's main directory:

```
libman install @microsoft/signalr@latest -p unpkg -d wwwroot/js/
signalr --files dist/browser/signalr.js
```

The preceding command avoided installing the `@microsoft/signalr@latest` library and then only added the necessary scripts to the application directories.

At this moment, the project is being created and prepared to receive implementations of real-time features. We must start by creating the Hub and configuring the application.

## Creating the Hub

The Hub is one of the most important components for implementing SignalR. It acts as a proxy that manages the connections of all clients to the server and allows both the client and the server to talk to each other to execute methods in real time.

For our **TaskManager** application, our first task will be to create a Hub and prepare it for communicating with clients. To do this, still in the terminal and the application directory, type the following command:

```
code .
```

This command will open an instance of VS Code in the application directory.

At the root of the project, create a folder called Hubs and then a file called TaskManagerHub.cs.

The project class will have two methods and will look like the code that follows:

```
public class TaskManagerHub : Hub
  {
    public async Task CreateTask(TaskModel taskModel)
    {
      // ..
    }

    public async Task CompleteTask(TaskModel taskModel)
    {
      // ..
    }
  }
```

The first detail to note is inherited from the Hub class. The Hub class is a superclass that abstracts all connection management and interaction with clients, available through the Microsoft. AspNetCore.SignalR package. All custom Hub classes must inherit from this class.

Next, we have the CreateTask and CompleteTask methods. These methods will be invoked through clients and at the same time will invoke methods on clients.

The CreateTask method receives as a parameter a class called TaskModel. This class has been broken into the Model/TaskModel.cs directory:

```
public class TaskModel
  {
    public Guid Id { get; } = Guid.NewGuid();
    public string Name { get; set; }
    public bool IsCompleted { get; set; }
    public TaskModel()
    {
```

```
      IsCompleted = false;
  }


  public TaskModel(string name) : this()
  {
    Name = name;
  }
  public TaskModel(string name, bool isCompleted)
  {
    Name = name;
    IsCompleted = isCompleted;
  }
}
```

As we can see, the TaskModel class only has a few basic properties such as Id, Name, and IsCompleted, which represent a task.

Communication between the client and the server is done through a transport strategy, as mentioned previously, and WebSockets will generally be used. The information transmitted is serialized in JSON or binary. However, binary data, commonly used for audio, images, and videos, is not supported. Only text data will be transmitted.

Now, let's look at the complete implementation of the CreateTask method:

```
public async Task CreateTask(TaskModel taskModel)
  {
    _taskRepository.Save(taskModel);
    await Clients.All.SendAsync(ClientConstants
      .NOTIFY_TASK_MANAGER, taskModel);
  }
```

The preceding code performs two basic procedures:

- **Persist a task**: The _taskRepository property is an interface that abstracts communication with a persistence layer. For this persistence project, it is being done in memory and the complete code for this implementation can be found in the book's GitHub repository (see the *Technical requirements* section).

- **Notify customers**: The Hub base class has a Client property with some functionality. In the code example, a notification is being made to all potential clients connected to Hub. The SendAsync method has 10 overloads of different variations. However, for the preceding code, two main parameters are being used. The first parameter concerns the name of the client method that will process the Hub's response, while the second parameter is the task object itself that will be sent to clients.

> **Constants are best practices**
>
> As we noted in the `SendAsync` method, the first parameter references a constant. This is good practice as it is necessary to know the name of the method that will process the communication made through the server. Since it's a string, it's easy to make mistakes. Use constants whenever necessary to center strings containing method names. This will facilitate maintenance and improvements.

With the Hub implemented, it will now be necessary to configure the application to handle communication through SignalR.

## Preparing the server application

The application needs to be configured to be able to handle connectivity between the client and the server. Without this step, the Hub will have no use.

To do this, we will need to change the code in the `Program.cs` file and add some important lines of code.

We must configure the SignalR services in the application container and map the Hub endpoint that will be used by the client to establish the connection.

At the end of the changes, the file should be similar to the following code:

```
using TaskManager.Hubs;
using TaskManager.Service;
using TaskManager.Service.Contract;
var builder = WebApplication.CreateBuilder(args);

// Add Razor Page services to the container.
builder.Services.AddRazorPages();

//Add SignalR Services
builder.Services.AddSignalR();

// ..
var app = builder.Build();

// Some codes have been omitted to facilitate learning
app.MapRazorPages();

// Add Hub Endpoint
app.MapHub<TaskManagerHub>("/taskmanagerhub");

app.Run();
```

It is very important to follow the order in which the settings were made. The `builder.Services.AddSignalR()` method was added before the `var app = builder.Build()` line. Likewise, the Hub route mapping is added right after the `app.MapRazorPages()` statement.

It is important to note the mapping of the Hub route, configured as `/taskmanagerhub`. The Hub route definition follows the same REST API pattern and this same route will be used so that client applications are able to establish connections with the server. The client will use the previously installed SignalR JavaScript SDK to connect to the Hub.

The Hub is configured and ready to receive connections. Now, it's time to configure the client.

## Preparing the client application

With the Hub configured, we must add the necessary features to the client application. To do this, we will use the `Pages/index.cshtml` page and create the JavaScript that will orchestrate all interactions between the client and the server.

Change the entire contents of the **Index.cshtml** page to the following code:

```
@page
@model IndexModel
@{
    ViewData["Title"] = "Home page";
}
<div class="text-center">
    <h1 class="display-4">SignalR Task Manager</h1>
</div>
<div class="task-form-container">
    <h2>Add a New Task</h2>
    <form method="post" class="task-form">
      <input type="text" id="taskName"
        placeholder="Enter task name"
        class="task-input"/>
      <input type="button" value="Add Task"
        id="addTaskButton" class="task-submit"/>
    </form>
</div>
<div class="tasks-container">
    <h2>Uncompleted Tasks</h2>
    <div class="tasks-list" id="uncompletedTaskList">
      </div>
    <h2>Completed Tasks</h2>
    <div class="tasks-list" id="completedTaskList">
      </div>
</div>
```

```
@section Scripts {
    <script src="~/js/signalr/dist/browser/signalr.js"
      asp-append-version="true"></script>
    <script src="~/js/index/index-page.js"
      asp-append-version="true"></script>
}
```

The HTML available is quite simple, just adding a form containing a field to name the task and a button that will be responsible for sending the new task to the server.

Additionally, there are two lists (completed tasks and uncompleted tasks) that will be displayed according to user interaction. We are not using any Razor Pages directives in the HTML elements, so it will not be necessary to make any changes to the Index.cshtml.cs file.

It is important to note that to facilitate the understanding of the concepts of client and server, together with SignalR, we are using a Razor Pages application. However, it is possible to benefit from another approach called SPA, which makes it possible to use Frameworks such as Angular, React, or VueJS to create applications in JavaScript and HTML that run on the client and interact with the server.

---

SPA

The **TaskManager** application uses Razor Pages to facilitate the explanation of SignalR concepts, concentrating the client and server in the same project. However, SignalR can be installed in a separate application that uses pure JavaScript, typescript, or any framework such as Angular, Vue.js, and so on. Furthermore, the SPA concept is a great practice for developing real-time functionalities. Otherwise, if there are several pages being loaded by the browser, with each new request, a new connection with the server is established. SPA makes it possible to render application pages dynamically while maintaining the same connection when using SignalR.

---

Note that the HTML code uses a @section Scripts {} directive, where the previously installed SignalR libraries and the JavaScript file that we will create are added. This section was defined in the Pages/Shared/_Layout.cshtml file, as we learned in *Chapter 2*.

Create an index-page.js file in the wwwroot/js/index directory. The entire content of this file is available in the application's source code in the book's repository.

Let's focus on the most important points for establishing a connection with the Hub. To do this, we will basically need three main steps:

1.   Create a connection object.

2.   Map the events.

3.   Start the connection.

These three steps are defined in the following code:

```
var connection = new signalR.HubConnectionBuilder()
    .withUrl(HUB_URL).build();
connection.on(NOTIFY_TASK_MANAGER_EVENT, updateTaskList);
connection.start().then(function () {
    addTaskButton.disabled = false;
}).catch(function (err) {
    return console.error(err.toString());
});
```

In the first line, we have the creation of the connection object using a SignalR object. Note that the withUrl(HUB_URL) method uses a constant that must contain the value of the Hub URL. As we are using Razor Pages, the client and server will be available through the same address, and in this case, we can enter a relative URL such as /taskmanagerhub. This URL is exactly the endpoint that was previously mapped on the server.

Next, we have the event implementation that will process the return from the server. In this case, we use the on method of the connection object. This method receives two parameters, the first being a string that represents the event. In this case, the NotifyTaskManager value was set to a constant. The updateTaskList method will process the return. We can use an inline function. However, to facilitate maintenance, we create a separate function that has the following signature:

```
function updateTaskList(taskModel) {
    //Code
}
```

This function could have any name and different types of parameters. However, the methods available in the Hub are sending the client a TaskModel object as a parameter. This object will be serialized in JSON or binary and SignalR will add it to the event corresponding to the processing of this return.

The updateTaskList function just gets the returned object and dynamically feeds the completed or incomplete task lists into the HTML using JavaScript.

> **Best practice**
> It is good practice to use objects as method parameters, both on the client and on the server. This prevents us from having to change method signatures in applications if output and input parameters are modified. The use of objects simplifies information traffic between the client and server.

It is important to note that the name of the event must be the same both on the client and on the server, hence the use of constants to facilitate maintenance and writing.

The third step is to start the connection through the Start method of the connection object. The Start method delivers a promise that is triggered after the connection is established. Additionally, it is possible to implement the catch method, for mapping and any possible error when trying to connect with the Hub.

Now it's time to add the click event to the **Add Task** button, which will be responsible for requesting the addition of a new task, according to the code that follows:

```
var addTaskButton = document
  .getElementById("addTaskButton");
addTaskButton.addEventListener("click", function (event) {
    let taskName = document.getElementById(TASK_NAME_ID);
    connection.invoke(HUB_ADD_TASK_METHOD,
      { name: taskName.value }).catch(function (err) {
        return console.error(err.toString());
    });
    taskName.value = "";
    taskName.focus();
    event.preventDefault();
});
```

The preceding code requests the server through the connection.Invoke() function, having the name of the method available in the Hub and a TaskModel object with the name defined through user input as parameters.

We currently have all the necessary requirements for the **TaskManager** application to have real-time functionality. Although it may seem complex, the approach is simple, requiring the client to be aware of the methods available on the server and the server to be aware of the events that can be executed on the client.

Let's analyze the application execution flow in more detail.

## Understanding the client and server communication flow

With the Hub and client properly configured, it's time to understand how the communication flow will work. The flow for creating a task is represented according to *Figure 4.3*:

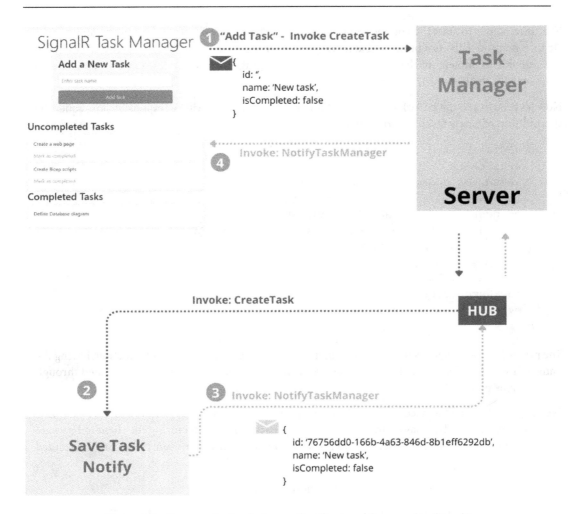

Figure 4.3 – Communication between the Client and Server using SignalR

The steps shown in *Figure 4.3* simply illustrate the entire communication flow of the application. Let's understand each of these steps:

1. After entering the task name, the user clicks the **Add Task** button. The button's click event requests the `CreateTask` method, available on the server, through the Hub, passing a `TaskModel` object with the `Name` property defined as a parameter. The invocation of the server-side method is done through the connection that was previously made to the Hub.

2. Upon receiving a request for the `CreateTask` method, the Hub then processes the task, adding it to a list in memory through the `Save` method, which adds values to the `Id` and `IsCompleted` properties.

3.  Then, the Hub invokes the `NotifyTaskManager` method on the client, passing it as a parameter from the created `TaskModel` object.

4.  The client executes the method responsible for processing the server notification. This method was implemented in the SignalR connection object and updates the application screen, displaying the list of created tasks and the list of completed tasks.

In this section, we learned the main concepts of SignalR for implementing real-time communication between client and server. These concepts can be used in different types of applications, such as chat apps, order status updates in an online store, and so on. However, there are cases wherein we must work with a constant data-sending model between the client and server and this depends on another synchronization model that can be implemented with SignalR through the use of streaming. This concept is widely used in dashboards and applications such as news feeds. In the next section, we will understand how streaming works.

## Working with streaming

In the context of SignalR, streaming is a powerful way of sending data from the server to the client and vice versa, in a continuous stream. Unlike traditional request/response models, where data is sent in a single batch, streaming allows for a constant flow of data, which is particularly useful for scenarios involving real-time updates, such as live feeds, dashboards, or even chat apps.

Streaming on SignalR is characterized by several important features that make it an exceptional choice for real-time applications. Through a continuous flow, data is sent as soon as it becomes available, which is crucial to creating a real-time user experience. This means users receive updates immediately, keeping them constantly informed.

Next, streaming operations in SignalR are inherently asynchronous, ensuring that the application remains responsive even when dealing with multiple streaming operations or large volumes of data. Lastly, SignalR supports bidirectional streaming, allowing not only server-to-client but also client-to-server data flows.

This flexibility opens up a wide range of possibilities for interactive applications where both the server and clients can initiate and participate in data exchanges, further enhancing the dynamic, real-time capabilities of applications built with SignalR.

The streaming strategy is a powerful solution. However, it is important to keep some limitations and challenges in mind:

*   **Network dependency and stability**: One of the main limitations of streaming on SignalR is its dependence on network quality. Since streaming involves a continuous flow of data, a stable and reliable network connection is crucial. Instabilities can cause a loss of connection, compromising the user experience.

- **Resource intensity**: Streaming can be more resource-intensive than traditional request/response interactions. Since the server must maintain an open connection and continually process and send data, this can increase CPU and memory usage. In high-volume scenarios or with a large number of connected clients, this can become a significant challenge for resource management and expansion strategies.

- **Complexity in implementation and maintenance**: Implementing streaming logic is generally more complex than dealing with standard request/response models due to the need to manage continuous connections and deal with asynchronous data streams. Additionally, it is challenging to debug streaming applications, especially when it comes to ensuring data integrity and dealing with network issues.

- **Scalability challenges**: Scaling real-time streaming applications can be challenging as the number of concurrent users increases and the load on the server can increase quickly.

- **Limited browser support and compatibility issues**: Although modern browsers generally support the technologies underlying SignalR, there may still be compatibility issues, especially with older browsers.

- **Security considerations**: With open and continuous connections, streaming applications may have different security considerations compared to traditional web applications.

Understanding these limitations provides better strategy definition and application design to take advantage of the best benefits available in SignalR.

## Implementing basic streaming

We already understand the most important concepts of SignalR, such as how the Hub and the communication between the client and the server work. However, it is important to implement a simple application example to understand the streaming approach.

There's nothing better than making an application to capture the concepts we're learning. Therefore, follow these steps to implement an application that uses streaming:

1. Access your operating system's terminal navigate to a directory of your choice and create a folder with the following instructions:

   ```
   mkdir SignalRStream
   cd SignalRStream
   ```

2. Now, follow these steps to create the application:

   I.    Run the following command to create the project:

   ```
   dotnet new webapp -o SignalRStreamingApp
   ```

II.    Then, access the created application directory and open Visual Studio code:

```
cd SignalRStreamingApp
code .
```

III.   In the same way as we did in the **TaskManager** project, the first task will be to create a
       Hub. Create a new folder called Hubs and then a class called StreamHub.cs:

```csharp
using Microsoft.AspNetCore.SignalR;
using System.Threading.Channels;
namespace SignalRStream.Hubs;

public class StreamHub : Hub
{
    public ChannelReader<int> Countdown(int count)
    {
        var channel = Channel
          .CreateUnbounded<int>();
        _ = WriteItemsAsync(channel.Writer, count);
        return channel.Reader;
    }

    private async Task
      WriteItemsAsync(ChannelWriter<int>
      writer, int count)
    {
        for (int i = count; i >= 0; i--)
        {
            await writer.WriteAsync(i);
            await Task.Delay(1000); // Simulates some delay
        }
        writer.TryComplete();
    }
}
```

IV.    This code has a Countdown method that returns a stream of integers counting down
       from a specified number.

V.     Now let's change the Program.cs file by adding SignalR functionalities in the same
       way as we did in the **TaskManager** project. The class should look like the following code:

```csharp
using TaskManager.Hubs;
using TaskManager.Service;
using TaskManager.Service.Contract;
```

```
var builder = WebApplication.CreateBuilder(args);
builder.Services.AddRazorPages();
//Add SignalR
builder.Services.AddSignalR();
var app = builder.Build();

if (!app.Environment.IsDevelopment())
{
    app.UseExceptionHandler("/Error");
    app.UseHsts();
}

app.UseHttpsRedirection();
app.UseStaticFiles();
app.UseRouting();
app.UseAuthorization();
app.MapRazorPages();

// Add Hub Endpoint
app.MapHub<StreamHub>("/streamHub");
app.Run();
```

VI.    Add the signalR client library using the libman application:

```
libman install @microsoft/signalr@latest -p unpkg -d
wwwroot/js/signalr --files dist/browser/signalr.js
```

VII.   Now we need to create a script to establish the connection to the Hub. To do this, create a file called index-stream.js in the wwwroo/js directory. This file must contain the following code:

```
const connection = new signalR.HubConnectionBuilder()
    .withUrl("/streamHub")
    .build();

connection.start().then(function () {
  connection.stream("Countdown", 10).subscribe({
    next: (count) => {
      logStream(count);
    },
    complete: () => {
      logStream("Stream completed");
    },
    error: (err) => {
```

```
            logStream(err);
        }
    });
}).catch(err => logStream(err.toString()));

function logStream(status) {
    let li = document.createElement("li");
    let ul = document.getElementById("ulLog");

    li.textContent = status;
    ul.appendChild(li);
}
```

The preceding code aims to connect the client application to the server, using the same approach learned in the previous session. In this example, first, there is the connection to the Hub. This is accomplished by creating the connection using the new `SignalR.HubConnectionBuilder()` line of code.

Then, when starting the connection, the streaming approach is used, initiated by the `connection.stream(..)` method. The `stream` method depends on two arguments, the first being the name of the method that will be requested on the server, called **Countdown**, previously created in the `StreamHub.cs` file. The second parameter is an integer value, where the countdown implemented in the server's `Countdown` method will start. It is important to note that the number of parameters required by the stream method, in addition to the name of the function defined as a string, will vary according to the number of parameters implemented on the server.

The stream method has a nested method called `subscribe`, which has an implementation to obtain responses from the server. The `subscribe` method has an object that contains three main callback methods: `next`, `complete`, and `error`. Each of these events is executed at a certain point in the streaming. The `next` method is used for the response sent from the server. The `complete` method is used when the streaming flow is finished and the error method is used if an error occurs. All three subscribe methods use a `logStream` javascript function implemented in the `index-stream.js` file that adds a list element to the HTML containing the response to events.

VIII. Next, we need to change the `Pages/Index.cshtml` file to the following code:

```
@page
@model IndexModel
@{
    ViewData["Title"] = "Home page";
}

<div class="text-center">
    <h1 class="display-4">Stream</h1>
```

```
    <ul id="ulLog"></ul>
</div>

@section Scripts {
  <script src=
    "~/js/signalr/dist/browser/signalr.js"
    asp-append-version="true">
  </script>
  <script src="~/js/index-stream.js"
    asp-append-version="true"></script>
}
```

IX.    Now, just run the application using the following command:

```
dotnet run
```

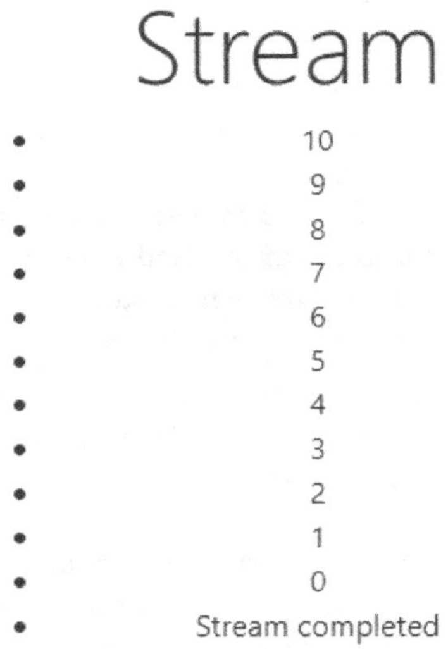

# Stream

-       10
-       9
-       8
-       7
-       6
-       5
-       4
-       3
-       2
-       1
-       0
-       Stream completed

Figure 4.4 – SignalR streaming app

As seen in *Figure 4.4*, we have a countdown starting from the number **10** and, at the end, there is a **Stream Completed** message, which determines the end of the streaming. In this example, the next and complete events from the subscribe method were used. This way, we can work with constant interaction between the client and the server using streaming, bringing greater power to our applications.

The application is very simple and basically generates a list of numbers obtained through the connection to the Hub, with a small delay to simulate latency.

The stream approach is very interesting for transporting small blocks of information and allowing active processing in parts, ensuring a better user experience.

We already understand the main features available in SignalR, but now let's learn what is needed to host applications on a server.

# Hosting the ASP.NET Core SignalR application

Like any web-based application, we must make them available through a server after the development stage. Applications developed in ASP.NET Core SignalR have the same characteristics and with all the power of the .NET platform, there is the possibility of hosting on internal servers and different cloud providers.

We will discuss more about hosting applications in *Chapter 10*. For now, we will just learn what is necessary to generate a hostable package for a SignalR application.

## The basics of hosting a SignalR application

Hosting an ASP.NET Core SignalR application isn't drastically different from hosting a regular ASP. NET Core web app. However, due to the real-time nature of SignalR, there are specific considerations to keep in mind.

It is important to define what the hosting model will be. In general, currently public clouds are selected, such as Azure, AWS, or GCP (Google). However, let's understand each type of hosting available for ASP.NET Core 9 applications:

- **Traditional hosting (IIS, Nginx, and Apache)**: These are standard web servers that can also serve SignalR applications. They mainly act as reverse proxies, forwarding client requests to the SignalR application.

- **Cloud hosting**: Cloud platforms offer robust and scalable hosting environments. **Azure App Service**, for example, provides an easy-to-use hosting model for ASP.NET Core applications, including those using SignalR.

- **Containers (Docker and Kubernetes)**: For those looking for more control over their hosting environment, containerization offers a way to package the SignalR application with all its dependencies, ensuring consistency across different environments.

After defining the hosting server, the process of hosting the application follows approximately four steps:

1. **Publishing the application**: Use Visual Studio or the .NET CLI to publish your application, generating a deployable unit. This task can be done by running the following command as an example that compiles the application in the Release mode and generates publication files in the Published folder:

```
dotnet pubilish -c Release -o ./Published
```

2. **Configuring the server**: Whether it's IIS, a Linux server with Nginx/Apache, or a cloud service, you will need to configure the server or service to host your application. This includes installing the necessary .NET runtimes, in the case of IIS or Nginex/Apache servers, and configuring the web server or cloud service.

3. **Configuring reverse proxy (if necessary)**: For IIS, Nginx, and Apache, ensure they are configured to correctly forward requests to your ASP.NET Core application. This is crucial for SignalR as it relies on persistent connections.

4. **Deploying the application**: Upload or deploy the published application to your hosting environment. This can be done via FTP, Web Deploy, or CI/CD pipelines if you are using cloud services or containerization.

Hosting SignalR applications presents unique challenges due to their nature of maintaining persistent connections to clients and can significantly burden server resources.

It is important to be aware of the connection limits of your server or hosting plan, as each will have a maximum number of simultaneous connections it can support. In environments where load balancing is employed, the use of sticky sessions is recommended to preserve the integrity of connections, ensuring that a client communicates consistently with the same server instance.

Additionally, as the number of concurrent connections increases, you may need to expand your application, involving deploying multiple instances of your application and distributing traffic between them. This would let you increase your ability to effectively manage a larger volume of concurrent connections. This approach helps maintain the optimal performance and reliability of your SignalR application under heavy load.

However, we understand that SignalR applications add the option of developing real-time applications using ASP.NET Core 9 and their hosting does not present major differences from traditional web-based applications.

In *Chapter 10*, we will explore in greater detail how we can host any type of web-based application dynamically, using the best practices available.

## Summary

In this chapter, we learned vital skills for creating dynamic real-time applications. We learned about the powerful features of ASP.NET Core 9 SignalR, its architectural model and fundamentals, and supporting technologies, as well as creating a real-time task management application. Furthermore, we explained the concepts of streaming in SignalR and covered the main activities required to host SignalR applications on servers.

In the next chapter, we will explore working with data and persistence by learning the aspects of data management and persistence in ASP.NET Core 9 applications, using technologies such as Entity Framework Core. We will delve deeper into your understanding of database interactions and state management. These are essential components for any web-based application.

## Get This Book's PDF Version
## and Exclusive Extras

**UNLOCK NOW**

Scan the QR code (or go to packtpub.com/unlock). Search for this book by name, confirm the edition, and then follow the steps on the page.

*Note: Keep your invoice handly. Purchase made directly from packt don't require one.*

# Part 2:
# Data and Security

When developing modern web solutions, we must deal with data persistence models and, of course, security. In this part, we will cover the principles, patterns, and best practices for connecting applications developed in ASP.NET Core 9 to databases such as SQL Server. We will learn about the entity-relational and NoSQL persistence models. We will learn how ASP.NET Core 9 provides powerful tools for interacting with data access layers and we will learn about the use of technologies such as EntityFramework Core and Dapper. In addition to interacting with data, we will learn about aspects related to application security, understanding the use of authorization and authentication, and how to implement applications that restrict access to information using ASP.NET Core Identity.

This part has the following chapters:

- *Chapter 5, Working with Data and Persistence*
- *Chapter 6, Enhancing Security and Quality*

# 5

# Working with Data and Persistence

Every application, at some point, will consume data, whether through services or even in a data source, such as a SQL Server database or MySQL. Interacting with the database is an important feature, and ASP.NET Core 9 offers mechanisms such as Entity Framework Core and easily integrates with other database interface providers, such as Dapper, a library optimized for abstracting data access in a simple way.

In this chapter, we're going to cover the following main topics:

- Connecting to a SQL database
- Understanding SQL, NoSQL, ORM, and Micro ORM
- Working with Entity Framework core and Dapper

We will explore communication between web applications and databases using technologies such as Entity Framework and Dapper, in addition to understanding important concepts such as the use of ORM and different data persistence models.

## Technical requirements

This chapter has some prerequisites in order to get the most out of it. Therefore, you will need to install Docker and Azure Data Studio.

All source code and examples for this chapter can be found in the GitHub repository at `https://github.com/PacktPublishing/ASP.NET-Core-9.0-Essentials/tree/main/Chapter05`.

## Docker installation

We will use Docker as the basis for running a SQL database server. Using Docker will avoid the problems associated with installing databases on different operating systems as it is a portable option.

To install Docker, follow the instructions for your operating system.

### Windows

Run the following command as an administrator on the terminal:

```
winget install -e --id Docker.DockerDesktop
```

### Mac

Access the following link and follow the tutorial for installation according to your processor: https://docs.docker.com/desktop/install/mac-install/#install-and-run-docker-desktop-on-mac.

### Linux

Docker supports **Ubuntu**, **Debian**, and **Fedora**. Use the instructions according to your platform at https://docs.docker.com/desktop/install/linux-install/.

## Azure Data Studio

Azure Data Studio is a specialized database editor and will be used to perform database operations, such as table creation, inclusion, and record querying.

Its installation is simple, and it supports different operating systems: https://learn.microsoft.com/en-us/azure-data-studio/download-azure-data-studio?tabs=win-install%2Cwin-user-install%2Credhat-install%2Cwindows-uninstall%2Credhat-uninstall#download-azure-data-studio.

# Connecting to a SQL database

In each chapter, we have learned about different aspects involving ASP.NET Core 9 and how this platform provides a large number of resources for the development of the most diverse types of applications. Each application has a purpose, which is to process data that generates information for users. However, at some point, your application will end up interacting with a data persistence model.

**Data persistence** occurs in several ways, but in general, it is the serialization of information allocated in memory to the disk, which can be in the form of files, and commonly takes place using a data persistence platform, such as a **Database Management System (DBMS)** or non-relational data. We will discuss these two persistence models in more depth soon.

Most applications use a persistence model based on databases such as SQL Server, Oracle, and MySQL. Each DBMS has models of administration, typing, and organization of resources; however, they share the same purpose of persisting data in a tabular format and use **Structured Query Language (SQL)** to manipulate and manage all persisted data.

ASP.NET Core 9 can communicate with different types of DBMS, but we will focus on the SQL Server database.

For an application to connect to a database, the following are necessary:

- A database driver (a NuGet package)
- A connection string
- Access to the desired resource

With this model, we can connect to any database that has a NuGet package ported to the .NET platform, such as the `System.Data.SqlClient` package for SQL databases, allowing applications to easily implement a persistence model.

Now that we know the principles related to the interaction between applications and data persistence, let's learn how the ASP.NET Core 9 platform communicates with a SQL Server database.

## Preparing SQL Server

In current versions of the .NET platform, they work mainly with the **dependency injection (DI)** design pattern, which allows the use of a technique called **inversion of control (IoC)**, causing classes and their dependencies to be managed by the .NET dependency container.

> **DI in .NET**
>
> The DI pattern design's main objective is to abstract the management of class instances and their respective dependencies. It is a common practice in most high-performance solutions. If you want to learn more about DI, visit `https://learn.microsoft.com/en-us/aspnet/core/fundamentals/dependency-injection?view=aspnetcore-9.0`.

Through DI, we can register a class to control the connection to the database. We will work with this approach in the topic where we will learn about using the Entity Framework in the *Working with EF Core and Dapper* section.

For now, it is important to understand the fundamentals of communicating between an application and the database. We will use SQL Server as the DBMS and for this, you must consult the *Technical requirements* section and install the Docker Engine. How Docker works is beyond the scope of this book. However, its use will allow you to continue with the examples described in this chapter without any compatibility problems.

Let's start configuring the database:

1.  The first step is to run a Docker container to run SQL Server. We will use the following command to start an instance of SQL Server:

    ```
    docker run -d -e "ACCEPT_EULA=Y" -e "MSSQL_SA_
    PASSWORD=Password123" -p 1433:1433 mcr.microsoft.com/mssql/
    server:2019-latest
    ```

    Let's review the preceding command:

    -   `docker run`: This uses the Docker Engine to run a container.

    -   `-d`: This parameter is used to execute the command in the background.

    -   `-e`: These are definitions of environment variables, used when starting the container. In this case, the `ACCEPT_EULA` variable is configured to agree with Microsoft's terms and the `MSSQL_SA_PASSWORD` parameter is where a password is defined for the SA user, the default SQL user administrator.

    -   `-p`: This defines the port of the host machine that will be used to communicate with port 1433 of the container. In this scenario, we're defining the host and container ports as the same, 1433.

    -   `mcr.microsoft.com/mssql/server:2019-latest`: This is the type and version of the Docker image that will be run.

    Docker does all the magic of downloading the SQL Server image onto your machine and running it in a virtualized way. The preceding command will return a hash code indicating that the image is running.

2.  Now, run the following command:

    ```
    docker ps
    ```

3.  The running image will be listed as shown in *Figure 5.1*, and the number of images listed may be different if you already use Docker.

Figure 5.1 – Docker image running

**Learn more about Docker**

To learn more about Docker, take a look at the following official documentation: `https://docs.docker.com/`.

4.  Now that we have the image running, open **Azure Data Studio**, installed as described in the *Technical requirements* section, and click the **Create a connection** button, as highlighted in *Figure 5.2*:

Figure 5.2 – Creating a connection to the database

5.  Fill in the fields as follows:

    *   **Server**: `localhost,1433`
    *   **Authentication type**: `SQL Login`
    *   **User name**: `sa`
    *   **Password**: `Password123`

6.  Keep the other parameters as they are, then click **Connect**. In some cases, a popup will be displayed informing you about the use of certificates. Just click the **Enable Trust server certificate** button. This certificate is automatically created by Azure Data Studio, so don't worry.

7.  After making the connection, you will have access to the server, which only has the standard databases. Click on the **New Query** option and you will see a new tab, as shown in *Figure 5.3*, that we will use to create a database and a table.

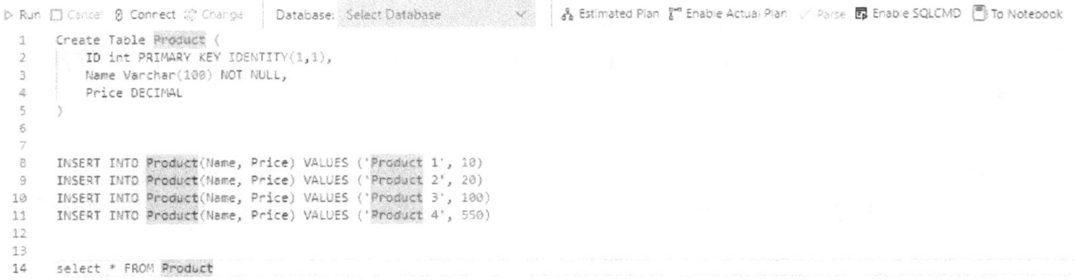

Figure 5.3 – New Query tab

8. Now, in the book GitHub repository, in the *Chapter 5* folder, copy the code from the `InitialDb.sql` file and paste it into the **New Query** tab, created previously, in Azure Data Studio.

9. Then click the **Run** button. The `DbStore` database and the `Product` table will be created, and some products will be inserted as an example of data.

Now that we have prepared the SQL database, it's time to create a simple console application, make the connection, and list the data from the product table.

## Using the SQL client

As mentioned previously, the .NET platform has more modern ways of establishing a connection to the database and we will talk more about this subject in the *ORM and Micro ORM* section. However, it is important that you understand the fundamentals of communication between an application and a database.

To do this, we will create a console application and add the necessary NuGet package to connect to the previously prepared SQL Server.

Then, we'll open the terminal in a folder of your choice and execute the following commands in sequence:

```
dotnet new console -n MyFirstDbConnection
cd MyFirstDbConnection
dotnet add package System.Data.SqlClient
code .
```

With the project ready, we will need to carry out the following steps:

1. Create a connection to the database. We will use the `SqlConnection` class.

2. Open the connection.

3. Create a SQL command that will be executed. We will use the `SqlCommand` class.

4. Read data based on the SQL command. We will use the `SQLDataReader` class.

5. Display the data on the screen.

6. Close the connection.

In just six steps, we will be able to interact with a data source. The code in the `Program.cs` file must be identical to the following:

```
using System.Data.SqlClient;
SqlConnection sql = new SqlConnection("Server=localhost,
    1433;Database=DbStore; user id=sa;
    password=Password123");

try
{
    sql.Open();
    Console.WriteLine("Connection Opened");
    SqlCommand cmd = new SqlCommand(
        "select * from Product", sql);
    SqlDataReader reader = cmd.ExecuteReader();
    while (reader.Read())
    {
        Console.WriteLine($"{reader[0]} - {reader[1]}
            - {reader[2]:C2}");
    }
}
catch (Exception ex)
{
    Console.WriteLine(ex.Message);
}
finally
{
    sql.Close();
    Console.WriteLine("Connection Closed");
}
```

Let's discuss the most important details of this implementation.

The first step was to create the database connection class, `SqlConnection`, which receives a connection string as a parameter in the constructor. The connection string can be understood as the address of the database server. In this case, this address is made up of three basic properties: `Server`, `user id`, and `password`. The default connection port is `1433`, which can be omitted, but you must explicitly define it if the connection port is different. These are the same parameters used previously to connect to the database through Azure Data Studio through the UI.

The connection string offers several other types of parameters to determine how the connection will be made. The version we are currently using is the simplest.

> **Connection String**
>
> As mentioned, the connection string is made up of different parameters, including sensitive data such as username and password. For this reason, it is good practice to keep connection string management out of the source code, to prevent vulnerabilities and to prevent sensitive data from being available in the application's version control. We will learn secure credential management approaches in *Chapter 9*. More details about connection strings can be found in this great reference: `https://www.connectionstrings.com/sql-server/`.

After creating the `SqlConnection` object, it is time to open the connection using the `sql.Open()` code. Next, the `SqlCommand` class is created, where the constructor receives an SQL string and also the database connection object.

The SQL code used performs a simple query on the `Product` table, obtaining all available rows and columns.

`SqlCommand` has different methods, such as `ExecuteNonQuery`, that are generally used to execute commands that change the database, such as `Insert`, `Delete`, and `Update`, or `ExecuteReader`, which is being used in this example to obtain data from the Product table. The `ExecuteReader` method returns an object of type `SqlDataReader`, which abstracts the rows and columns into an object, where it is possible to perform interactions and access table information.

All this abstraction work is done by the `System.Data.SqlClient` library, which has access to the SQL Server database connection driver and provides several classes for manipulating data.

After obtaining the data by executing the `ExecuteReader` method, we finally iterate on the returned object by displaying the data obtained from the database.

All code is protected by a `try..catch..finally` block to guarantee error handling and, above all, to close the connection at the end of use.

We can analyze the result of listing the database records in *Figure 5.4*:

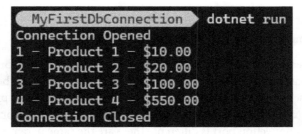

Figure 5.4 – Displaying records in the Product table

Despite being a simple application, we learned important concepts and fundamentals related to interactions between applications and databases. We use SQL Server as a base, but the lessons learned apply to other data sources, such as MySQL or Oracle, varying, of course, the connection, command, and reading objects.

Furthermore, we prepared the basis of the environment for the remainder of the chapter, where we will explore other concepts, starting with the differences between relational and non-relational databases, in addition to understanding what ORM and Micro ORMs are.

# Understanding SQL, NoSQL, ORM, and Micro ORM

With the emergence of different application structures and needs, different ways of managing data have also been developed. Choosing the right database and interaction methods has a significant impact on application performance, scalability, and maintainability.

Likewise, with the increase in systems complexity, new technologies for manipulating data obtained through DBMSs have also emerged, such as **Object-relational mapping** (**ORM**) and micro ORM. Each of the technologies has benefits for certain contexts, and it is important to know them correctly as there are no silver bullets.

## SQL versus NoSQL

The complexity of applications and different data management needs have led to several challenges for companies, such as having suitable performance for managing large amounts of data, which leads to maintainability and scalability challenges.

Along with these variables, keeping the servers running perfectly is expensive. **Relational Database Management System** (**RDBMS**) were the main means of tracking organizations' information, and their approach in a relational model that prioritizes the integrity and relationship between information has defined how development teams handle data manipulation for years.

**Relational databases** have tables that represent a type of information. This information is distributed in columns, representing the characteristics of a piece of data. Complete data is determined in a row of a table. Tables can have relationships with other tables, associating different data to compose information. That's why they are called relational models. The example in *Figure 5.5* shows some tables and their relationships, representing a data abstraction from a bank account application:

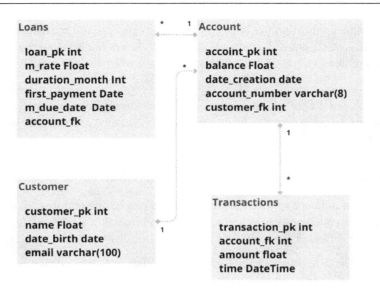

Figure 5.5 – Basic bank account data model

In the figure, you can see that a customer has an account that has transactions. This is a basic representation of this context. But in large contexts, this relational structure model leads to different challenges for companies and follows the application development model based on how data should be persisted.

Relational databases provide flexibility; however, basing applications on the data model shown in *Figure 5.5* leads to several challenges.

Modern systems need to have flexibility and elasticity, and in some cases must be technology agnostic.

With the emergence of the cloud, the possibility of having elastic resources also emerged. However, maintaining a cluster of data and synchronizing and managing it is not an easy or cheap task, even in cloud environments. Nowadays, through **Platform as a Service (PaaS)**, such activities are abstracted by cloud providers; however, they come at a cost.

With the evolution of technology, other types of persistence models and different opportunities for applications and companies have emerged. One of the big terms generally misunderstood in the technical community a few years ago was the term **NoSQL**, which means **non-relational database** or **not-only SQL**.

This persistence model has a different approach to the traditional relational model. NoSQL databases have a more flexible data structure that does not have many restrictions about how data will be persisted.

For many years, NoSQL was seen as the new persistence model for DBMSs, causing companies to try to migrate to this model without fully understanding the fundamentals and using relational database approaches in NoSQL structures.

This way of interacting with a different source of data persistence had several benefits, including making developers, engineers, and companies change their perspective on application development, but focused on the business instead of how the data should be persisted.

In *Figure 5.6*, we can see most of the differences between relational databases and NoSQL databases.

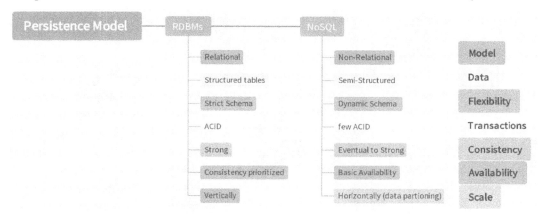

Figure 5.6 – Biggest differences in relational databases and NoSQL

The NoSQL approach offers different types of data persistence that bring several benefits to applications. The most common are as follows:

- Key-value stores (Redis, Memcached)
- Document databases (MongoDB, Couchbase)
- Column-family databases (Cassandra, HBase)
- Graph databases (Neo4j, OrientDB)

Likewise, the data manipulation model for NoSQL is different from relational databases, and query methods vary depending on the NoSQL database type and may not be as standardized as SQL.

Furthermore, it is important to understand that NoSQL databases often prioritize scalability, performance for specific query patterns, and flexibility to handle evolving data structures.

But when should we use one approach over the other?

Let's analyze the following table to understand the differences between persistence approaches:

| Feature | RDBMS | NoSQL |
|---------|-------|-------|
| Structure | Rigid, predefined schemas | Flexible, adaptable, schemas can be schema-less or defined on-the-fly |
| Scalability | Usually scales vertically (increase hardware power) | Often designed for horizontal scaling (adding more servers) |
| Consistency | Strong ACID guarantees | Eventual consistency is common for faster writes |
| Querying | Powerful, expressive SQL queries | Varies by database type, potentially less powerful than SQL for complex relationships |
| Use cases | Data with rigid schemas, complex relationships, strong consistency needs | High-volume data, rapidly changing data models, high performance, specific query patterns, distributed systems |

Table 5.1 – Comparison between data persistence models

As shown in *Table 5.1*, RDBMSs excel in predictable and structured data models, where data accuracy and relationships are key. NoSQL stands out in scenarios where flexibility, massive scalability, and high performance for specific needs take priority. Both are excellent proposals for different types of applications, with their varied applicability, such as an application persisting data in SQL Server and using Redis to manage the cache of some information, avoiding constant access to the database. Both approaches are used for the same application.

Fortunately, ASP.NET Core 9 allows us to work with different types of data models because it is extensible and dynamic. Let's delve a little deeper into two important concepts for manipulating data in relational databases, which are ORMs and Micro ORMs.

## ORM and Micro ORM

ORM is a technique that acts as a bridge between the world of **object-oriented programming (OOP)** and the relational world of databases. OOP models data as objects with properties and behaviors, while databases work with tables, rows, and columns.

As we learned at the beginning of the chapter, we use objects such as `SqlConnection`, `SqlCommand`, and `SqlDatReader` to read data in SQL Server. This is a simple approach, but as businesses become more complex, it can be a big problem to work with obtaining and mapping data to apply the required business rules in the application.

In the example of the `Products` table, we implemented in the *Using the SQL Client* section, a SQL query was used to obtain all existing records. In real, large-scale applications, it is impractical for any interaction by users to be necessary to obtain all records from a table. This could cause serious performance problems in the application.

It is necessary to insert, delete, and update data, and even customize searches through filters, meaning that a SQL command is written for each situation. Furthermore, for data to be processed efficiently, it is necessary to abstract what persistence is and what the business domain is. In C#, we can work with the concept of **object orientation** at a high level and, in this context, ORM emerges as a powerful technique that allows us to focus on the business, in addition to other flexibilities.

The implementation of an ORM on the .NET platform is called **Entity Framework (EF)**. EF provides all the high-level mechanisms for manipulating and translating data either from objects to databases or from databases to C# objects.

With EF, we don't need to worry about writing SQL queries for the various operations in a database. EF also has other features, such as **migrations**, which allow you to update the database according to the developed code model, providing a great solution for database versioning.

To better understand how ORM works, look at *Figure 5.7*:

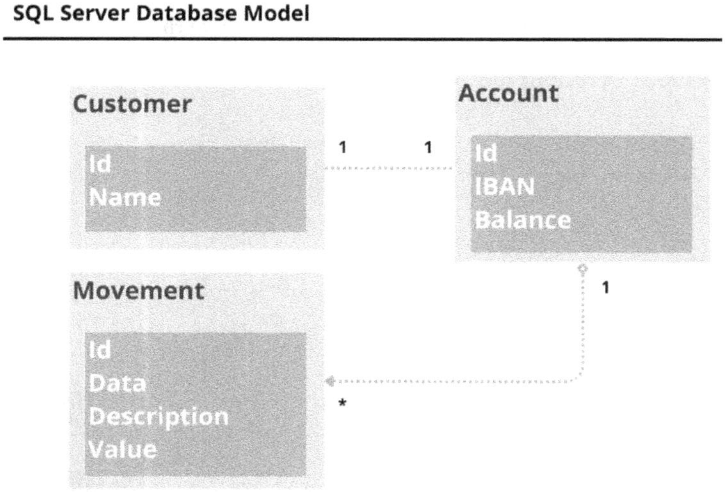

**SQL Server Database Model**

Figure 5.7 – Simple data model of a banking system

We know that it is possible to obtain data in a C# application, as we learned previously. To translate the data objects shown in *Figure 5.7*, it would be necessary to create three C# classes: `Customer.cs`, `Account.cs`, and `Movement.cs`. However, for each of the classes, it would be necessary to write different SQL queries to perform any operations on the database. Furthermore, for each business need, it would be necessary to map the data to C# classes and vice versa to persist data.

This means that to obtain customer data, such as their accounts and transactions, it would be necessary to carry out at least three database queries, interact with `SqlDataReader` objects, and create the respective C# objects. Although it is not a very complex job, as the software becomes more complex, with various changes, this model becomes problematic.

Imagine changing the name of the `Description` column in the `Movement` table to `Event`. It would even be necessary to change all the SQL queries created in C#, in addition to the mappings. When it comes to more complex data models, maintenance difficulties and possible problems grow exponentially.

When working with an ORM, this entire task is abstracted and less complicated. Fortunately, EF provides a great solution for this scenario, requiring the following:

- **Connection string**: Database address and access credentials
- **DbContext object**: Orchestrator of the connection to the database and management of objects and mappings
- **DbSet**: Domain objects that will be mapped to database objects

EF Core manages all the communication with the database, mapping, and migrations, allowing developers to focus on the business.

The `DbContext` class for the example in *Figure 5.7* would look like this:

```
public class BankingDbContext : DbContext
  {
    public BankingDbContext (DbContextOptions
      < BankingDbContext > options)
      : base(options)
    {
    }

    public DbSet<Customer> Customers { get; set; }
    public DbSet<Account> Accounts { get; set; }
    public DbSet<Movement> Movements { get; set; }
  }
```

We will implement this class in more detail in the next section. At this point, it is important to understand that all the tables that will be managed by `DbContext` are properties of the class `BankingDbContext` with the type `DbSet`.

The mapping of database objects is generally done by conventions, where EntityFramework Core compares the property names and types against the table column names and types in the database, but can be easily customized using specialized attributes or classes.

> **Conventions in EF Core**
>
> To learn more about conventions, visit `https://learn.microsoft.com/en-us/ef/core/modeling/#built-in-conventions`.

With mapping database conventions, we can obtain all the customers in the database through the `BankingDbContext` class, as follows:

```
public async Task<ICollection<Account>>
    GetAllAccountsAsync()
{
    return await _context.Accounts.ToListAsync();
}
```

As you can see in the previous code, the `GetAllAccountsAsync` method searches for all the accounts in the database. The EF Core `ToListAsync` method will query the database asynchronously, returning a list of `Account` objects.

The preceding code shows a simple and powerful approach using ORM, without needing to manage the connection or write SQL commands, as they are generated by EF, in addition to there being no need to map database objects into classes. All these functionalities are already abstracted.

In this way, ORMs provide several benefits:

- *Reduced boilerplate code*: ORMs automatically generate much of the repetitive SQL code (`SELECT`, `INSERT`, `UPDATE`), allowing developers to focus on application logic, not data access code.

- *Enhanced productivity*: Working with objects is often more intuitive for developers who are used to OOP principles, speeding up development.

- *Increased maintainability*: ORMs provide a certain level of abstraction between your application code and the specific database, making it easier to switch database providers or refactor your data model with less impact on your codebase.

However, ORM technologies have pros and cons to consider:

- *Performance overhead*: In some cases, the SQL queries generated by an ORM might not be the most efficient. Experienced developers can often write more performant SQL by hand.

- *Potential abstraction issues*: ORMs can hide some of the underlying database concepts, which can be beneficial, but might make optimization or troubleshooting more challenging for those unfamiliar with database fundamentals.

EF Core is in version 8 and, over the years, it has been improved, with different features added. However, we still recommend using the best technology offered to us wisely.

Although ORM technologies are becoming increasingly modern, there is still a concern about performance, especially when you have a complex data model, with several levels of relationships between objects. ORMs are often not capable of generating extremely performant queries, and, in some cases, it is necessary to use other resources, such as the Micro ORM approach learned at the beginning of the chapter.

In this context of facilitating work between the application and database objects, the concept of Micro ORM emerged.

**Micro ORMs** are conceptually very similar to the ORM model. However, micro ORMs abstracts the database mapping objects into C# classes but prioritize performance. In some cases, they even provide some automatic generation of queries.

Some differences between Micro ORM and ORM are as follows:

- *Footprint*: Micro ORMs have a much smaller code base and fewer dependencies, resulting in significantly less overhead.

- *Complexity*: Micro ORMs offer a basic set of features for mapping and executing queries, leaving behind many of the complexities found in traditional ORMs.

- *Control*: With less abstraction, developers have more direct control over the SQL queries being executed.

- *Features*: Micro ORMs typically lack these features often found in larger ORMs:

  - Extensive object relationship management

  - Change tracking

  - Automatic schema migrations

  - Identity maps (entity tracking to prevent duplicate payloads)

There are some Micro ORM technologies commonly used by the .NET community, the most famous of which is called Dapper.

> **Dapper is open source**
>
> The Dapper library is open source and is constantly being updated. There is a comparison between different ORM engines, including EF Core, on GitHub: `https://github.com/DapperLib/Dapper`.

Using a Micro ORM does not preclude using an ORM. They can coexist in an application, depending on the need and context. It is important to keep in mind that this approach allows us to bring greater quality to our applications.

In the next section, we will cover, in a practical way, the use of EF Core and Dapper based on the previously mentioned *bank account* concept.

Now that we understand what an ORM and a Micro ORM are, the time has come to implement solutions using these approaches.

# Working with EF Core and Dapper

ORM and Micro ORM are widely techniques used in modern applications due to their various benefits. As we have learned, ASP.NET Core 9 has several options for working with data models from different technologies. We will learn how to use EF Core as an ORM, and we will also use Dapper as a Micro ORM.

## EF Core

Based on the example of the bank account data model, we have tables *Customer*, *Account*, and *Movement*, we will create a project to connect to the SQL database we configured at the beginning of the chapter, which is running in a Docker container.

The complete solution code will therefore be available in the GitHub repository mentioned in the *Technical requirements* section.

For this project, we will use a Minimal API project and, to do this, open the terminal in administrator mode and execute the following command:

```
dotnet new webapi -n WorkingWithOrm
cd WorkingWithOrm
```

Now, we need to add the EF Core libraries that will be necessary for the application to connect to the SQL server database. Additionally, we will need to install an EF CLI tool. This tool will be used to apply some updates to the database.

Run the following commands in the terminal:

```
dotnet tool install -global dotnet-ef
dotnet add package Microsoft.EntityFrameworkCore
dotnet add package Microsoft.EntityFrameworkCore.SqlServer
dotnet add package Microsoft.EntityFrameworkCore.Design
```

The first command installs the EF CLI tool, and the following commands are the EF libraries that will be used to connect the application to the database.

> **EF Core database providers**
>
> EF Core has the ability to work with different databases; it is not restricted to SQL Server. More details about the available providers can be found at `https://learn.microsoft.com/en-us/ef/core/providers/?tabs=dotnet-core-cli`.

The project is now ready to be configured, and we will perform the following steps:

1. Configure the connection string.
2. Create model classes.
3. Create a class that inherits from `DbContext`.
4. Configure the `DbContext` created in the ASP.NET Core 9 DI container.
5. Add migrations.
6. Update the database.

As you perform these steps, you will notice some differences from implementing communication with the database in the traditional approach using `SqlConnection`, `SqlCommand`, and `SqlDataReader`.

Open the project in Visual Studio Code with the following command in the terminal:

```
code .
```

The complete project has the structure shown in *Figure 5.8*:

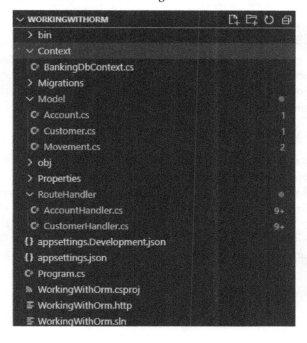

Figure 5.8 – Banking project project structure

To configure the connection string, we will use `appsettings.json`. It is important to mention that information containing user credentials should not be available directly in a code repository. The best practice is to use secrets or even a configuration server such as **Azure App Configurator** to manage this information. We'll talk more about good security practices in *Chapter 6*.

For teaching purposes, we will add the connection string to the `appsettings.json` file:

```json
{
    "Logging": {
      "LogLevel": {
        "Default": "Information",
        "Microsoft.AspNetCore": "Warning"
      }
    },
    "AllowedHosts": "*",
    "ConnectionStrings": {
     "BankingDbContext": "Server=localhost;
       Database=dbBanking;User Id=sa;
       Password=Password123;
       TrustServerCertificate=True"
    }
}
```

We are using the same connection string as the database server running through Docker, with an additional default, `Database=dbBanking`, which will be used for this application. The JSON `ConnectionStrings` object is an ASP.NET Core 9 convention, with each property of this object representing a different connection string.

EF Core does all the work of managing the connection and mapping database entities into C# objects, as well as generating SQL commands. For this to be possible, there is a base object that we must use to map the domain classes. This base object is called `DbContext`.

`DBContext` implements the **Unit of Work** design pattern, managing all states of the objects manipulated in memory and persisting changes when necessary.

> **Unit of Work pattern**
>
> The Unit of Work design pattern is used in different contexts, favoring the separation of responsibilities, such as separating all the business rules of an application from the responsibility of communicating with and manipulating data in a database.
>
> Learn more about the Unit of Work pattern at `https://learn.microsoft.com/en-us/archive/msdn-magazine/2009/june/the-unit-of-work-pattern-and-persistence-ignorance`.

According to the project structure shown in *Figure 5.8*, we will create a class called BankingDbContext. cs that will have the following code:

```
namespace WorkingWithOrm.Context;
using Microsoft.EntityFrameworkCore;
using WorkingWithOrm.Model;

public class BankingDbContext : DbContext
{
    public BankingDbContext(DbContextOptions
      <BankingDbContext> options) : base(options)
    {
    }

    public DbSet<Account> Accounts { get; set; }
    public DbSet<Customer> Customers { get; set; }
    public DbSet<Movement> Movements { get; set; }
}
```

For the application we are creating, the class is quite simple. Let's explore the most important points of this code:

- DbContext: The BankingDbContext class inherits from the DbContext superclass, which has the necessary abstractions for communication between the application and the database, state management, mapping, and the generation of SQL commands.

- BankingDbContext constructor: The class constructor receives, as a parameter, the generic DbContextOptions<BankingDbContext> class, which allows us to pre-define configurations that will be used in the DI container to create an instance of the DbContext object. The constructor can also receive a connection string; however, it is good practice to use the C# options pattern.

- DbSet: Each property of the DbSet type represents a table in the database, and it is these properties that provide information to EF Core to transform data from tables into objects and vice versa.

> **C# options pattern**
>
> The **options pattern** is widely used in the .NET platform with the aim of providing strongly typed access to groups of related settings.
>
> Learn more about the options pattern at https://learn.microsoft.com/en-us/ aspnet/core/fundamentals/configuration/options?view=aspnetcore- 9.0#the-options-pattern.

The BankingDbContext class is now complete and provides everything needed to interact with the SQL database. The mapping model used, in this case, is based on the EF Core convention, which infers the name of the table and columns from the name of the class and its properties.

Let's look at the Account.cs class:

```
public class Account
{
    public int Id { get; set; }
    public string Name { get; set; }
    public decimal Balance { get; set; }
    public int CustomerId { get; set; }
    public virtual Customer? Customer { get; set; }

    public virtual ICollection<Movement>? Movements
        { get; set; }
}
```

Based on this class and the EF Core convention, it is expected that there will be a table named Account and columns called Id, Name, Balance, and CustomerId in the database.

But there is, in addition, a property called Customer and a collection of Movement objects. Due to the existence of the CustomerId property, EF infers that there is a relationship with the Customer table, which has a foreign key (<TableName>+Id) in the Account table. Likewise, because there is a Movement collection, EF infers that the Account class may have one or more Movements in the Movement table.

However, if it is necessary to follow different naming standards from database to database, the names of tables, columns, primary keys, and so on can be mapped directly into the DbContext class using the fluent API. This can be done using data annotation in the domain classes, or even by implementing a specific mapping class for each entity using the IEntityTypeConfiguration<TEntity> interface.

The following code example represents a custom or manual mapping of the Customer class to the tbl_customer table. In order to customize the mapping of classes in database entities, it is necessary to override the OnModelCreating method, inherited from the DbContext class:

```
override protected void OnModelCreating(
  ModelBuilder modelBuilder)
  {
    modelBuilder.Entity<Customer>(obj => {
      obj.ToTable("tbl_customer");
      obj.HasKey(c => c.Id).HasName
        ("pk_customer_id");
      obj.Property(c => c.Name).HasColumnName
        ("customer_name").HasMaxLength(100).IsRequired();
```

```
        obj.HasMany(c => c.Accounts)
          .WithOne(a => a.Customer)
          .HasForeignKey(a => a.CustomerId);
    });
  }
```

As you can see in the code, it is possible to define all the attributes required for the correct mapping of entities.

With the `BankingDbContext` class finalized, we must configure it in the DI container and configure the connection string.

We will add the following line to the `Program.cs` file:

```
// Code omitted for readability
builder.Services.AddDbContext<BankingDbContext>(options =>
  options.UseSqlServer(builder.Configuration
    .GetConnectionString("BankingDbContext")));

var app = builder.Build();
// Code omitted for readability
```

We use the `AddDbContext<BankingDbContext>` extension method to configure the connection string that will be used for the connection. Note that we are using the `options` property, which is expected in the `DbContext` constructor, and through the use of the `UseSqlServer` extension method, we are recovering the connection string that we configured in the `appsettings.json` file.

The application is practically ready to communicate with the database; however, it will still be necessary to add migrations and update the database.

Open the terminal in the project directory and run the following command:

```
dotnet ef migrations add InitialDatabase
```

This command uses the EF CLI tool that we installed previously, adding migrations with the name `InitialDatabase`.

The objective of migrations is to allow the application and the database to remain synchronized in the objects that are used. In real applications, changes to the database, such as creating new tables or adding or removing columns, can happen constantly. These changes impact both the database in question and the application that consumes the objects in this database. When adding a migration, such as in the preceding command, we are taking a picture of the domain model that the application uses, and EF Core generates the scripts that will be applied to the database to keep it up to date.

Migrations create a set of classes in the project. These classes must not be changed manually. As we can see in *Figure 5.9*, three files were added to the application's `Migrations` folder:

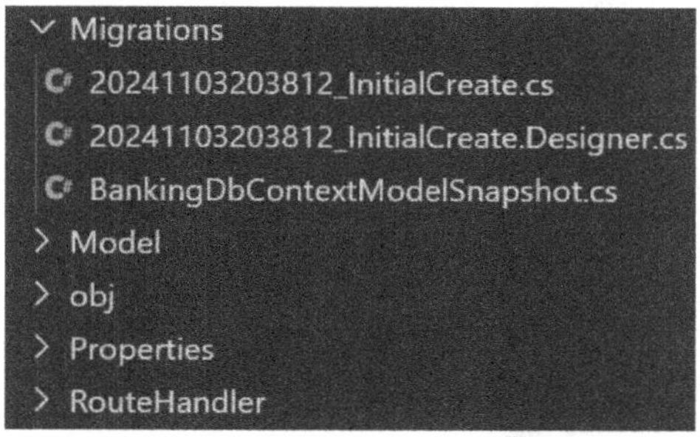

Figure 5.9 – Initial database migration files

When observing a snippet of code extracted from the `InitialDatabase.cs` suffix file, we observe that they are resource creation scripts in the database:

```
...
protected override void Up(MigrationBuilder
  migrationBuilder)
  {
    migrationBuilder.CreateTable(
      name: "Customers",
      columns: table => new
      {
          Id = table.Column<int>(type: "int",
            nullable: false)
            .Annotation("SqlServer:Identity", "1, 1"),
          Name = table.Column<string>(
            type: "nvarchar(max)", nullable: false)
      },
      constraints: table =>
      {
        table.PrimaryKey("PK_Customers", x => x.Id);
      });
...
```

With each change in your application's domain model, a new migration must be added. This way, you will maintain a history of changes, and this will facilitate the maintenance and evolution of the database and the application.

Now, you will need to update the database. So far, we have not run any SQL scripts on SQL Server, much less created the database. Instead of opening Azure Data Studio to perform this task, we will use the EF Core CLI tool to update the database according to the version mapped in the application.

To do this, run the following command in the terminal, in the project directory:

```
dotnet ef database update
```

The CLI tool will connect to SQL Server and execute scripts to create the database and tables mapped in the application. *Figure 5.10* displays the created objects:

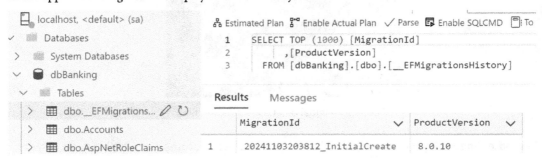

Figure 5.10 – Objects created in the database using the EF CLI tool

All communication with the database has been properly configured. The time has come to add the APIs to interact with the database. Therefore, create the following routes in the `Program.cs` file:

```csharp
app.MapGet("/customers", async (CancellationToken
  cancellationToken, BankingDbContext dbContext) =>
  {
    var customers = await dbContext.Customers
      .ToListAsync(cancellationToken);
    return Results.Ok(customers);
      });

    app.MapGet("/customers/{id}", async (int id,
      BankingDbContext dbContext,
      CancellationToken cancellationToken) =>
      {
        var customer = await dbContext.Customers
          .FindAsync(id, cancellationToken);
        return Results.Ok(customer);
      });

    app.MapPost("/customers", async (
      [FromBody] Customer customer,
      BankingDbContext dbContext,
      CancellationToken cancellationToken) =>
      {
        await dbContext.Customers.AddAsync(
```

```
        customer, cancellationToken);
    await dbContext
      .SaveChangesAsync(cancellationToken);
    return Results.Created();
  });
```

The above routes perform operations on the Customer table. Notice the first Get method. This method receives as a parameter an instance of the `BankingDbContext` object that is automatically resolved through the .NET Core dependency injection DI context.

Then, using the `dbContext.Customers.ToListAsync(cancellationToken)` code, all existing customers in the database are retrieved. We only use the `Customers DbContext` and `DbSet`, and EF Core takes care of creating the SQL query to select the records. There is no need to open connections, create commands, or even map manually. Everything is done transparently.

The `Post` method performs the following operations:

- `dbContext.Customers.AddAsync`: The `Customer` object is passed as a parameter in the request body. This is then added to `DbSet` in the same way as we would add an item to a list.

- `dbContext.SaveChangesAsync`: When executing this method, `dbContext` updates the database. This means that if there were other operations on the `DbSets`, such as removal, updates, or additions, this information would only be updated in the database after executing the `SaveChanges` or `SaveChangesAsync` methods.

---

**Asynchronous processing and cancellation token**

Asynchronous processing is a fundamental aspect of modern web application development. In ASP.NET Core 9, asynchronous methods allow the server to handle more requests simultaneously by not blocking threads during operations such as database queries, file access, or consuming HTTP resources. This approach allows the application to scale and respond quickly under load. The `async` and `await` keywords make it possible to write asynchronous code that is easy to maintain and read, and the .NET platform abstracts the complexity of managing asynchronous mechanisms.

In conjunction with asynchronous methods, it is a good practice to use cancellation tokens, which allow applications to properly handle the cancellation of requests, making applications more responsive and resilient. The cancellation token associated with an asynchronous method propagates a cancellation signal throughout all of the application's asynchronous operations, allowing them to terminate early and free up resources. ASP.NET Core 9 and C# simplify asynchronous programming and the use of cancellation tokens, providing a robust framework that ensures applications remain responsive even under varying loads.

For more information about asynchronous programming and token cancellation, visit `https://docs.microsoft.com/en-us/dotnet/csharp/programming-guide/concepts/async/` and `https://learn.microsoft.com/en-us/dotnet/standard/threading/cancellation-in-managed-threads`.

With this, we can run the application to interact with the database in a simple way, making it possible to perform any operations using **Language Integrated Query** (**LINQ**), such as advanced filters or obtaining records ordered by specific columns.

The use of an ORM provides several benefits for high-level applications and, likewise, several challenges when we delegate the management of data management complexity to the ORM. This makes them slow, since, despite several innovations and improvements, in many cases, they are not the best choice when it comes to performance.

In this case, Micro ORMs are great options; they have similar performance to traditional approaches and mapping capabilities like ORMs. Therefore, let's explore how Dapper can be used to add more features to the database communication model.

## Dapper

**Dapper** is a Micro ORM that gives us the ability to interact with the database in a performative way while mapping database entities into C# objects.

It is a simple-to-use yet powerful library. Its mapping model is interesting and flexible, allowing you to create different types of query result projections quickly and effectively.

Dapper and EF Core are not mutually exclusive technologies, and using both approaches in a project can provide great benefits.

Let's add the Dapper library to the project created previously by executing the following command in the terminal, in the application directory:

```
dotnet add package Dapper
```

All the prerequisites required to work with Dapper have already been implemented in the project, the main one being the connection string that we configured in the appsettings.json file.

Let's change the Program.cs file to add two new routes that use Dapper to perform a query where we can obtain all the customers in the database and query a customer by Id:

```
builder.Services.AddScoped(_ => new SqlConnection(builder
  .Configuration.GetConnectionString("BankingDbContext")));
var app = builder.Build();
// Codes omitted for readability
app.MapGet("GetAllCustomersUsingDapper", async(SqlConnection
connection) =>
{
  var customers = await connection.QueryAsync<Customer>
    ("SELECT Id, Name FROM Customers ORDER BY Name");

  return Results.Ok(customers);
```

```
});

app.MapGet("GetCustomerByIdUsingDapper",
  async(int id, SqlConnection connection) =>
{
    var customer = await connection
      .QueryFirstOrDefaultAsync<Customer>("SELECT Id,
    Name FROM Customers WHERE Id = @Id", new {
      Id = id });

    if (customer is null) return Results.NotFound();
    return Results.Ok(customer);
});
```

Let's explore the preceding code:

- In C# and ASP.NET Core 9, the _ => new syntax is known as discarded lambda and is used when there is no need to use the input parameter of the lambda expression.

- SqlConnection: We are adding the SqlConnection object to the DI container using the same connection string used by the DbContext. We are using the AddScoped method, which means that each time the SqlConnection object is used during a request, it will be reused.

- QueryAsync: We are getting all the customers from the database using a simple SQL query. The desired columns have been added to the SQL command, along with an ORDER BY NAME statement. QueryAsync is a SqlConnection extension method and, when it obtains the result, it will automatically map the data to C# objects based on the names of the properties and columns.

---

**Get all the data from the database**

Generally, it is not recommended to fetch all the records from a database in a single query as there may be thousands or millions of records in the database tables, which can cause performance problems. Keep in mind that the example proposed here is intended to facilitate understanding of the concept and should not be used in production applications. The recommended solution is to use pagination. Pagination involves breaking data into small, manageable chunks. To learn more, the following page contains implementation examples: https://learn.microsoft.com/en-us/ef/core/querying/pagination.

- `QueryFirstOrDefaultAsync`: In the same way as the previous method, a query is made in the database and if the record is found, it will be returned and mapped to a Customer object. If the record is not found, then it returns the value `Null`. The important point in the SQL query is the use of the `@Id` parameter. Dapper methods can substitute named parameters in the string. So, after defining the SQL command with the parameters, we must define an object that contains the named properties of the same parameters as the parameters defined in the SQL command. In the code example above, the defined parameter is named `@Id`, which requires that the object passed as a parameter has a property named Id, like the snippet `new {Id = id}`. Using an object allows us to define more than one parameter if necessary.

The use of SQL commands, in this case, allows us to create more performant queries for different purposes. Likewise, Dapper can be used to add, change, and remove records in the database.

In this case, we do not need to manage the SQL connections that are controlled by the DI container, and we benefit from the ORM's automatic mapping approach.

> **Dapper SqlBuilder**
>
> Dapper also has an extension that makes it easier to write SQL commands in the format needed by the Micro ORM called Dapper SQL Builder. It is a very useful extension, even when it is necessary to manipulate SQL strings according to some conditions.
>
> You can find out more about the Dapper SQL Builder extension by visiting `https://github.com/DapperLib/Dapper/tree/main/Dapper.SqlBuilder`.

As we have seen, both ORM and Micro ORM are great allies in the communication model with the database and can be used together, providing different benefits in different contexts.

This flexibility of ASP.NET Core 9 allows us to create different types of applications, from the simplest to the most complex, and interact with databases using best practices.

## Summary

In this chapter, we learned about data persistence in ASP.NET Core 9, exploring how applications interact with databases to store and manage critical information. You've compared the strengths of relational (SQL) and non-relational (NoSQL) databases, allowing you to choose the right fit for your project. Additionally, you've seen how ORMs such as EF Core simplify development by mapping objects to database records, and you've learned about the benefits of Micro ORMs such as Dapper for fine-grained control over performance-critical database operations.

We'll take another step toward developing high-quality applications by learning about security best practices in *Chapter 6*. We'll explore essential best practices and strategies for defending your applications against vulnerabilities. You'll learn how to ensure user data protection, authentication security, and overall application integrity – vital foundations for building robust, reliable web applications.

## Get This Book's PDF Version and Exclusive Extras

UNLOCK NOW

Scan the QR code (or go to `packtpub.com/unlock`). Search for this book by name, confirm the edition, and then follow the steps on the page.

*Note: Keep your invoice handly. Purchase made directly from packt don't require one.*

# 6

# Enhancing Security and Quality

In the rapidly evolving digital world, where new cyber threats emerge with alarming frequency, web-based application security is not just a feature but a fundamental necessity. So that applications are prepared for various existing vulnerabilities, software engineers must consider security as part of the entire development flow of web-based solutions so that they can protect data, guarantee integrity and availability, and minimize threats that can compromise an organization.

In this chapter, we'll learn about basic security principles that every web developer should master, especially regarding how ASP.NET Core 9, as a powerful platform, can help us create secure, high-level applications.

First, we'll explore the essential principles of web security, understanding that security must be taken into consideration in all phases of developing a web solution.

Next, we'll address the concepts of authentication and authorization, both of which are commonly used when users and applications, as well as applications and external applications, interact with each other. Once we have a better understanding of authorization and authentication flows, we'll use the ASP.NET Core Identity framework to add security to an API project and learn about some important approaches that are available in ASP.NET Core 9 that allow us to strengthen security mechanisms in our applications.

In this chapter, we'll cover the following topics:

- Understanding the security principles of web-based applications
- Comparing authorization and authentication
- Working with the ASP.NET Core Identity framework
- Strengthening application security

For us to have a great learning experience in this chapter, we must prepare our environment with some tools that will be essential for us to fully utilize the concepts that will be introduced.

## Technical requirements

To complete this chapter, the following tools must be present in your development environment:

- **Docker**: Docker Engine must be installed on your operating system and have a SQL Server container running. You can find more details about Docker and SQL Server in *Chapter 4*.

- **Postman**: We'll use this tool to execute requests that are sent to the APIs of the developed application.

- **Azure Data Studio**: We'll use this tool to connect to a SQL Server database so that we can execute SQL scripts.

The code examples for this chapter can be found in this book's GitHub repository: `https://github.com/PacktPublishing/ASP.NET-Core-9.0-Essentials/tree/main/Chapter06`.

## Understanding the security principles of web-based applications

Every year, new approaches to developing solutions emerge for the most diverse types of environments and devices. With this comes various challenges. Developing web applications that previously focused on technologies such as HTML, CSS, JavaScript, and a programming language of choice is no longer a reality.

Software engineers began to serve other contexts outside the environment of a programming IDE, often working with iInfrastructure, adding to a multitude of frameworks and tools that emerged along with the DevOps cCulture approach, and constant value delivery.

The DevOps culture has brought a new working model where teams avoid silos and work together while exchanging knowledge and, consequently, learning. Therefore, a subject that is becoming increasingly present in the lives of solution developers is **security**. The term security has long ceased to be an isolated subject directed only at a cybersecurity team. It is now essential from the first stages of design and must be considered in all aspects of a solution.

Paying attention to threats in applications and data control and management has become paramount and is even a strategic factor for companies and customers that use applications. There are many security standards and policies from a data processing perspective, such as the **General Data Protection Regulation (GDPR)** in Europe.

Security is very important and ASP.NET Core 9 offers several mechanisms that we can use to deal with the challenges proposed by avoiding threats and maintaining secure and reliable applications.

However, we must understand how security aspects are applied to web applications and common vulnerabilities, as well as how ASP.NET Core 9 works to prevent threats from occurring in applications.

## Security topics in web applications

As we've already learned in previous chapters, in general, a web application has two main components: the frontend, which is responsible for interacting with the user, and the backend, which is responsible for processing the application's business rules, providing control, and interacting with the data layer.

Most web applications, whether they're client-server ones or **single-page applications** (**SPAs**), use the aforementioned approach in some way. As shown in *Figure 6.1*, several components are part of how the frontend and backend interact, such as the communication protocol, requests, responses, HTTP headers, the browser, the application server, the database, the TCP protocol, credentials, cookies, and local storage (browser), among others:

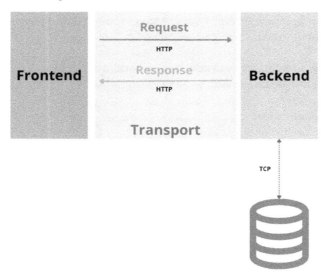

Figure 6.1 – Components of a SPA

As we can see, several components communicate with each other. Similarly, several vulnerabilities can compromise the integrity of your application. In some cases, an information leak can have serious consequences for an organization.

As a premise, software engineers must have a security aspect set out from the initial design stage that can often be associated not only with communication protocols and interactions between systems but also with code development.

Let's say that, during the development process, a software engineer made a very important change that was supposed to fix a critical problem in the application. To quickly perform the correction, the software engineer created communication with the database using SQL commands and string concatenation. After carrying out the tests, the engineer submitted the code to the Git repository so that the system could be updated. There was no code review and within a few minutes, the fix was in the production environment.

So, what's wrong in this scenario? Initially, the software engineer acted correctly in providing a quick response to the problem that was found in the application and corrected it, and everything returned to normal. However, the approach they used to communicate with the database contained a vulnerability that could be exploited by malicious users by utilizing what's known as **SQL injection attacks**.

Let's look at an example of some code that's vulnerable to SQL injection attacks:

```csharp
using System;
using System.Data.SqlClient;

public class VulnerableDataAccess
{
  private string connectionString = "TheConnectionString";
  public void GetUserData(string username)
  {
    string query = "SELECT * FROM Users WHERE
    Username = '" + username + "'";

    using (SqlConnection connection = new
      SqlConnection(connectionString))
    {
    SqlCommand command = new SqlCommand(query,
      connection);
    try
    {
      connection.Open();
      SqlDataReader reader = command.ExecuteReader();

      while (reader.Read())
      {
        Console.WriteLine(String.Format("{0}, {1}",
          reader["Username"], reader["Email"]));
      }
      reader.Close();
    }
    catch (Exception ex)
    {
      Console.WriteLine(ex.Message);
    }
    }
  }
}
```

In the preceding code, the SQL query has been constructed by directly concatenating a user's input (username) into the SQL string. This is a dangerous practice because it allows an attacker to alter the intended SQL query by injecting SQL code into the `username` variable. For example, if a user enters something like `'; DROP TABLE users; --`, the resulting SQL query would be as follows:

```
SELECT * FROM Users WHERE Username = ''; DROP TABLE Users; --'
```

This would execute the `DROP TABLE` statement, potentially destroying data.

So, a simple change such as this, even with great intentions, could have a big impact. Likewise, simple processes can avoid this situation by implementing a code review, a practice where members of the engineering team analyze the code that should be incorporated into the main code to search for any flaws, evaluate code patterns and complexity, and more. The code can only be incorporated into the main code if it meets the quality and security criteria.

Furthermore, while integrating the new code into the main code, automated processes can be executed, where it would be possible to add **static code analysis** mechanisms. If there are any invalid security and quality criteria, the application can't be delivered to the productive environment. We'll learn more about automated processes in *Chapter 10*.

---

**Static code analysis**

Static code analysis acts on security checks, coding standards, and cyclomatic complexity analysis, among other aspects, adding value to the application development process associated with automation techniques that involve **continuous integration** (**CI**) and **continuous delivery** (**CD**). There are several tools available in the market for static code analysis, with the most famous being **SonarQube** (https://hub.docker.com/_/sonarqube). It has a community version and can be hosted in any environment. However, it does have some limitations regarding how many lines of code can be analyzed. Alternatively, there's a version that's delivered as a **Software-as-a-Service** (**SaaS**) offering called **Sonar Cloud** (https://www.sonarsource.com/products/sonarcloud/).

Adding static analysis to the development flow is an excellent practice.

---

In this chapter, we'll explore other ways we can make our applications more secure and talk about various vulnerabilities. But first, let's understand a common security model that's used by most applications that's based on two basic processes: authentication and authorization.

# Comparing authorization and authentication

As we've been learning, the security aspect is important throughout the application development flow. Despite having good intentions, we can include vulnerabilities in our code that directly affect our users, applications, and companies.

However, in addition to the code, some features require security processes. For example, this is the case for some service platforms, such as email managers, which allow users to access their messages privately once they've gained access by logging in.

The login functionality is very important and, although it seems like a simple process, it requires a lot of attention. Otherwise, depending on the application, there may be consequences.

What would happen if there was a vulnerability upon logging into an online banking platform? It would probably be a big problem for the users of this bank (and also for the bank).

Modern systems work with identity management for different aspects. As discussed in previous chapters, web applications can make requests to different APIs. APIs allow companies to provide business as services, which allows for diverse integrations between different applications. With this, it's possible to have applications with different types of functionalities that add value to the user, such as map APIs, payment gateways, and even APIs that provide AI functionalities.

For applications and APIs to communicate securely, an identity-based security mechanism is necessary. With this, we can find out who is demanding some type of information and why.

This security mechanism is divided into two concepts: **authentication** and **authorization**.

In general, we know that this approach involves a login flow. However, it's essential to understand the difference between authentication and authorization.

## Authentication

Authentication aims to answer the question, *Who are you?*:

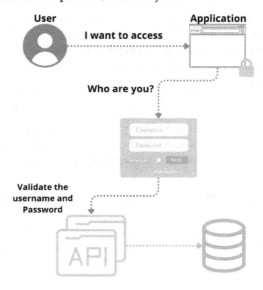

Figure 6.2 – The authentication flow

*Figure 6.2* shows an authentication flow where, through a login form, a user's credentials are provided, such as their email and password.

By posting this information to the server by clicking the **log in** button, the application starts identifying this user by using the credentials provided.

If the user is found according to these credentials, then the application is aware of who wants to access the system.

However, this is just one part of the process. Now that the application has identified the user, it's important to understand what this user can do. This is done during the authorization process.

## Authorization

Authorization aims to answer the question, *What can this user do?*:

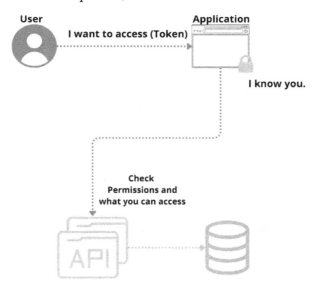

Figure 6.3 – Checking permissions with the authorization flow

After identifying the user, the application starts identifying the user's permissions, as shown in *Figure 6.3*.

Authorization defines the scope in which this user can act, whether in managing some information or accessing a certain type of data, among other aspects. The authorization flow often identifies the user through roles, where it's possible to group access levels within the scope of the application.

It's very common to use roles because it's possible to group the different permissions that a user can have within an application.

In general, the authentication and authorization processes are simple. However, to be able to implement them securely, there are some standards that we must be aware of: the **OAuth 2.0** and **Open ID Connect (OIDC)** protocols.

## Understanding OAuth 2.0 and OIDC

Imagine a high-security building. Here, authorization can be thought of as acquiring permission to enter, while authentication verifies your identity.

OAuth 2.0 focuses on authorization, allowing users to grant access to their data on one platform (such as a social media account) to another, without the need for them to share their actual passwords. In other words, we allow other applications to access a certain scope of our information without us having to provide certain credentials, such as what happens when we log in to some platform using credentials from Microsoft, Google, Facebook, and so on.

The basic OAuth 2.0 flow can be defined as follows:

1.  The user logs in to a new application using their social media account.

2.  The application redirects the user to the social media platform (the authorization server).

3.  After logging into the social media account, the user grants the application permission to use their data (such as their name, email, profile photo, and more).

4.  The authorization server generates special tokens for the application. Tokens are used to gain access to user data (access tokens). In some cases, refresh tokens are used to provide access to new tokens.

5.  The application uses the access token to retrieve your data from the social media platform securely.

This process involves negotiating two different applications that share user information, without the need to enter their credentials for each new application, increasing security and convenience.

On the other hand, OIDC builds on OAuth 2.0, adding an authentication layer. It leverages the OAuth authorization framework to verify a user's identity through trusted providers such as Google or Facebook.

Let's see how OIDC complements OAuth 2.0:

1.  Some applications provide the ability to log in using other social media platforms. In this case, during the OAuth 2.0 flow, instead of logging into the new application, you're redirected to your social media login page (the OpenID provider).

2.  The user authenticates with their social media credentials, proving their identity to the OpenID provider.

3.  With the user's consent, the OpenID provider shares their basic profile information (such as name and email) with the new application via an ID token.

OIDC enables features such as **single sign-on** (**SSO**), allowing you to access multiple applications using the same login credentials (think of logging into multiple websites with your Google account).

Although OAuth 2.0 and OIDC flows are similar and interconnected, they serve different purposes:

- **Focus**: OAuth 2.0 acts on authorization (granting access to data), while OIDC acts on the authentication layer (verifying user identity).

- **Sharing information**: OAuth 2.0 mainly deals with access tokens, while OIDC introduces ID tokens containing user profile information.

We can think of OAuth 2.0 as a key that opens the door to a house, while OIDC provides identity verification so that this key can be received.

This flow is quite common in several applications we use, as shown in *Figure 6.4*:

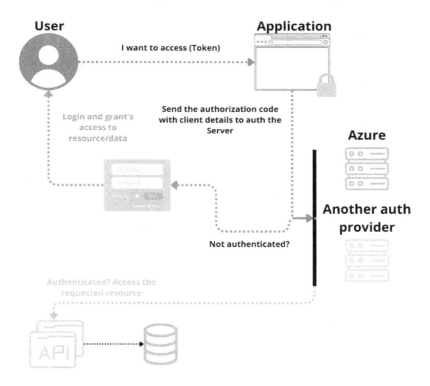

Figure 6.4 – Basic OAuth 2.0 flow

The authorization and authentication flows are constantly used by applications, allowing both to identify who the users are and define the type of permissions that these users can execute in a web system or API.

Despite this straightforward explanation of the OAuth 2.0 and OIDC protocols, as well as concepts of authorization and authentication, the task of implementing this approach isn't simple and depends on some important mechanisms to ensure these functionalities are running correctly.

Due to this, ASP.NET Core 9 has abstractions that support the development of identity management while following the standards outlined so far. The abstraction that implements these resources is known as ASP.NET Core Identity. It has been evolving with each new version of the framework and allows teams to use security best practices in their authorization and authentication flows, as well as integrate with other identity providers while allowing customizations to be made. We'll learn more about this approach in the next section.

# Working with the ASP.NET Core Identity framework

Modern applications interact with different types of technologies, protocols, and standards. As we've been learning, security is extremely important at any level of a solution's implementation flow. A book could easily be dedicated to the subject of authorization and authentication.

However, the ASP.NET Core 9 platform has been evolving every year and as a result, the identity management model has undergone several improvements, in addition to some dependencies being eliminated.

To be able to implement authorization and authentication in our applications, we have ASP.NET Core Identity. It's a membership system that adds capabilities to web-based applications developed in ASP. NET Core 9 and operates in both authentication and authorization flows.

The set of features available in ASP.NET Core Identity includes APIs, a UI, databases between user identity management and credentials, and the ability to grant and revoke permissions. This is in addition to features such as integration with external logins, **two-factor authentication** (**2FA**), password management, being able to block and activate accounts, and providing authentication in applications.

Before we learn how to integrate an application with ASP.NET Core identity, let's learn more about its structure.

## Understanding the ASP.NET Core Identity architecture

ASP.NET Core Identity has an architectural structure that's divided into the following layers:

- **Identity manager**: These are service classes that are responsible for implementing the business logic that involves identities. We can find classes such as `UserManager` for user management and `RoleManager` for role management.

- **Identity store**: The identity store is the domain entity that represents each piece of data in a database. We can see the identity store as a table in the database that's mapped to a class such as `UserStore` or `RoleStore`, among others.

- **Data access layer**: These are classes that have the necessary logic to interact with the database so that they can persist and retrieve identity-related information.

- **Data source**: The data source is the data mechanism that will be used for persistence. By default, ASP.NET Core Identity uses **SQL Server**. However, there are other databases available, and there's the possibility of customizing other data sources.

These four layers have well-defined responsibilities and are fully extensible, bringing flexibility to development and allowing the identity mechanism to be customized according to the context required in an organization.

ASP.NET Core Identity manages both authentication and authorization and works with the following types of data:

- **Users**: These represent users in the application. This entity has some basic attributes implemented, but they can easily be extended.

- **User claims**: These are a set of statements (claims) about a user. Claims add information to the user's identity.

- **User logins**: These provide information about authentication with external providers such as Facebook, Google, Microsoft, and others, if your application has any integration with these providers.

- **Roles**: These are authorization groups.

Based on the information that's managed by the ASP.NET Core Identity platform, we have what we need to implement authorization and authentication flows in our applications. However, this is a robust and highly customizable framework that allows various customizations to be implemented across identity types.

---

**Customizing Identity**

If you want to customize Identity, please consult the official documentation: `https://learn.microsoft.com/en-us/aspnet/core/security/authentication/customize-identity-model?view=aspnetcore-9.0`.

---

Now that we know more about the architectural structure of ASP.NET Core Identity, it's time to add it to an application.

## Getting started with integrating ASP.NET Core Identity

Now that we have greater knowledge about some of the security perspectives that are part of the context of an application, it's time to use ASP.NET Core Identity to add authorization and authentication flows.

As a basis, we'll use the source code available in this book's GitHub repository, as mentioned in the *Technical requirements* section, where you'll be able to download the complete solution. The project we'll be using is a version of the API project that we created in *Chapter 5* since all assumptions related to database configurations have been created. Therefore, we'll leverage the API structure and database structure created earlier. The objective is to implement Identity.

---

**Database settings**

When starting a new project, you'll need to configure **EntityFrameworkCore** and connect the application to a database, as we learned in *Chapter 5*. This way, you'll be able to follow along and configure ASP.NET Core Identity with ease.

---

For this application, which is a web API that connects to a SQL Server database, we'll use the same model we learned about in *Chapter 5* and use **EntityFrameworkCore**. To do so, we'll need to add one more library: **Microsoft.AspNetCore.Identity.EntityFrameworkCore**. This library allows Identity to work with Entity Framework Core.

Ensure this library has been added to your project by opening the `WorkingWithIdentity.csproj` file or running the following command in your terminal, inside the application directory, to install it:

```
dotnet add package Microsoft.AspNetCore.Identity.EntityFrameworkCore
-v 8.0.2
```

---

**Creating the WorkingWithIdentity.csproj project**

The `WorkingWithIdentity.csproj` project is a web API that will be protected with ASP.NET Core Identity and is available in this book's GitHub repository, as described in the *Technical requirements* section. However, if you want to create the project for yourself, follow these steps:

1. Open your operating system's terminal and access the folder where the project should be created.

2. Run the following command to create the project:

```
dotnet new webapi -n WorkingWithIdentity
```

3. Access the new project folder:

```
cd WorkingWithIdentity
```

4. Add the following NuGet packages, all of which are necessary for using the SQL Server database:

```
dotnet add package Microsoft.EntityFrameworkCore
```

```
dotnet add package Microsoft.EntityFrameworkCore.SqlServer
```

```
dotnet add package Microsoft.EntityFrameworkCore.Design
```

5. Make sure you have the **dotnet-ef** tool installed. To do so, run the following command:

```
dotnet tool install --global dotnet-ef
```

By default, the project already contains the **Microsoft.AspNetCore.Identity** library since we added it when we created the project. However, we still need to follow a few more steps to configure the project. Let's start by configuring the database context so that the stores and Identity models can be mapped by **EntityFramework**.

## Configuring the database context

For ASP.NET Core Identity to be able to manage **users**, **roles**, **claims**, and **tokens**, we must configure the application by adding this capability to the DbContext class, which is responsible for interacting with the SQL Server database.

To do this, we must change the BankingDbContext class, available in the Context directory of the reference project in this chapter's repository.

The first step is to change the inheritance class to IdentityDbContext<IdentityUser>, which is located in the Microsoft.AspNetCore.Identity.EntityFrameworkCore namespace. Once we've done this, we'll have the following updated class:

```
namespace WorkingWithIdentity.Context;
using Microsoft.AspNetCore.Identity;
using Microsoft.AspNetCore.Identity.EntityFrameworkCore;
using Microsoft.EntityFrameworkCore;
using WorkingWithIdentity.Model;

public class BankingDbContext : IdentityDbContext<IdentityUser>
{
    public BankingDbContext(DbContextOptions
      <BankingDbContext> options) : base(options)
    {
    }


    public DbSet<Account> Accounts { get; set; }
    public DbSet<Customer> Customers { get; set; }
    public DbSet<Movement> Movements { get; set; }
}
```

As we learned in *Chapter 5*, the DbContext class is an abstraction of **Entity Framework Core** that allows the application to interact with the database, where each entity in the database is represented by properties of the DbSet type. This allows classes to be mapped to entities and vice versa.

By changing the inheritance of the BankingDbContext class to IdentityDb Context<IdentityUser>, we're reusing the default DbContext implementation from ASP.NET Identity Core. This contains the DbSet type for mapping the Identity tables that will be part of the database.

To ensure that all the database settings are available in the application, open the `Program.cs` file and make sure that the following line of code exists in the file:

```
builder.Services.AddDbContext<BankingDbContext>(
  options =>   options.UseSqlServer(builder
  .Configuration.GetConnectionString("BankingDbContext")));
```

It's very important to configure the `DbContext` class in the ASP.NET Core dependency injection container. In this case, we added the `BankingDbContext` class to the dependency injection context while also configuring the use of SQL Server, whose connection will be based on the `ConnectionString` value, which is passed as a parameter to the `UseSqlServer` method. This `ConnectionString` is obtained through the application settings, which in this case can be found in the `appsettings.json` file.

At this point, we have all the necessary configurations so that ASP.NET Core Identity is configured in the data layer. In the next section, we'll update the database so that we can add the necessary tables for identity management.

## Updating the database

In *Chapter 5*, we created an API that simulates digital bank operations and connected it to a database using Entity Framework Core. For this example, we'll use the same database – that is, **dbBanking**. Currently, it has the following data structure:

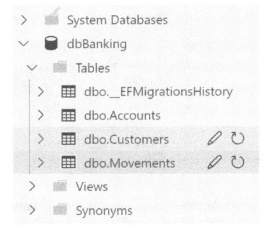

Figure 6.5 – The structure of the dbBanking database

The **dbBanking** database consists of four tables, three of which are part of the application context – that is, **dbo.Accounts**, **dbo.Customers**, and **dbo.Movements**. The fourth table, **dbo.EFMigrationsHistory**, is responsible for managing the status of changes that are made to the database using migrations.

> **Database migrations**
>
> In *Chapter 5*, we explored how migrations work, their importance during application development, and changes that can be made dynamically to the database. If you want to learn more about how ASP.NET Core 9 migrations works, please refer to `https://learn.microsoft.com/en-us/ef/core/managing-schemas/migrations/?tabs=dotnet-core-cli`.

The **dbo.EFMigrationsHistory** table contains the history of the first entities that were created for the bank API. You can check the history that's been generated through the code in the application's directory structure, in the **Migrations** folder, as shown in *Figure 6.6*:

Figure 6.6 – Migrations classes for the API

These classes are automatically generated by the Entity Framework Core command-line tool and should not be changed manually.

After making changes to the `DbContext` class and adding the ASP.NET Core Identity models, we must change the database. To do so, we'll create a new migration.

To do this, open a terminal of your choice, access the root directory of the **WorkingWithIdentity** application, and execute the following command:

```
dotnet ef migrations add IdentityModels
```

The preceding command uses Entity Framework Core's `ef` tool and adds a migration named `IdentityModels`.

Again, when opening the project's **Migrations** folder, we can analyze which new classes were created, as shown in *Figure 6.7*:

```
∨ Migrations
    C⁺ 20241103203812_InitialCreate.cs
    C⁺ 20241103203812_InitialCreate.Designer.cs
    C⁺ 20241103214158_IdentityModels.cs
    C⁺ 20241103214158_IdentityModels.Designer.cs
    C⁺ BankingDbContextModelSnapshot.cs
```

Figure 6.7 – Migration classes for the Identity model

Now that we have the migration structure for the database, we must update **dbBanking** so that it includes the Identity tables. To do this, in your preferred terminal, run the following command in the project directory:

```
dotnet ef database update
```

The preceding command reads the migrations available in the project, analyzes the migration history in the **dbo.EFMigrationsHistory** table in the database, and applies the updates, which in this case involve creating the tables necessary for ASP.NET Core Identity to work correctly. We'll see the new tables that have been created:

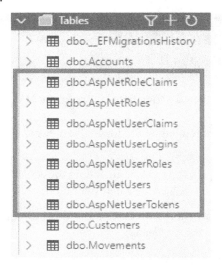

Figure 6.8 – The database now contains ASP.NET Core Identity tables

With that, all basic ASP.NET Core Identity settings related to the data model have been added successfully. However, we still need to add some other configurations to the project so that the application is capable of handling authorization and authentication. So, in the next section, we'll add ASP.NET Core Identity services to the application's dependency injection context.

## Adding ASP.NET Core Identity services and routes

Asp.Net Core Identity contains the necessary abstractions to deal with authorization and authentication mechanisms using the services available in the dependency injection container, in addition to wheels for authentication and token generation.

However, it's necessary to activate these abstractions explicitly. To do so, we must add a few lines of code to the application. Open the `Program.cs` file so that we can edit them. At this point, we must follow these steps:

1. Adding the required Identity namespace – that is, `using Microsoft.AspNetCore.identity;`.

2. Add the authentication services that are responsible for determining the identity of users to the dependency injection container, as well as the authentication method. In this case, we'll be using a bearer token: `builder.Services.AddAuthentication().AddBearerToken();`.

3. Add the authorization services to the dependency injection container by running `builder.Services.AddAuthorization();`.

4. Add the Identity APIs and configure data access through Entity Framework Core by running `builder.Services.AddIdentityApiEndpoints<IdentityUser>().AddEntityFrameworkStores<BankingDbContext>();`.

5. Map the Identity endpoints using `app.MapIdentityApi<IdentityUser>();`.

6. Add each request authentication middleware to the application's request processing pipeline, using the settings defined by `AddAuthentication()` to validate and define the user's identity: `app.UseAuthentication();`.

7. Add middleware that checks authorization policies against the identity of the authenticated user to determine whether the user is allowed to proceed with the current request: `app.UseAuthorization();`.

By making these changes, we'll have the following complete code in the `Program.cs` file:

```
using Dapper;
using Microsoft.AspNetCore.Identity;
using Microsoft.Data.SqlClient;
using Microsoft.EntityFrameworkCore;
using Microsoft.EntityFrameworkCore.SqlServer;
using WorkingWithIdentity.Context;
using WorkingWithIdentity.Model;
using WorkingWithIdentity.RouteHandler;

var builder = WebApplication.CreateBuilder(args);

builder.Services.AddAuthentication().AddBearerToken();

// Adding the Authorization Services from the Asp.Net Core
Identity
builder.Services.AddAuthorization();
// Configure the Database access for the Asp.Net Core Identity
builder.Services.AddIdentityApiEndpoints
```

```
  <IdentityUser>()
    .AddEntityFrameworkStores<BankingDbContext>();

builder.Services.AddEndpointsApiExplorer();
builder.Services.AddSwaggerGen();

builder.Services.AddDbContext<BankingDbContext>
  (options => options.UseSqlServer(builder
    .Configuration.GetConnectionString(
      "BankingDbContext")));

builder.Services.AddScoped(_ => new SqlConnection
  (builder.Configuration.GetConnectionString(
    "BankingDbContext")));

var app = builder.Build();

// Configure the HTTP request pipeline adding the ASP.NET Core
Identity routes
app.MapIdentityApi<IdentityUser>();

// Configure the HTTP request pipeline.
if (app.Environment.IsDevelopment())
{
    app.UseSwagger();
    app.UseSwaggerUI();
}

app.UseHttpsRedirection();

app.RegisterAccountRoutes();
app.RegisterCustomerRoutes();

app.MapGet("GetAllCustomersUsingDapper", async(SqlConnection
connection) =>
{
  var customers = await connection
    .QueryAsync<Customer>("SELECT Id,
    Name FROM Customers ORDER BY Name");

    return Results.Ok(customers);
});

app.MapGet("GetCustomerByIdUsingDapper",
```

```
    async(int id, SqlConnection connection) =>
  {
      var customer = await connection
        .QueryFirstOrDefaultAsync<Customer>(
        "SELECT Id, Name FROM Customers WHERE
        Id = @id", new { id });

      if (customer is null) return Results.NotFound();
      return Results.Ok(customer);
  });
  app.UseAuthentication();
  app.UseAuthorization();
  app.Run();
```

**Register account and customer routes**

The routes that are responsible for processing requests for the Account and Customers APIs were registered through the app.RegisterAccountRoutes and app.RegisterCustomerRoutes extension methods, as highlighted in the preceding code.

This is a good practice for correctly separating responsibilities, as well as improving the maintainability of the Program.cs file code.

To create these extension methods, two classes were created, as shown here:

```
public static class AccountRoutes
{
  public static void RegisterAccountRoutes(this
    IEndpointRouteBuilder routes)
  {
    var group = routes.MapGroup("/accounts");
    // GET: /accounts
    group.MapGet("/", async (BankingDbContext dbContext) =>
    {
      return await dbContext.Accounts.Include(a =>
        a.Customer)
        .Include(a => a.Movements)
        .ToListAsync();
    });
  // other methods
  }
}
```

```
}

public static class CustomerRoutes
{
  public static void RegisterCustomerRoutes(this
    IEndpointRouteBuilder routes)
  {
    var group = routes.MapGroup("/customers");

    // GET: /customers
    group.MapGet("/", async (BankingDbContext dbContext) =>
    {
      return await dbContext.Customers.ToListAsync();
    });

    // other methods
  }
}
```

The extension classes that were created here have a static method that's responsible for registering the routes of the respective entities. This is a practice that makes code more organized and easier to read and maintain. To learn more about creating extension methods, go to `https://learn.microsoft.com/en-us/dotnet/csharp/programming-guide/classes-and-structs/how-to-implement-and-call-a-custom-extension-method`.

When analyzing the preceding code, it's very important to consider the order of the highlighted lines of code; otherwise, the objects and route mappings won't work correctly.

So far, the solution code presents a configuration model that already allows us to benefit from the authorization and authentication features of ASP.NET Core Identity. However, there are some cases where there's a need to customize access types based on user roles. Fortunately, ASP.NET Core 9 offers a powerful feature that allows us to segregate the type of access to application resources, as we will see in the next section.

## Role-based authorization

To have greater control over the user authorization flow in the application, we can implement **role-based authorization**. This role-based control allows you to segregate the type of access to parts of your application based on the roles that have been assigned to users. Imagine a scenario where there are two roles: **Administrator** and **Reader**. By using the role-based authorization approach, you can ensure that only users authorized to certain areas of the application can access specific resources or perform specific actions in an application.

In ASP.NET Core 9, the role-based authorization approach can be implemented by defining policies, which extend role-based authorization with more complex logic, offering fine-grained control over user permissions.

Once a policy has been defined, it can be applied to controllers, actions, or even Razor Pages to enforce the desired authorization behavior. Policies make your authorization logic more modular and reusable. This is especially useful in larger applications, where access control can become complex.

For example, consider a scenario where you want to create a policy that only allows users with the **Admin** role to access certain administrative resources. Also, you might want to create another policy that only allows users with the **Manager** role to be employed for over 1 year so that they can access specific reports. These policies can be defined in the `Program.cs` file and then applied to controllers or actions using the [**Authorize**] attribute.

Let's look at a simple example of a policy that could be added to a `Program.cs` file:

```
builder.Services.AddAuthorization(options =>
{    options.AddPolicy("AdminOnly",
     policy => policy.RequireRole("Admin"));
});
var app = builder.Build();
app.UseAuthorization();
 app.MapGet("/admin", [Authorize(Policy = "AdminOnly")]
   () => {
     return Results.Ok("Welcome, Admin!");
});
app.Run();
```

In the preceding code, we configured a policy called `AdminOnly` that sets a rule where the user has the `Admin` role. The [`Authorize`] attribute is then applied to an endpoint and uses the policy we created earlier, restricting access to users who meet the policy criteria.

Now, let's look at a more complex example. Here, a custom policy has been defined that checks the user's role and provides an additional claim that requires the user's employment duration to be 1 year:

```
builder.Services.AddAuthorization(options =>
{
    options.AddPolicy("EmployeeWithExperience",
    policy =>
    {
        policy.RequireRole("Manager");
        policy.RequireClaim("EmploymentDuration", "1Year");
    });
});
var app = builder.Build();
app.UseAuthorization();
app.MapGet("/reports",
  [Authorize(Policy = " EmployeeWithExperience ")]
  () => {    return Results.Ok("Access granted to experienced
managers.");
});
app.Run();
```

In this example, the `EmployeeWithExperience` policy requires that the user has the `Manager` role and owns a claim named `EmploymentDuration` with a value of `1Year`. This policy applies to the `/reports` endpoint, restricting access to managers only.

Role-based authorization and policies give you a powerful way to manage access to your application's resources, allowing you to build complex authorization logic that goes beyond simple role checks and incorporate additional conditions and claims as needed.

Now that we know more about ASP.NET Core Identity, have integrated it into our application, and know how to segregate access to application resources by implementing authorization policies, it's time to add restrictions to the application's routes.

## Securing APIs with ASP.NET Core Identity

At this point, the application has been fully integrated with ASP.NET Core Identity. Now, we'll run it so that we can analyze the results. Open a terminal of your choice and access the application directory. Then, run the following command:

```
dotnet run
```

An address in `http://localhost:<port>` format will be provided. The port number may be different from the one shown in this example, but the execution will be the same. Access the `http://localhost:<port>/swagger/index.html` address; you should see the following output:

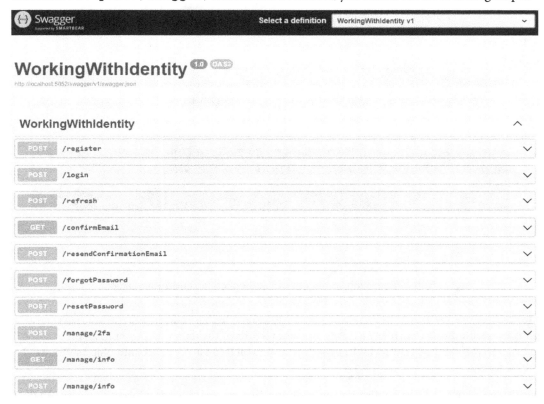

Figure 6.9 – Banking API integrated with ASP.NET Core Identity

As we can see, new routes were added to the API. These routes are the APIs that are provided by ASP.NET Core Identity. Each API allows us to manage the application's users and add different capabilities, such as password recovery, user creation, or password reset.

However, upon attempting to execute an endpoint, such as performing a **GET** request on the **/accounts** API, we realized that we were able to obtain a valid response. To perform the test, simply open the **GET** method of the **/accounts** API, click the **Try Out** button, and then the **Execute** button. We should get the following response:

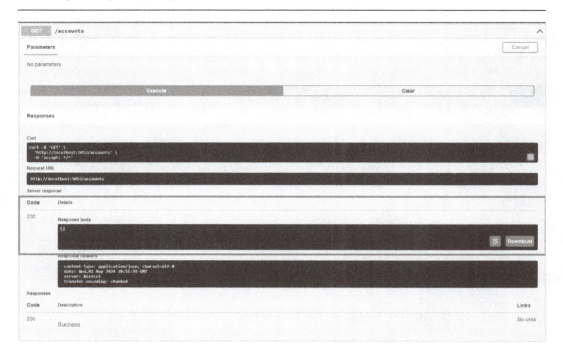

Figure 6.10 – Requesting an API without authentication and authorization

As we can see, we have an HTTP status code of **200**, which means that the request was successful, even if the result didn't return any existing account records in the database. If you have any records registered in this table in your local database, the result will be an array of account objects serialized in JSON format.

However, we want to add authentication and authorization processes to the application's APIs. To do so, we must make some changes to the source code.

As we know, each API has its routes registered in the Program.cs file. These routes act as entry points for requests. Since we want to protect each route so that only known and authorized users can consume the API, we must add a configuration to the routes so that when someone attempts to request the API without being authenticated, the request must return an HTTP **401** status code, informing the API consumer that there's a need for authentication.

In the next section, we'll learn how to protect routes and prevent unauthorized requests.

## Securing application routes

Even if all authentication and authorization settings are present in the application, it's necessary to determine what should be protected and what shouldn't.

One of the ways we can ensure that a given API method is protected by authentication and authorization middleware is by adding an explicit configuration to the routes.

In the application that we're working on, the API routes were implemented in separate files as **extension methods**, as a good practice. So, let's make the necessary change in the `AccountHandler.cs` file, located in the application's `RouteHandler` directory.

To do this, we'll configure the `/accounts` route so that it only accepts requests if the user is authenticated. Let's look at the changed code:

```
app.MapGet("/accounts", async (BankingDbContext
   dbContext) => {
      var accounts = await dbContext.Accounts.ToListAsync();
      return Results.Ok(accounts);
}).RequireAuthorization();
```

Here, we added the `RequireAuthorization()` method call. We've already learned that authorization is a process that validates a user's permissions, while authentication involves identifying the user. In this case, if the user isn't authenticated, they can't be authorized.

Again, in a terminal of your choice, inside the application directory, execute the following command:

```
dotnet run
```

Next, we'll request the `/accounts` route. However, let's execute the **Postman** application first. Follow the steps:

1. Go to **File | New | HTTP**.
2. A new tab will open where you can make a request.
3. Add the URL of the running application – that is, `http://localhost:<port>/accounts` – and check whether the selected method is **GET**.
4. Then, click on the **Send** button. We'll get the following output:

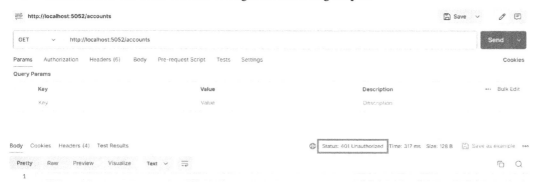

Figure 6.11 – Requesting the protected route

*Figure 6.11* highlights the return of the request with an HTTP status code of 401, which means that the request wasn't authorized.

For a successful request for this route to be made, we must log in and configure the request with the authenticated user's information.

Before logging in, we must create a user in the application. To do this, perform the following steps:

1.  Create a new HTTP request in Postman.

2.  Set the request type to **POST**.

3.  Add `http://localhost:<port>/register` as the route. This is the default route for creating ASP.NET Core Identity users that will be added to the application.

4.  At this point, we need to define the body of the request. To do this, click on the **Body** tab, select the **raw** option, and add the JSON shown in *Figure 6.12*:

Figure 6.12 – Configuring the body of the register user request

5.  You can change the properties of the JSON object to your liking.

6.  Finally, click the **Send** button to make the request.

Upon being executed, we should get a response similar to the one shown in *Figure 6.13*:

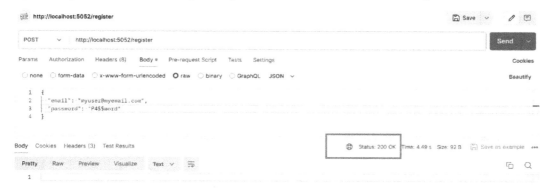

Figure 6.13: Registering a new user using ASP.NET Core Identity

*Figure 6.13* displays an HTTP status code of 200, informing us that the request was successful and that a new user has been registered in the database.

At this point, we must log in. We'll do so using Postman. Create a new HTTP request and perform the following steps to configure the request:

1.  Set the request type to **POST**.

2.  Set the URL to `http://localhost:<port>/login`.

3.  Select the **Body** tab, then the **raw** option, and add the following JSON:

    ```
    {
        "email": "myuser@myemail.com",
        "password": "P4$$word"
    }
    ```

4.  Click the **Send** button.

5.  Make sure you've added the JSON parameters according to the user data you created in your environment.

6. Upon performing the request, you should see the following response:

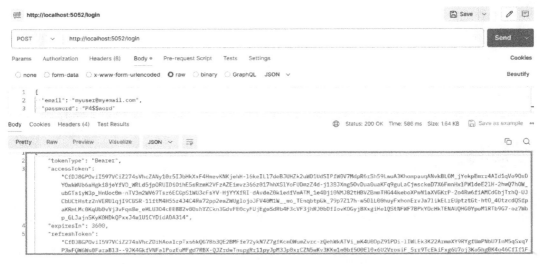

Figure 6.14 – Getting a login response

In response to the login request, we can see that a JSON object with some important properties has been returned:

- tokenType: This value will always be Bearer, which indicates that this response provides a Bearer token in the form of an opaque accessToken, as we configured in the Program. cs file.

- accessToken: This is the token that's generated for the authenticated user. It must be sent as part of the authorization request header.

- expiresIn: A value in seconds that represents the expiration time of accessToken.

- refreshToken: If set, we can obtain a new access_token value upon expiration by using a refresh endpoint without having to re-enter user credentials.

The values displayed in *Figure 6.14* will be different for each request and don't represent a **JWT**. The **access token** is generated and encrypted in a proprietary way in this version of ASP.NET Core Identity and doesn't follow a known convention. However, it's possible to change to a **JWT** if you wish, as well as other configuration parameters of the token generation process.

**ASP.NET Core Identity configurations**

ASP.NET Core Identity offers different authentication options, including JWT (`https://jwt.io/introduction`), cookies, and other settings. To learn more about the different configuration options, go to `https://learn.microsoft.com/en-us/dotnet/api/microsoft.aspnetcore.identity.identityoptions?view=aspnetcore-9.0`.

However, the token-based approach we're using, even though it doesn't involve a JWT, uses the same configuration process as a request being made with the authenticated user's credentials. In the next section, we'll use the **access token** value to make a request on the `/accounts` route and obtain a valid response.

## Requesting an API with the access token

The access token contains the authenticated user's information in encrypted form.

For us to make a valid request on the `/accounts` route, we'll need to pass the token as a parameter in the request header. So, copy the access token value and, in Postman, open the tab that contains the request, as shown in *Figure 6.11*, for the `/accounts` route. Then, perform the following steps:

1.  In the **GET** request tab for the `/accounts` route, click on the **Authorization** tab.
2.  For **Type**, select the **Bearer Token** option.
3.  In the **Token** field, paste the value of the access token that you obtained via the login request.
4.  Click the **Send** button.

As shown in *Figure 6.15*, an empty array is returned since no accounts have been registered in the database. Note that the HTTP status code is **200**, which means that it was a successful request:

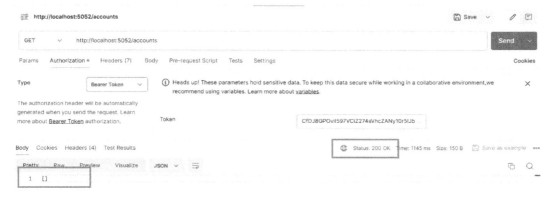

Figure 6.15 – Successful accounts request

So far, the application is working as expected. However, it's important to understand how this authorization process works.

When requesting the account route again, we inform the access token, as configured previously. Despite Postman having a user-friendly UI, when selecting the authentication type and entering the access token, Postman automatically adds an HTTP header. HTTP headers are key/value pairs that are part of requests and responses.

For this request, the header was created with the authorization key and the access token value. You can check this header by clicking on the **Headers** tab and viewing the hidden headers, as shown in *Figure 6.16*:

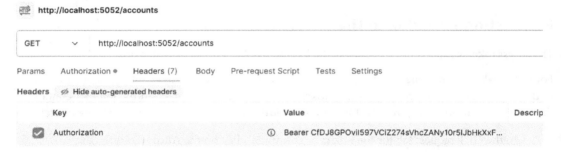

Figure 6.16 – The authorization HTTP header

When making the request, the authentication and authorization **middleware** comes into action. The authentication middleware reads the token that was informed in the authorization header and fills in the user credentials for the request in the **HttpContext.User** object, which is part of the request. This object allows us to access information such as **claims**, which contain data such as the user's name and email, and **roles**, which allow us to determine the user's access type, such as admin, member, and so on.

**The ASP.NET Core 9 HttpContext object**

In ASP.NET Core, `HttpContext.User` is a core property that represents the user security context associated with an HTTP request. This property is an instance of `ClaimsPrincipal`, a .NET class that contains the user's identity in the form of claims. `HttpContext.User` is a key element in handling user authentication and authorization in an ASP.NET Core application.

During the authentication process, when a request arrives at the application, the authentication middleware reads the authentication tokens or cookies attached to the request, validates them, and constructs a `ClaimsPrincipal` object. The `ClaimsPrincipal` object can contain one or more instances of `ClaimsIdentity`.

Each `ClaimsIdentity` instance can contain multiple claims. A claim is a statement about a subject that's been made by an issuer and can represent the user's identity attributes, such as name, role, email, and more.

This process allows the use of `HttpContext.User` in application-wide authorization checks to determine whether the current user has permission to perform certain operations to ensure that only properly authenticated and authorized users can access certain resources or perform specific actions.

The following code shows the use of `HttpContext.User` when executing an action. This object is automatically populated by the execution pipeline through middleware:

```
public IActionResult ExampleAction() {
    var user = HttpContext.User;
    if (user.Identity.IsAuthenticated)        {
        // Do something for authenticated users
        var userName = user.Identity.Name;
        // Get the user's name
        return Content($"Welcome, {userName}");
    }
    else
    {
        // Handle non-authenticated users
        return Unauthorized("You must be logged in to access
this.");
    }
}
```

You can learn more about `HttpContext` at https://learn.microsoft.com/en-us/aspnet/core/fundamentals/http-context?view=aspnetcore-8.0#httpcontext-user.

Authorization middleware analyzes whether the requested route requires authorization. If so, it decrypts the token, analyzes whether it's a valid token, and allows the request on the route to be made correctly.

> **What is middleware?**
>
> During the execution flow of a request in ASP.NET Core 9, several types of processes are carried out, such as identifying the route to be executed, among other functionalities. This flow is called a pipeline. In some cases, there's a need to add functionality to the execution pipeline. This is done through middleware, something we implemented by adding the `app.UseAuthtentication()` and `app.UseAuthorization()` method calls to the `Program.cs` file, which allows us to pre-process the request for authentication and authorization requirements. Through middleware, it's possible to add functionality to both requests and responses.
>
> We'll learn more about middleware in *Chapter 8*.

With each API request, the token is sent so that the user information and their respective accesses are loaded during the request execution flow. This is a characteristic of cloud-native applications. The stateless approach allows applications to be scalable and resilient and ensures the server doesn't retain any information about a client's state between requests, eliminating the need to manage session state. This leads to easier scaling and load balancing, makes it easier to scale servers when the need arises to handle high user demand, and allows each server instance to be able to handle any request without needing to know the context of previous requests.

By not relying on server-side state, developers can avoid issues related to session management, such as session persistence, synchronization across distributed systems, and resource locking.

Modern applications must have security as a premise by design, and the implementation of authentication and authorization has several advantages within the context of applications. However, other aspects related to security are linked not only to the functionalities available to users but also to the application's source code. In the next section, we'll learn how to reinforce security in applications.

# Strengthening application security

For us to be able to create secure web-based applications, we must go beyond implementing the use of a security layer based on authentication and authorization, something we implemented when using ASP.NET Core Identity.

ASP.NET Core 9 allows us to deal with security as a premise when developing applications, providing tools and mechanisms that facilitate the implementation of features that minimize possible loopholes, something that can generate attacks from malicious users.

Let's learn about some good security practices that should be part of every software engineer's toolbox. We'll start by understanding how we can improve the process of managing sensitive configurations in our development environment.

# Managing secrets properly

Every application has configurations and some of these can be sensitive, such as database connections, encryption keys, and even security keys for accessing external resources.

So far, we've learned that it's good practice to keep such settings separate from the C# source code and that we can manage settings through files such as `appsettings.json` and even environment variables. ASP.NET Core 9 allows us to handle external configuration management.

Keeping the settings hard-coded is a bad practice since to change any hard-coded parameter, we must recompile the application. In addition, there's the possibility of malicious users decompiling the application if they have access to the binaries, and then obtaining sensitive data.

> **Obfuscator**
>
> Code obfuscation refers to the process of transforming application source code into a form that's difficult for humans to understand but can still be executed by a computer. This technique is primarily used to protect intellectual property by making it difficult for attackers or unauthorized users to reverse engineer the code and understand its logic.
>
> The process of obfuscation involves several techniques, such as renaming variables and methods to meaningless symbols, removing metadata, encrypting strings, and altering the control flow to make the code more complex. For more information, go to `https://learn.microsoft.com/en-us/visualstudio/ide/dotfuscator/?view=vs-2022`.

Imagine a situation where our application uses an API key to connect to a payment gateway to process transactions from an online store, or even the database connection string. If this key is exposed, malicious users can potentially manipulate transaction data, access sensitive information, and even delete your database.

You might be thinking that since your code is in a private repository, and all settings are being kept in `appsettings.json` files, this problem is solved.

Of course, since it's a private repository, the chances of an attacker gaining access to the data aren't very high. However, consider that your company may work with employees and third-party companies that can access the data in your repository.

While it's good practice to manage settings in `appsettings.json` files, this isn't a good approach for sensitive information. With this, we avoid synchronizing the source code of applications with external repositories containing information that shouldn't be shared.

Fortunately, ASP.NET Core 9 implements the best development practices and provides secret management in your local environment. Proper secret management ensures that sensitive data, such as API keys, isn't hard-coded into your application's source code but is stored and accessed securely, protecting your infrastructure and data integrity.

The Secret Manager tool is included in the .NET Core SDK, so you typically don't need to install anything else if you have the SDK.

To start using Secret Manager, you need to initialize it for your project. Navigate to the project's `WorkingWithIdentity` directory, which we worked on previously, in the Command Prompt or terminal where your `.csproj` file is located. Then, run the following command to initialize secret storage:

```
dotnet user-secrets init
```

The preceding command adds a `UserSecretsId` element within a `PropertyGroup` value to your `.csproj` (project file). This ID uniquely identifies your project's secrets.

You can verify the addition of the `UserSecretsId` element by opening the `.csproj` file in your code editor, as shown in *Figure 6.17*:

```
<PropertyGroup>
  <TargetFramework>net9.0</TargetFramework>
  <Nullable>enable</Nullable>
  <ImplicitUsings>enable</ImplicitUsings>
  <UserSecretsId>51843fb9-c6b0-4766-bc62-2114d83fdf7d</UserSecretsId>
</PropertyGroup>
```

Figure 6.17 – The UserSecretsId element configured in the .csproj file

Next, we'll configure the connection string with the SQL Server database. To do this, we must add some new code by executing the following command:

```
dotnet user-secrets set "ConnectionStrings:BankingDbContext" "YOUR
DATABASE CONNECTION STRING"
```

**Secrets naming convention**

The notation commonly uses colons ( : ) to separate different levels of a hierarchy in the key names of secrets. This structure not only helps in organizing the keys logically but also aligns with how the ASP.NET Core 9 configuration system retrieves values from various configuration sources, such as `appsettings.json`, environment variables, and Secret Manager.

In the `WorkingWithIdentity` application, we have the following configuration in the `appsettings.json` file:

```
"ConnectionStrings" {
        "BankingDbContext": "..."
}
```

The preceding JSON represents a property of the `object` type called `ConnectionStrings` that has a string property called `BankingDbContext`.

Based on this, the secret is called `ConnectionStrings:BankingDbContext`. Here, `ConnectionStrings` is the top-level category and `BankingDbContext` is the actual key containing the respective secret – in this case, the SQL Server database connection string. This notation helps to logically group related settings.

Since this is a convention used by ASP.NET Core 9, there's no need to change the application's source code to obtain the database connection string.

When using environment variables (which don't allow colons in variable names on some operating systems), colon separators are typically replaced with double underscores (__). So, if you were defining these secrets via environment variables in a production environment, you would define them like this:

```
ConnectionStrings__BankingDbContext
```

This naming convention ensures that when the ASP.NET Core configuration system reads the environment variables, it can reconstruct the hierarchy and treat them equivalently to secrets defined in `appsettings.json` or Secret Manager.

There's no need to change the application code to obtain the secret since this is a feature of ASP.NET Core 9 and works in the same way if you want to use environment variables.

The secret that's created is kept in the operating system; its location may vary from environment to environment. However, you can manage secrets using the `user-secrets` tool. For example, you can use it to list the secrets that exist on your local machine:

```
dotnet user-secrets list
```

You can use the following command to remove a specific secret:

```
dotnet user-secrets remove "ConnectionStrings:BankingDbContext"
```

You can even clear all secrets:

```
dotnet user-secrets clear
```

All secrets information is kept in your operating system. When integrating the source code with your remote code repository, the secrets won't be shared.

Keep in mind that the Secret Manager tool is intended for development purposes only. For production environments, you should use a secure vault such as **Azure Key Vault**, **AWS Secrets Manager**, or another secure means of managing sensitive configuration data. We'll learn more about configuration management in *Chapter 9*.

Now that we know how to better manage application secrets, let's learn about other good security practices, including the use of **Hypertext Transfer Protocol Secure (HTTPS)** and **Cross-Origin Resource Sharing (CORS)**.

## Enforcing HTTPS and working with CORS

HTTPS enforcement is important for ensuring secure communication between clients and servers by encrypting data transmitted over the network. As we've already learned, ASP.NET Core 9 provides us with integrated middleware to enforce HTTPS, which can be configured to redirect all HTTP requests to HTTPS.

To enforce HTTPS in an ASP.NET Core 9 application, simply add the following line of code to the `Program.cs` file to add a middleware to the application's execution pipeline:

```
// Enforce HTTPS
app.UseHttpsRedirection();
```

It's important to know that adding the middleware that enforces the use of HTTPS is a configuration step for the application. Likewise, you must also configure your web server (for example, IIS, NGINX, Azure App Services, and so on) to enforce HTTPS and obtain a valid SSL/TLS certificate from a trusted certificate authority.

In addition to enforcing HTTPS, you can configure **CORS**, a feature that's implemented by browsers to restrict web applications running on one origin from accessing resources on a different origin without explicit permission. It's more common to see this type of behavior in SPA applications that use technologies such as **Angular**, **React**, or even pure **JavaScript**. When making an HTTP request through JavaScript, it's executed in the browser, which, through the security mechanism, doesn't allow a request on one origin server to be made to another server where the resource is hosted. Fortunately, ASP.NET Core 9 provides middleware to configure and manage CORS policies, allowing you to specify which origins, headers, and methods are allowed. This feature is interesting because we can only respond to certain requests based on a specific origin.

To enable and configure CORS in an ASP.NET Core 9 application, you can add the following code to the `Program.cs` file:

```
var builder = WebApplication.CreateBuilder(args);

// Add services to the container.
builder.Services.AddRazorPages();

// Configure CORS policy
builder.Services.AddCors(options =>
{
    options.AddPolicy("AllowSpecificOrigin",
        builder =>
        {
            builder.WithOrigins("https://myapp.com")
                .AllowAnyHeader()
                .AllowAnyMethod();
        });
});

var app = builder.Build();

// Enforce HTTPS
app.UseHttpsRedirection();

// Use CORS policy
app.UseCors("AllowSpecificOrigin");

app.UseStaticFiles();
app.UseRouting();
app.UseAuthorization();
app.MapRazorPages();
app.Run();
```

Let's understand the preceding code:

- `builder.Services.AddCors(options => { ... })`: This line adds CORS services to the application's dependency injection container. The `options` parameter, which is of the `Action<CorsOptions>` type, allows you to configure CORS policies.

- `options.AddPolicy`: In this line, we're adding a new policy named `AllowSpecificOrigin`. The `builder` parameter in the Lambda expression is an instance of the `CorsPolicyBuilder` class, which provides methods to configure the policy.

- `builder.WithOrigins("https://myapp.com")`: The `WithOrigins` method defines the origins that are allowed to access the application's resources. In this case, any requests coming from `https://myapp.com` will be allowed by this CORS policy.

- `AllowAnyHeader()`: The `AllowAnyHeader` method allows any HTTP headers in the request, allowing the specified origin to include any headers without being blocked by the CORS policy.

- `AllowAnyMethod()`: This method defines that any HTTP methods (`GET`, `POST`, `PUT`, `DELETE`, and others) can be used in the request.

- `app.UseCors("AllowSpecificOrigin")`: This triggers the CORS middleware in the request pipeline, referencing the previously created policy globally to all HTTP requests of the application.

> **Learn more about CORS**
>
> As defined earlier, CORS is an HTTP header-based mechanism that lets you tell the browser which origins can load resources. ASP.NET Core 9 has an excellent framework for implementing CORS in your applications. To learn more, go to `https://learn.microsoft.com/en-us/aspnet/core/security/cors?view=aspnetcore-9.0`.

The preceding example illustrates the use of CORS in an ASP.NET Core 9 application. However, apart from the origin, it doesn't have restrictions on the use of HTTP headers or methods. In some cases, it will be necessary to explicitly define the HTTP headers and methods that an origin can access.

However, the features available in ASP.NET Core 9 give us great flexibility in defining different policies for different origins, creating more restricted and specific rules for CORS. This is an important mechanism since the browser uses it to allow SPAs or other applications running on the client to be able to consume external resources appropriately.

CORS is not a security mechanism, but its use is recommended. In the next section, we'll talk about some security mechanisms we can use to prevent vulnerabilities in applications.

## Preventing common vulnerabilities

When we talk about vulnerabilities in applications, several topics can be taken into consideration, such as source code, servers, credential management, protocols used, and encryption, among others.

Some common vulnerabilities are already well known, but if they aren't addressed in applications, they can cause some problems for organizations. ASP.NET Core 9 offers mechanisms for dealing with several common threats in web applications:

- SQL injection
- **Cross-site scripting (XSS)**
- **Cross-site request forgery (CSRF)**

Let's learn how to prevent each of these vulnerabilities.

## SQL injection

SQL injection is a common attack where an attacker inserts malicious SQL code into an SQL query.

To prevent SQL injection, always use parameterized queries or ORM frameworks such as Entity Framework, which handle query parameters safely and help us avoid string concatenation. We learned about this in the *Security topics in web applications* section.

## XSS

XSS attacks occur when an attacker injects malicious scripts into a web page. To prevent XSS, always encode or escape user input before rendering it in the browser. This way, if there's any code injection in an input, for example, it will be encoded with special characters. ASP.NET Core 9 provides built-in helpers to sanitize the output, as shown in the following example:

```
@{
var inputSimulator = "<script>
  alert('Injected Code');</script>";
}
<p>@inputSimulator</p>
// output: &lt;script&gt;alert('Injected Code');&lt;/script&gt;
```

In the preceding example, the JavaScript code was encoded, preventing the injected code from being sent and executed since, after encoding, it becomes just a string. To learn more about the vulnerabilities associated with XSS, go to https://learn.microsoft.com/en-us/aspnet/core/security/cross-site-scripting?view=aspnetcore-9.0.

## CSRF

CSRF is a type of security attack in which a malicious website tricks a user's browser into performing actions on another website where the user is authenticated, without the user's knowledge. This can lead to unauthorized actions such as changing settings, transferring funds, or making purchases. ASP.NET Core provides built-in anti-forgery tokens to prevent CSRF attacks. These tokens are automatically included in forms and validated on the server.

To use anti-forgery tokens in a simplified way in Razor Pages or MVC, add the following code to your form:

```
<form method="post">
@Html.AntiForgeryToken()
<!-- Form fields -->
<input type="submit" value="Submit" />
</form>
```

At this point, we must add the `ValidateAntiForgeryToken` attribute to the action that will process the form request, as shown here:

```
[ValidateAntiForgeryToken]
public IActionResult SubmitForm()
{
    // Process the form submission
    return View();
}
```

ASP.NET Core 9 also ¢provides other mechanisms for dealing with this vulnerability. You can learn more at `https://learn.microsoft.com/en-us/aspnet/core/security/anti-request-forgery?view=aspnetcore-9.0`.

As we've learned, applications can contain several vulnerabilities that aren't only associated with the source code but also with the hosting server, communication protocol, and many others.

In any case, the ASP.NET Core 9 platform provides several mechanisms and best practices that, combined and related to the requirements of the applications, allow us to minimize risks and keep our solutions robust, secure, and reliable while following the best practices of modern applications. As we progress through this book, we'll learn about more mechanisms and approaches we can use to create increasingly robust applications.

## Summary

In this chapter, we learned about the principles of web application security and how they influence the development model and the interaction with users and other applications. In addition, we learned about the authorization and authentication processes, comparing the flows of these processes and getting to know standards such as OAuth 2.0 and OIDC. To reinforce our knowledge about authentication and authorization, we worked with ASP.NET Core Identity, which provides all the mechanisms that support user authentication and authorization in an application, integrated with a database for managing identities securely. To do so, we consumed information securely by providing tokens provided by ASP.NET Core Identity. Finally, we discussed how to strengthen the security of applications, understood secret management, and learned about techniques such as the use of CORS to prevent common vulnerabilities in web applications.

In the next chapter, we'll learn how to add more capabilities to applications, understand how to implement best practices, and learn how to use caching and monitoring.

## Get This Book's PDF Version and Exclusive Extras

**UNLOCK NOW**

Scan the QR code (or go to packtpub.com/unlock). Search for this book by name, confirm the edition, and then follow the steps on the page.

*Note: Keep your invoice handly. Purchase made directly from packt don't require one.*

# Part 3:
# Applying Best Practices

In this section, we assume that you are more familiar with the ASP.NET Core 9 platform and most of the powerful features available in this technology. As we advance in the knowledge of the platform and the need to develop increasingly rich solutions, we must stick to best practices. Therefore, we will cover topics related to the addition of features that interact with the application, including the challenge strategy, resilience, and best practices. We will also learn how to implement monitoring (Logging and Tracing), allowing software engineers the ability to deal with bug fixes, optimizations, and proactive actions. We will also explore the use of Middleware to customize the interaction flow in the application.

This part has the following chapters:

- *Chapter 7, Adding Capabilities to Applications*
- *Chapter 8, Enhancing Applications with Middleware in ASP.NET Core 9*
- *Chapter 9, Managing Application Settings*

# 7

# Adding Capabilities to Applications

ASP.NET Core 9 provides different features and tools that enable us to develop powerful web-based solutions. However, we often need more specialized features in order to provide a better end-to-end experience. In this chapter, we will learn good practices related to web applications such as adding caching, using asynchronous mechanisms, resilience mechanisms, and logging. We will explore essential best practices for developing applications with ASP.NET Core 9, covering the correct use of asynchronous mechanisms, HTTP requests, and application instrumentation through logs.

We will focus on the following topics in this chapter:

- Working with ASP.NET Core 9 best practices
- Improving performance with a cache strategy and making the application resilient
- Understanding and implementing logging and monitoring

## Technical requirements

To support the learning of this chapter, the following tools must be present in your development environment:

- **Docker**: Docker Engine must be installed on your operating system and have a SQL Server container running. You can find more details about Docker and the SQL Server container in *Chapter 5*.
- **Postman**: This tool will be used to execute requests to APIs of the developed application.
- **Redis Insight**: This tool is used to connect to a Redis Server database (`https://redis.io/insight/`).

The code examples used in this chapter can be found in the book's GitHub repository: `https://github.com/PacktPublishing/ASP.NET-Core-9.0-Essentials/tree/main/Chapter07`.

# Working with ASP.NET Core 9 best practices

So far, we have already learned about several features and benefits of ASP.NET Core 9 in creating quality web systems. Of course, just like any other software development technology, there is no restriction on the way we will handle our code. In this way, we have the freedom to create solutions and new standards with the aim of meeting a specific need.

However, relying on good practices can not only expand our capacity to develop quality applications but also avoid wasting several hours to achieve a goal.

In this case, we will address some good practices necessary to bring greater quality to our applications, starting with the correct use of **HTTP requests**.

## HTTP request best practices

The HTTP request is a fundamental component when working with web applications. Proper handling of HTTP requests can significantly impact the performance and reliability of your application.

We have already learned about the types of HTTP verbs and status codes in *Chapter 3*. However, each HTTP method provided by the application must be treated appropriately, to avoid inconsistencies in the application and avoid vulnerabilities.

Furthermore, the way HTTP requests are made directly impacts the experience of users or consumers of your solution.

Let's understand some good practices related to HTTP requests.

### Validate and sanitize input

Always validate and sanitize input to prevent security vulnerabilities such as SQL injection and **cross-site scripting (XSS)**.

> XSS
>
> XSS is a security vulnerability where the attacker injects scripts into web pages. To know more, go to `https://learn.microsoft.com/en-us/aspnet/core/security/cross-site-scripting?view=aspnetcore-9.0`.

Consider a scenario where a user submits a form with a username. To prevent harmful data from being processed, you should validate the input to ensure it meets the expected criteria and sanitize it to remove any malicious content:

```
public IActionResult Submit(string username)
{
    if (string.IsNullOrEmpty(username))
    {
        return BadRequest("Username is required.");
    }
    username = HttpUtility.HtmlEncode(username);
    // Proceed with processing the username
    return Ok();
}
```

The preceding code demonstrates a simple validation of the username parameter, `if (string. IsNullOrEmpty)`, avoiding using it incorrectly. The `HttpUtility.HtmlEncode(username)` method is used to convert characters such as <, >, &, and so on into an HTML-encoded format.

### Use asynchronous methods

During the execution flow of an HTTP request, we must avoid making the processing actions synchronous. Otherwise, this could degrade the user experience and cause some problems for the application, such as the following:

- **Thread blocking**: Synchronous methods block the thread while waiting for I/O operations (such as database queries, file access, or network requests) to complete. In an ASP.NET Core application, the thread pool is a limited resource.

- **Thread pool exhaustion**: When an application heavily relies on synchronous methods, the thread pool can become exhausted, especially under high load, which occurs when all available threads are blocked and no new threads are available to handle incoming requests.

It is a recommendation and good practice to use asynchronous methods to improve performance and scalability. For example, when using the `HttpClient` object to make a request in an API, use the `HttpClient.SendAsync` method instead of `HttpClient.Send`.

Asynchronous programming allows your application to handle multiple tasks simultaneously without waiting for each task to complete before starting the next one. This is similar to how a chef in a busy kitchen might prepare multiple dishes at once, rather than finishing one dish before starting another.

We will cover the use of asynchronous programming in more detail in the *Asynchronous requests and I/O optimization* section. Now, let's understand another good practice in relation to HTTP requests, regarding caching and compression.

## Caching and compression

Requests via the HTTP protocol have some attributes, including headers and body. During communication between an application and the backend, this information is transmitted, and the headers are used both by the client (in this case, the browser) and by the backend.

There are several types of HTTP headers, including those associated with caching and compression.

By utilizing caching and response compression, we can reduce bandwidth usage and improve load times. Browsers also identify these headers, avoiding unnecessary requests to the server.

Caching and dating compression work similarly to how a library might keep frequently borrowed books readily accessible or how a vacuum-sealed package takes up less space. These practices reduce the load on your server and speed up responses to user requests.

Let's analyze the following code snippet extracted from a `Program.cs` class:

```
// Add services to the container. builder.Services.
AddResponseCaching();
app.UseResponseCaching();
app.Use(async (context, next) => {
  context.Response.GetTypedHeaders().CacheControl =
    new Microsoft.Net.Http.Headers.CacheControlHeaderValue
    {
       Public = true, MaxAge = TimeSpan.FromMinutes(10)
    };
    await next();
});
```

Let's understand the preceding code. When you add `app.UseResponseCaching` to the application's **middleware** pipeline, it performs the following functions:

- **Checks for Cache-Control headers**:

  - The middleware checks whether the incoming request can be cached based on the presence of Cache-Control headers

  - If a valid Cache-Control header is found and it allows caching, the middleware proceeds to handle the request

- **Stores responses in the cache**:

  - If the response to the request can be cached, the middleware stores the response in the cache

  - Subsequent requests that match the cache criteria will be served directly from the cache, bypassing the need to generate the response again

- **Serves cached responses**:

  - For requests that match previously cached responses, the middleware serves the cached response

  - This reduces the processing time and load on the server, as the response is retrieved directly from the cache

The app.Use(async (context, next) method adds the necessary parameters for the Cache-Control header to the middleware pipeline, such as the cache duration time. This is necessary so that the client can know how the response should be cached.

The cache is managed in the application's memory and, therefore, it is not interesting to keep the cache for a large amount of time in memory, which could cause problems. However, it is good practice to use it. We will go into more detail about cache usage in the next section, *Improving performance with a cache strategy and making the application resilient*.

To further improve response performance, we can perform compression automatically with a few lines of code.

For this purpose, we must add the Microsoft.AspNetCore.ResponseCompression NuGet package to the project. You can do this by typing the following command in your application's project directory:

```
dotnet add package Microsoft.AspNetCore.ResponseCompression
```

In any case, it is important that you understand how to use this functionality in your applications.

After adding the NuGet package, we must add the compression services to the Program.cs file. When doing so, we have the following modified file taking into account caching and compression:

```
var builder = WebApplication.CreateBuilder(args);
// Add services to the container.
builder.Services.AddResponseCompression(options =>
{
    options.EnableForHttps = true;
    // Enable compression for HTTPS requests
    options.Providers.Add<GzipCompressionProvider>();
    // Add Gzip compression
    options.Providers.Add<BrotliCompressionProvider>();
    // Add Brotli compression
});

builder.Services.Configure<
  GzipCompressionProviderOptions>(options =>
{
    options.Level = System.IO.Compression
```

```csharp
        .CompressionLevel.Fastest;
    // Set compression level for Gzip
});

builder.Services.AddResponseCaching();

var app = builder.Build();

// Configure the HTTP request pipeline.
if (!app.Environment.IsDevelopment())
{
    app.UseExceptionHandler("/Home/Error");
    app.UseHsts();
}

app.UseHttpsRedirection();
app.UseStaticFiles();

app.UseRouting();

app.UseResponseCompression(); // Use response compression middleware
app.UseResponseCaching(); // Use response caching middleware

app.Use(async (context, next) =>
{
  context.Response.GetTypedHeaders().CacheControl =
    new Microsoft.Net.Http.Headers.CacheControlHeaderValue
  {
    Public = true,
    MaxAge = TimeSpan.FromMinutes(10)
  };
  await next();
});

app.UseAuthorization();

app.MapRazorPages();
app.MapControllers();

app.Run();
```

The preceding code can be explained as follows:

- **Add response compression middleware**:

  - The `builder.Services.AddResponseCompression` method is used to add response compression services to the **Dependency Injection (DI)** container.

  - `options.EnableForHttps` is set to `true` to enable compression for HTTPS responses.

  - `options.Providers.Add<GzipCompressionProvider>()` and `options.Providers.Add<BrotliCompressionProvider>()` are used to add support for **Gzip** and **Brotli** compression providers.

- **Configure compression options**:

  - `builder.Services.Configure<GzipCompressionProviderOptions>(options => options.Level = System.IO.Compression.CompressionLevel.Fastest)` is used to configure the compression level for Gzip. You can adjust the compression level based on your needs (`Optimal`, `Fastest`, or `NoCompression`).

- **Use middleware**:

  - `app.UseResponseCompression()` adds the response compression middleware to the request pipeline.

> **The order of middleware is important**
>
> When combining response caching and compression, the order of the middleware is important. Make sure compression middleware is included before caching middleware. This way, responses are compressed before being cached, ensuring that cached responses are already compressed and ready to be served efficiently.

With these practices, you can reduce the size of responses, leading to better performance and faster loading times for users.

The time has come to understand asynchronous requests in more detail.

## Asynchronous requests and I/O optimization

Asynchronous programming is a fundamental aspect of modern web development, enabling non-blocking operations that improve application responsiveness and scalability.

The great complexity of asynchronous programming is abstracted by the resources available in C#, making applications and functionalities even more powerful. But to better understand the importance of this asynchronous process, let's analyze the following example.

Imagine you are waiting in line at a coffee shop. If the barista had to wait for each cup of coffee to finish brewing before starting the next one, the line would move very slowly. Instead, the barista starts preparing the next drink while the previous one is being prepared. Similarly, asynchronous programming allows your application to start other tasks while waiting for a previous task to complete.

Web applications can respond to a large number of requests from users at a given time. ASP.NET Core 9 is optimized enough to manage requests and memory efficiently. However, if you choose to use a synchronous approach, which is also possible, some problems may be caused. Let's see how we can develop asynchronous methods.

### Use async and await keywords

In C#, the `async` and `await` keywords let you write asynchronous code that is easier to read and maintain.

For example, in the context of an ASP.NET Core application, using `async` and `await` allows your server to handle more requests simultaneously by not blocking threads during I/O operations, as demonstrated in the following code:

```
public async Task<IActionResult> GetDataAsync()
{
    var data = await _dataService.GetDataAsync();
    return Ok(data);
}
```

Let's look at the details highlighted in the code:

- `async`: This is the keyword used to indicate that the method is asynchronous. When declaring an asynchronous method, it is mandatory to use at least one `await` keyword to perform asynchronous operations in the method body.

- `Task<IActionResult>`: This specifies that the method returns a task that will eventually be completed with `IActionResult`. The `Task` type represents an asynchronous operation in C#. `IActionResult` is a common return type in ASP.NET Core MVC that represents the result of an action method. The return type could be any type of class or structure, for example, returning an integer such as `Task<int>`.

- `await`: The `await` keyword is used to asynchronously wait for the `GetDataAsync` method to complete. This means that the method will return a task and execution will be paused until the task is completed, without blocking the thread.

- `_dataService.GetDataAsync()`: This line calls an asynchronous `GetDataAsync` method on the `_dataService` object. `_dataService` is presumably an instance of a service class that handles data retrieval.

C# has several asynchronous methods and you can identify them by using the `async` suffix, added to the name of the methods as a convention.

> **Asynchronous programming**
>
> Asynchronous programming in C# has several other details and ways of application, and it is not possible to consider them as part of this book. However, to continue your learning, I suggest this great content from Microsoft Learn: `https://learn.microsoft.com/en-us/dotnet/csharp/asynchronous-programming/`.

With some simple changes, using the features available in ASP.NET Core 9, we have the ability to implement asynchronous requests with some keywords.

These resources can be used in conjunction, for example, with Entity Framework Core.

We can implement asynchronous data access using Entity Framework Core with methods such as `ToListAsync()` and `SaveChangesAsync()`.

The asynchronous data access lets your application perform other operations while waiting for data from the database, as exemplified in the following code, where an asynchronous query is made to obtain all records from the `Customers` table through Entity Framework:

```
public async Task<List<Customer>> GetCustomersAsync()
{
    return await _dbContext.Customers.ToListAsync();
}
```

Consider the use of asynchronous programming in the design of your applications.

Although the ASP.NET Core 9 platform provides us with several mechanisms to create robust applications, it is important to keep in mind that the use of best practices for HTTP requests, compression, and information caching, in addition to the asynchronous programming model, must be taken into consideration in all applications developed. This guarantees the best experience for users and integrated systems, in addition to ensuring that applications can be optimized enough to support large demands correctly.

In the next section, we will see in more detail the use of caching strategies and how to make applications resilient.

# Improving performance with a cache strategy and making the application resilient

In the *HTTP request best practices* subsection of the *Working with ASP.NET Core 9 best practices* section, we learned about some mechanisms capable of bringing several improvements to our applications. Some approaches were discussed, including a brief introduction to the use of caching.

To expand our knowledge and add techniques to our robust application development model, we will explore the use of caching strategies and how to make our applications resilient, a fundamental requirement for modern solutions.

Let's start with first understanding the different types of caching strategies.

## Caching strategies

Caching is a powerful technique to improve application performance by storing frequently accessed data in a temporary storage location. This reduces the need to retrieve data from the original source repeatedly.

In the *Caching and compression* subsection, a code was demonstrated that enabled the application to manage a cache, adding functionality to ASP.NET Core 9 middleware, used during request processing. For this case, the **in-memory** cache strategy was used, which stores data in memory for quick access. This is suitable for small to medium-sized datasets that are frequently accessed.

However, for more robust applications, another strategy called the **distributed cache** is necessary.

A distributed cache uses some type of resource specialized in distributed caching, such as Redis.

**Redis** is a powerful technology for large datasets or when running in a distributed environment.

---

**What is Redis?**

**Remote DIctionary Server** (**Redis**) is an open source, in-memory data structure store. It is known for its high performance, flexibility, and support for diverse data structures.

Redis stores data in memory, which makes it extremely fast compared to disk-based databases, and also supports data persistence on disk periodically.

Redis' persistence model is key/value, supporting data structures such as strings, hashes, lists, sets, sorted sets, bitmaps, HyperLogLogs, and geospatial indexes. This flexibility allows for diverse use cases.

Redis is a resource widely used by several applications; if you want to know more, go to this link: `https://redis.io/`.

---

Several modern applications, hosted mainly in cloud environments, use Redis as a solution for distributed caching, in addition to being fully integrated with ASP.NET Core 9.

So that we can better understand how Redis works when integrated with ASP.NET Core 9, let's implement an application.

It is important to take into account the requirements mentioned in the *Technical requirements* section. Let's learn how to integrate Redis into our application.

## Integrating Redis in our application

We will start by creating an application. Therefore, open the terminal in a directory of your choice and perform the following steps:

1. Create a new ASP.NET Core 9 project by running the following commands:

   ```
   dotnet new webapi -n DistributedCacheExample
   cd DistributedCacheExample
   ```

2. Add the Redis cache package:

   ```
   dotnet add package Microsoft.Extensions.Caching.
   StackExchangeRedis
   ```

3. Now, run the following command to open Visual Studio Code in the application directory:

   ```
   Code .
   ```

4. Open the appsettings.json file and change the content to the following code:

   ```
   {
     "ConnectionStrings": {
       "Redis": "localhost:6379"
     }
   }
   ```

   The preceding JSON defines a connection string for the Redis server that we will create later.

5. Open the Program.cs file and change all its contents with the following code:

   ```
   using Microsoft.Extensions.Caching.Distributed;

   var builder = WebApplication.CreateBuilder(args);

   // Add services to the container.
   builder.Services.AddControllers();
   builder.Services.AddEndpointsApiExplorer();
   builder.Services.AddSwaggerGen();

   // Configure Redis distributed cache
   builder.Services.AddStackExchangeRedisCache(options =>
   {
     options.Configuration = builder
       .Configuration.GetConnectionString("Redis");
     options.InstanceName = "myPrefix_";
   });
   ```

```
var app = builder.Build();

// Configure the HTTP request pipeline.
if (app.Environment.IsDevelopment())
{
    app.UseSwagger();
    app.UseSwaggerUI();
}

app.UseAuthorization();
app.MapControllers();
app.Run();
```

You should already be used to most of the code described previously. The builder.Services.AddStackExchangeRedisCache method adds the default required objects, as part of the added library **Microsoft.Extensions.Caching.StackExchangeRedis**, to manage the cache when configuring the DI container.

We have two main configurations:

- options.Configuration: This is where the connection address to the Redis server is provided

- options.InstanceName: This is an optional parameter that defines a prefix for the cache keys

The foundation of the application has been configured, and now it's time to implement a controller that will interact with Redis.

## Working with cache in the controller class

To do this, still in Visual Studio Code, follow the following steps to create the controller:

1. If it does not exist, in the root of the project, create a folder named Controllers.

2. Add a class called CacheController in the Controller folder

3. Modify all content of the previously created class with the following code:

```
using Microsoft.AspNetCore.Mvc;
using Microsoft.Extensions.Caching.Distributed;
using System.Text.Json;
using System.Text;

namespace DistributedCacheExample.Controllers;
    [ApiController]
    [Route("api/[controller]")]
    public class CacheController : ControllerBase
```

```
{
    private readonly IDistributedCache _cache;
    public CacheController(IDistributedCache
      cache)
    {
        _cache = cache;
    }

    [HttpGet("{key}")]
    public async Task<IActionResult>
      Get(string key)
    {
        var cachedData = await _cache
          .GetStringAsync(key);
        if (string.IsNullOrEmpty(cachedData))
        {
            return NotFound();
        }

        var data = JsonSerializer
          .Deserialize<MyData>(cachedData);
        return Ok(data);
    }

    [HttpPost]
    public async Task<IActionResult>
      Post([FromBody] MyData data)
    {
        var cacheKey = data.Key;
        var serializedData = JsonSerializer
          .Serialize(data);
        var options = new
          DistributedCacheEntryOptions()
          .SetSlidingExpiration(TimeSpan
          .FromMinutes(5))
          .SetAbsoluteExpiration(TimeSpan
          .FromHours(1));

        await _cache.SetStringAsync(cacheKey,
          serializedData, options);
        return CreatedAtAction(nameof(Get),
         new { key = cacheKey }, data);
    }
```

```
    }

    public class MyData
    {
        public string Key { get; set; }
        public string Value { get; set; }
    }
```

The preceding code creates an API called `Cache` containing **GET** and **POST** methods. Let's analyze the important points of the code in more detail:

- `Microsoft.Extensions.Caching.Distributed`: This is a namespace that references the NuGet package containing the dependencies necessary for handling the cache in the `CacheController` class.

- `private readonly IDistributedCache _cache`: This is a private property of the class that abstracts a cache handling object.

- `public CacheController(IDistributedCache cache)`: As a dependency, the class constructor has the `IDistributedCache` interface that will be injected by DI and assigns the instance to the class's `_cache` property.

- `var cachedData = await _cache.GetStringAsync(key)`: During the execution of the `Get` method, the `_cache` object, which abstracts a connection to the Redis server, will search for a string using the key and return it in the request; otherwise, it will return a `NotFound()` status.

- `Post` method: The `Post` method receives as a parameter an object of the `MyData` type, a class created at the end of the file. When obtaining the `MyData` object, the `Key` property will be used as the cache key, `var cacheKey = data.Key`. Then, the `MyData` object is serialized into JSON, `JsonSerializer.Serialize(data)`. Subsequently, an object of the `DistributedCacheEntryOptions` type is created, where expiration parameters for information in the cache are specified. Finally, the cache persisted in Redis by running `await_cache.SetStringAsync(cacheKey, serializedData, options)`.

**SetSlidingExpiration and SetAbsoluteExpiration**

The `.SetSlidingExpiration(TimeSpan.FromMinutes(5))` and `.SetAbsoluteExpiration(TimeSpan.FromHours(1))` methods are used to configure cache entry expiration options in `DistributedCacheEntryOptions`. These methods help manage how long the cached data should be kept in the cache.

`SlidingExpiration` specifies the amount of time a cache entry can be inactive (not accessed) before it is removed from the cache. The expiration time is reset every time the cache entry is accessed.

`AbsoluteExpiration` specifies the maximum time a cache entry should be kept in the cache, regardless of how often it is accessed. The cache entry will be removed from the cache after the specified time has elapsed, no matter how many times it has been accessed.

With the application developed, we must create a Redis server, and for this, we will use Docker to run it:

1.  In the application directory, open the terminal and run the following command:

    ```
    docker run --name redis -d -p 6379:6379 redis
    ```

    If this is your first time running Redis on your machine, wait for it to download and then the server will start.

2.  Still in the application terminal, use the following command to run it:

    ```
    dotnet run
    ```

3.  After running the application, open Postman and create a new request by accessing the **File | New Tab** menu.

4.  Then, define the request type as **GET**, and in the URL field, enter the URL made available in the terminal after executing the application with the suffix `/api/Cache/DataInCache`. *Figure 7.1* demonstrates an example of the request configuration:

Figure 7.1 – Configuring the API request on Postman

> **API URL port**
>
> The number 5277 added to the URL shown in *Figure 7.1* represents the API execution port. This value may vary from environment to environment. Make sure to enter the execution port available in your terminal after executing the docker run command.

5.  The DataInCache value represents the key we want to get the cached value from. However, when clicking on the **Send** button in Postman, we have the following return (*Figure 7.2*):

Figure 7.2 – Requesting data in cache

As shown in *Figure 7.2*, the HTTP status and JSON return in the response body represent the 404 not found state.

The API return is correct, as the GET method tries to obtain a value from the cache, and if not found, an HTTP status of 404 is returned.

6.  Still in Postman, open a new tab (**File | New Tab**), set the request type as **POST**, and define the API URL with the following suffix: /api/Cache.

7.  Then, click **Body**, select the **raw** option, and add the following JSON:

```
{
    "key": "DataInCache",
    "value": "Value in cache"
}
```

The entire configuration of this request is demonstrated in *Figure 7.3*:

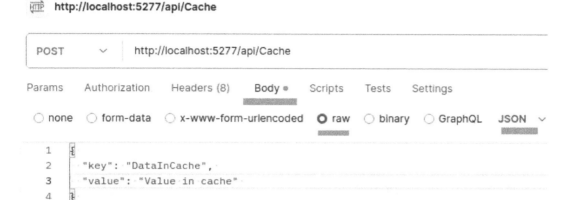

Figure 7.3 – Post request configuration

The **POST** request, demonstrated in *Figure 7.3*, will make a call to the API's POST method, which will add the value defined in the request body to the Redis cache.

8.  Click the **Send** button to make the request and you should receive the HTTP 201 status code in return, indicating that the information was created in the cache.

9.  If you want to confirm the cached value, in Postman, open the previous tab containing the GET request and you should receive the HTTP 200 status code in return, along with the JSON object that represents the cached data.

Another way to check the values available in the Redis cache is to use a UI tool such as Redis Insight, mentioned in the *Technical requirements* section, which we'll configure now.

## Configuring Redis Insight

Let's configure Redis Insight to connect to the Redis server running on Docker by following these steps:

1.  On the application's main screen, click on the **Add connection details manually** option, as shown in *Figure 7.4*:

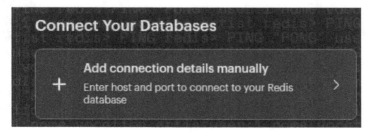

Figure 7.4 – Configuring the Redis connection

2.  On the next screen, we must add the connection parameters to the Redis server. As this server is running through Docker, the default parameters will be used, already available on the screen:

    • **Host**: This defines the Redis server address.

    • **Port**: This defines the server execution port.

    • **Other parameters**: Not important at this time. However, in productive environments, the host address, port, user, and password may be different and necessary.

3.  For our example, just keep the default values and click the + **Add Redis database** button.

    Once the connection is created, the list of servers connected to Redis Insights will be displayed, as shown in *Figure 7.5*:

Figure 7.5 – Connected Redis cache in the Redis Insight tool

4.  Click on the created connection displayed in the list of connections. Then, click on the magnifying glass icon, as highlighted in *Figure 7.6*, to view the data available in the cache:

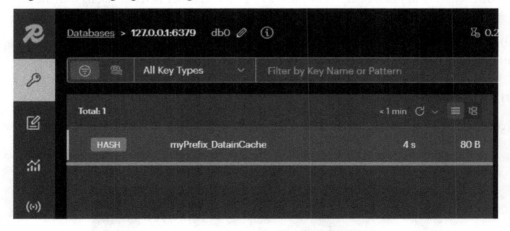

Figure 7.6 – List of data in the cache

If you cannot view any information when clicking the magnifying glass icon, it means that the previously added key has expired. In this case, just make another POST request to add another key and view it in Redis Insight.

This is a simple example created so that we can learn how to communicate with the cache and add information to memory. In this case, we are using Redis, a powerful distributed data management resource, as a server for the information that will be kept in memory.

In real scenarios, this approach can be used in conjunction with a database. This way, before executing a request to the database, the existence of information in the cache will be checked. If it exists, it will not be necessary to make a call to the database, optimizing processes.

As we learned, caching is a powerful solution for making our applications more performant and available.

Now that we have learned how to quickly retrieve information from a cache server, we will understand how to make our applications more resilient in the next topic.

## Resilience mechanisms

To build robust applications, it is essential to implement resilience mechanisms that deal with transient failures and ensure continuous availability.

Think of resilience mechanisms as safety nets that catch us if something goes wrong. They help your application recover from unexpected crashes and maintain a smooth user experience.

The most common resilience strategies are as follows:

- **Retry pattern**: Automatically retries a failed operation a specified number of times before giving up. This is useful for dealing with transient faults.

- **Circuit breaker pattern**: Prevents an application from performing an operation that is likely to fail. It stops the flow of requests to a service when a failure is detected, allowing the system to recover.

In order to have the ability to implement these patterns in our applications, we will use a library called **Polly**.

---

Polly

Polly is a library that is part of the .NET Foundation used to add various resilience features to applications. It is constantly updated by the open source community and used in various applications in production environments. To learn more about Polly, go to `https://github.com/App-vNext/Polly`.

---

To use Polly in our applications, we just need to add it to the project through the following command executed in the application's project directory:

```
dotnet add package Polly.Core
```

Let's analyze the implementation of the retry strategy in the following code example:

```
var retryPolicy = Policy.Handle<Exception>().RetryAsync(3);

public async Task<IActionResult> GetDataWithRetryAsync()
{
    return await retryPolicy.ExecuteAsync(async () =>
    {
        var data = await _dataService.GetDataAsync();
        return Ok(data);
    });
}
```

As we can see in the preceding code, the implementation process is quite simple and integrates with the ASP.NET Core 9 development model. In this example, the objective is to obtain data from a service in a resilient way. Let's analyze the main points of the implementation:

- `var retryPolicy = Policy.Handle<Exception>().RetryAsync(3)` aims to create a retry policy. In this case, the policy is related to an exception. During execution, if an exception is identified, the request will be made again. Trials were configured to run a maximum of three times.

- The `return await retryPolicy.ExecuteAsync` command is a method that executes an action using the previously configured retry policy. All code executing the `GetDataAsync` method request is defined within the scope of the policy that automatically manages the retry mechanism.

It is very common to use the retry strategy when consuming external APIs. There may be intermittences or momentary unavailability and, in this case, `retry` helps to guarantee greater resilience in cases of momentary unavailability.

Let's look at an example of implementing the circuit breaker strategy:

```
var circuitBreakerPolicy = Policy.Handle<Exception>()
    .CircuitBreakerAsync(
        3, // Number of consecutive faults before breaking the circuit
        TimeSpan.FromMinutes(1) // Duration of the circuit break
    );

public async Task<IActionResult>
    GetDataWithCircuitBreakerAsync()
{
    return await circuitBreakerPolicy
        .ExecuteAsync(async () =>
        {
```

```
            var data = await _dataService.GetDataAsync();
            return Ok(data);
    });
}
```

Let's look at the details of the preceding code:

- `CircuitBreakerAsync`: This method creates an asynchronous circuit breaker policy.

- The circuit breaker will open (break the circuit) after three consecutive exceptions (faults).

- `TimeSpan.FromMinutes(1)`: Once the circuit is open, it will remain open for one minute. During this time, any attempt to perform the action will immediately throw `BrokenCircuitException` without performing the action.

  The circuit breaker has the following states:

  • **Closed**: The normal state where all calls are allowed.

  • **Open**: The state in which calls are blocked after a specified number of consecutive failures.

  • **Half-open**: After the open period, the circuit breaker allows a limited number of test calls to verify that the underlying problem has been resolved. If these calls are successful, the circuit returns to the closed state. If they fail, the circuit returns to the open state.

  • `circuitBreakerPolicy.ExecuteAsync`: This method executes the given asynchronous delegate (the code block inside) under the control of the circuit breaker policy.

  • If the `_dataService.GetDataAsync()` call succeeds, the method returns the data wrapped in an `OkObjectResult` (HTTP 200 response).

  • If the `_dataService.GetDataAsync()` call throws an exception, the circuit breaker policy handles it:

    ◆ If fewer than three exceptions have occurred consecutively, the circuit breaker remains closed, and the exception is propagated.

    ◆ After three consecutive exceptions, the circuit breaker opens for one minute. Any further calls within this period will immediately throw `BrokenCircuitException`.

The circuit breaker policy helps prevent repeated failures from overloading the system by interrupting the circuit after three consecutive failures and keeping it open for one minute. During this period, any attempt to call the data service will result in an immediate exception without attempting to execute the service call. This allows the system to recover and prevents cascading failures in dependent systems.

The circuit breaker and retry strategies are powerful resilience strategies that, despite appearing similar, have different objectives, as shown in *Table 7.1*:

| Aspect | Circuit Breaker | Retry |
|---|---|---|
| Purpose | Prevent overwhelming a failing service | Handle transient faults by retrying |
| Behavior | Stops requests after a certain number of failures and opens the circuit for a specified time | Retries the operation a specified number of times with a delay between retries |
| States | Closed, open, half-open | No states, just retries |
| Failure Handling | Fails fast once the circuit is open | Retries multiple times before failing |
| When to Use | When repeated failures need to be avoided to protect a system | When temporary faults are expected to be resolved with retries |
| Complexity | Higher, with state transitions and monitoring | Lower, with simple retry logic |
| Feedback to Users | Immediate failure feedback when the circuit is open | Delayed feedback after all retries fail |

Table 7.1 –The circuit breaker and retry objectives

In practice, these patterns are often used together to provide a robust fault-handling mechanism. For example, you can use a retry policy to handle transient failures, and if the attempts consistently fail, the circuit breaker can be used to prevent retries and allow the system to recover.

Polly offers several other resilience mechanisms that can be combined to make applications even more powerful.

The use of these strategies greatly contributes to the creation of robust solutions prepared for large-scale execution models, especially in cloud environments.

In any case, even by adding several mechanisms to avoid failures, they may arise. In this case, we must be able to obtain sufficient information to make corrections and keep applications free from non-conformities. For this, it is important to add logs in applications, and ASP.NET Core 9 provides a powerful mechanism for this, which we will learn about in the next section.

# Understanding and implementing logging and monitoring

Having optimized performance and resilience, we now turn to logging and monitoring, essential practices for maintaining and troubleshooting your ASP.NET Core 9 applications.

# Introduction to logging and monitoring

Logging and monitoring are crucial to understanding your application's behavior, diagnosing problems, and ensuring it runs smoothly. Logs provide visibility into application processes and help detect anomalies early.

Think of logging like keeping a diary and monitoring like installing surveillance cameras in your home. The diary helps you remember past events, while the cameras let you see what's happening in real time, maintaining safety and order.

## *Logging with ILogger*

.NET provides abstractions that allow ASP.NET Core 9 applications to handle different logging strategies. The **ILogger** and **ILoggerFactory** interfaces, provided by the **Microsoft.Extensions.Logging** namespace, are essential for implementing logging in your applications, allowing you to capture and record information about the operation of the application.

Logging provides insights into the behavior of your application and is essential for debugging and monitoring.

The ILogger interface in ASP.NET Core allows you to log information at various levels of details as described in the following points:

- **Trace**: Detailed information, typically of interest only when diagnosing problems
- **Debug**: Information useful for debugging the application
- **Information**: Informational messages that highlight the progress of the application
- **Warning**: Potentially harmful situations that are not errors
- **Error**: Errors that prevent the application from performing a function
- **Critical**: Critical errors causing complete failure of the application

The ILogger interface provides some useful methods:

- **Log methods**:
  - Log<TState>(LogLevel logLevel, EventId eventId, TState state, Exception exception, Func<TState, Exception, string> formatter): The core method to log messages. It allows you to specify the log level, event ID, state, exception, and a formatter function.

- **Convenience methods**:
  - LogTrace(string message, params object[] args): Logs a trace message.
  - LogDebug(string message, params object[] args): Logs a debug message.

- `LogInformation(string message, params object[] args)`: Logs an informational message.

- `LogWarning(string message, params object[] args)`: Logs a warning message.

- `LogError(string message, params object[] args)`: Logs an error message.

- `LogCritical(string message, params object[] args)`: Logs a critical error message.

- **Scope Method**:

  - `BeginScope<TState>(TState state)`: This method starts a logical operation scope. It returns an `IDisposable` interface that ends the scope on disposal. Scopes are useful for correlating a set of operations with a common context.

The following is an example of using the `ILogger` interface:

```
public class MyService
{
    private readonly ILogger<MyService> _logger;
    public MyService(ILogger<MyService> logger)
    {
        _logger = logger;
    }

    public void DoWork()
    {
        _logger.LogInformation("Starting work.");

        try
        {
            // Perform some work here
        }
        catch (Exception ex)
        {
            _logger.LogError(ex, "An error occurred while doing
work.");
        }

        _logger.LogInformation("Finished work.");
    }
}
```

The previous code uses several methods provided by the `ILogger` interface:

- `ILogger<MyService> _logger`: This declares a private `readonly` field, `_logger`, of the `ILogger<MyService>` type. The `ILogger<T>` interface is part of the .NET logging infrastructure, where `T` is the type that is being logged. By specifying `MyService`, the logger is associated with this class, which helps in identifying where the log messages are coming from.

- `MyService(ILogger<MyService> logger)`: The `ILogger<MyService>` instance is typically provided via dependency injection. This allows the logging infrastructure to be configured and managed centrally.

- `_logger.LogInformation("Starting work.")`: Log the information type with the string `Starting work`.

- `_logger.LogError(ex, "An error occurred while doing work.")`: Log the information type with the string `An error occurred while doing work`.

The `ILogger` interface offers a powerful abstraction for logging your application's execution data in a technology-agnostic manner, facilitating maintenance and extensibility.

Another powerful abstraction mechanism available in .NET is **ILoggerFactory**.

The `ILoggerFactory` interface is responsible for creating `ILogger` instances. It is generally used to create loggers for specific categories or to configure logging providers and settings.

The main methods are as follows:

- `CreateLogger(string categoryname)`: Creates an `ILogger` instance for the specified category. The category is usually the name of the class or component that the logger is associated with.

- `AddProvider (ILoggerProvider provider)`: Adds `ILoggerProvider` to the factory. This method is used to configure where and how log messages are sent, such as to the console, a file, or a remote log service.

- `To discard()`: Discards the logger factory and all loggers it created. Typically used to release any resources held by log providers.

We can use the `ILoggerFactory` interface as in the following example of code:

```
public class MyService
{
    private readonly ILogger _logger;
    public MyService(ILoggerFactory loggerFactory)
    {
        _logger = loggerFactory.CreateLogger<MyService>();
    }
```

```
public void DoWork()
{
    _logger.LogInformation("Starting work.");

    try
    {
        // Perform some work here
    }
    catch (Exception ex)
    {
        _logger.LogError(ex, "An error occurred while doing
work.");
    }

    _logger.LogInformation("Finished work.");
}
}
```

The big difference between using the ILoggerFactory interface and the ILogger interface is the creation of a new category of logs that will be used to group the application's log messages. The constructor receives an ILoggerFactory instance via dependency injection and then an ILogger instance is created for the MyService class. In this case, all log messages of this class will be grouped by the MyService category.

ILoggerFactory allows for centralized configuration of logging settings. This means you can set up logging providers, filters, and other settings in one place, typically during application startup, and apply these configurations across all loggers created by the factory. You can also dynamically create loggers for different categories or components within your application. This is useful for associating log messages with specific parts of the application, making it easier to filter and analyze logs.

Logs work with providers, which are different sources where the logs will be made available. An application may contain different types of providers for each purpose.

Each provider is centrally configured during application startup. This way, the ILogger and ILoggerFactory abstractions will use the configured providers for submitting the logs.

There are several types of providers that can be used in ASP.NET Core 9, such as providers for writing to the console, adding debug information, and even providers for writing logs to external services such as Azure Application Insights and Elasticsearch, among others.

Let's look at an example of log settings in the following code from a Program.cs class:

```
using Microsoft.Extensions.DependencyInjection;
using Microsoft.Extensions.Hosting;
using Microsoft.Extensions.Logging;
```

```
var builder = WebApplication.CreateBuilder(args);

// Add services to the container.
builder.Services.AddControllers();

// Configure logging
builder.Logging.ClearProviders();
// Optional: clear default providers
builder.Logging.AddConsole(); // Add console logging
builder.Logging.AddDebug(); // Add debug logging
builder.Logging.AddEventSourceLogger();
// Add event source logging

var app = builder.Build();
// Configure the HTTP request pipeline.
if (app.Environment.IsDevelopment())
{
    app.UseDeveloperExceptionPage();
}
else
{
    app.UseExceptionHandler("/Home/Error");
    app.UseHsts();
}

app.UseHttpsRedirection();
app.UseStaticFiles();
app.UseRouting();
app.UseAuthorization();
app.MapControllers();
app.Run();
```

As we can see in the preceding code example, different providers were added for writing logs. This means that when using a method such as _logger.LogInformation, _logger.LogError, these logs will be distributed to the configured providers.

Logs are a powerful tool, essential in any application, helping to detect failures and even optimize systems.

In *Chapter 8*, we will explore the use of logs in conjunction with middleware.

## Summary

During this chapter, we learned about implementing best practices in ASP.NET Core 9, working correctly with HTTP requests, adding comprehension to responses, and understanding the use of caching to bring better performance and resilience to applications. We also understood the concepts related to asynchronous requests and how we can use this approach in ASP.NET Core applications through the use of the `async` and `await` keywords. Finally, we learned about the importance of using application monitoring, taking advantage of internal mechanisms that abstract writing and logs, such as the use of the `ILogger` and `ILoggerFactory` classes, allowing us to have enough inputs to fix inconsistencies in applications and optimize them.

In the next chapter, we will learn how to expand the request pipeline of ASP.NET Core 9 applications through the use of middleware.

### Get This Book's PDF Version and Exclusive Extras

Scan the QR code (or go to `packtpub.com/unlock`). Search for this book by name, confirm the edition, and then follow the steps on the page.

*Note: Keep your invoice handly. Purchase made directly from packt don't require one.*

# 8

# Enhancing Applications with Middleware in ASP.NET Core 9

ASP.NET Core 9 offers a robust and flexible framework designed to handle high-demand web applications. A key component of this framework is middleware, which allows developers to interact directly with the request and response pipeline. Understanding and leveraging middleware can significantly enhance your application's capabilities. This chapter will dive deep into middleware, exploring its structure, implementation, and practical applications, such as global error handling, request limiting, and more.

In this chapter, we will focus on the following topics:

- Knowing the middleware pipeline

- Implementing custom middleware

- Working with factory-based middleware

- Adding capabilities to applications using middleware

- Creating an extension method for middleware registration

In this chapter, we will explore essential best practices for developing applications with ASP.NET Core 9, covering the correct use of asynchronous mechanisms, HTTP requests, and application instrumentation through logs.

## Technical requirements

To support the learning of this chapter, the following tools must be present in your development environment:

- **Docker**: The Docker engine must be installed on your operating system and have an SQL Server container running. You can find more details about Docker and SQL Server containers in *Chapter 5*.

- **Postman**: This tool will be used to execute requests to APIs of the developed application.
- **Redis Insight**: This tool is used to connect to a Redis Server database (`https://redis.io/insight/`).

The code examples used in this chapter can be found in the book's GitHub repository: `https://github.com/PacktPublishing/ASP.NET-Core-9.0-Essentials/tree/main/Chapter08`

## Knowing the middleware pipeline

During the previous chapters, we used several features of ASP.NET Core 9, including middleware.

Middleware is a pipeline model used during the execution flow of an ASP.NET Core 9 web application to handle requests and responses, and the applications developed in this book already use some standard middleware from the .NET platform, such as **Authentication**, **Authorization**, **Cross-Origin Resource Sharing** (**CORS**), and so on.

The ASP.NET Core request pipeline consists of a sequence of request delegates, called one after the other. *Figure 8.1* demonstrates the concept:

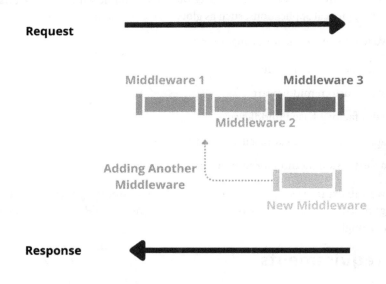

Figure 8.1 – ASP.NET Core 9 middleware pipeline

Request delegates are configured using the `Run`, `Map`, and `Use` extension methods typically configured in the `Program.cs` file.

Each extension method has a template for registering a request delegate:

- Run: The app.Run method is used to define an inline middleware that handles the request and completes the response, as in the following example code that implements an inline middleware:

```
app.Run(async context =>
{
    await context.Response.WriteAsync("Hello Inline middleware!");
});
```

- Map: The app.Map method is used to create a branch in the middleware pipeline. In the following code, requests to /SomeRoute are handled by this middleware branch. The middleware in the branch writes a message to the response:

```
app.Map("/SomeRoute", someRouteApp =>
{
    someRouteApp.Use(async (context, next) =>
    {
        Console.WriteLine("In SomeRoute middleware");
        await context.Response.WriteAsync("Hello from the SomeRoute
middleware!");
    });
});
```

- Use: The app.Use method is used to add middleware to the pipeline. The following code uses a middleware to log the request method and path before calling the next middleware in the pipeline. After the next middleware completes, it logs the response status code:

```
app.Use(async (context, next) =>
{
    // Log the request
    Console.WriteLine($"Request:
        {context.Request.Method}
        {context.Request.Path}");
    await next.Invoke();
    // Log the response
    Console.WriteLine($"Response:
        {context.Response.StatusCode}");
});
```

The use of middleware brings constant benefits to applications; we will understand in greater detail the use of different approaches, such as the creation of middleware classes.

Now, let's learn about how the middleware execution flow works.

## Understanding middleware flow

When the application receives a request, it goes through each middleware component in the order they are registered, and the following cases can be executed:

- **Process the request and pass it to the next piece of middleware**: It's like a relay race where each runner passes the baton to the next. Each piece of middleware does its part and then calls the next one in line to continue processing the request.

- **Process the request and break the chain, preventing other middleware from running**: Imagine a security checkpoint at an airport. If security finds a problem, they may stop you for additional checks, preventing you from proceeding. Likewise, the middleware may decide to handle the request completely and stop further processing.

- **Process the response as it moves up the chain**: This is like sending a package through multiple stages of inspection. Once the package reaches the final stage, it is inspected again at each stage on the way back, ensuring that everything is in order before being delivered.

The layered approach allows for powerful and flexible handling of HTTP requests and responses. Middleware can be used for a variety of tasks, such as logging, authentication, error handling, and more.

Furthermore, the order in which you register middleware is crucial, as it defines the flow of the request and response pipeline. We can see a representation of the middleware execution flow in *Figure 8.2*:

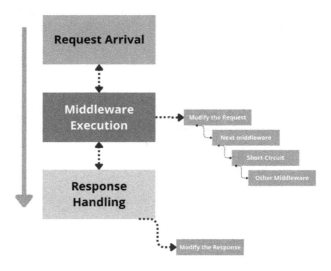

Figure 8.2 – Middleware execution flow

Let's see how the flow works in detail:

- **Request arrival**: When a request arrives at the server, it enters the pipeline and reaches the first middleware component

- **Middleware execution**: Each middleware can do the following:

  - **Modify the request**: Middleware can change aspects of the request, such as adding headers or changing the request path

  - **Move to next middleware**: After processing, the middleware can call the next middleware in the pipeline using `await next`, which we'll discuss in the *Implementing custom middleware* section

- **Short-circuiting the pipeline**: The middleware may decide not to call the next middleware, effectively ending request processing early

- **Response handling**: When the request reaches the end of the pipeline, the response goes back through the middleware components in reverse order

- **Modifying the response**: The middleware can change the response, such as adding headers, changing the status code, or logging information

---

**Middleware order**

ASP.NET Core 9 has, by default, some middleware available to handle requests and responses. However, the order in which this middleware is inserted completely changes the application's execution flow and, in some cases, can cause malfunctions. For example, it is important to add middleware authentication before middleware authorization; otherwise, how can you validate authorization without being authenticated?

In any case, in addition to standard middleware, there is an order of execution for customized middleware.

To learn more about middleware order, see the following link: `https://learn.microsoft.com/en-us/aspnet/core/fundamentals/middleware/?view=aspnetcore-9.0#middleware-order`.

---

By working on the middleware execution flow, we have the ability to add several powerful possibilities to our applications, and we will learn some more benefits in the next section.

## Benefits of middleware and best practices

Middleware plays a key role in ASP.NET Core 9 applications, offering a number of benefits that contribute to the robustness, maintainability, and extensibility of your application. Understanding these benefits allows you to use this resource effectively, so let's look at this in more detail:

- **Modularity**: Modularity means that middleware is an independent unit of functionality that can be easily added, removed, or replaced without affecting the rest of the application. This modularity allows developers to create reusable middleware components that can be shared between different projects or in different parts of the same project.

- **Composition**: Middleware can be composed in multiple orders to achieve different behaviors. This compositional nature allows you to tailor the request and response pipeline to the specific needs of your application.

Let's say you have three middleware components: one for logging, one for authentication, and one for handling errors. You can compose these middleware components in the desired order:

```
var builder = WebApplication.CreateBuilder(args);
var app = builder.Build();

app.UseMiddleware<ErrorHandlingMiddleware>();
app.UseMiddleware<AuthenticationMiddleware>();
app.UseMiddleware<RequestLoggingMiddleware>();

app.Run(async context =>
{
    await context.Response.WriteAsync("Hello,
      World!");
});

app.Run();
```

As you can see in the preceding code, the `app.UseMiddleware` method adds middleware to handle errors, authentication, and logging in the application. The `app.Run` method just creates a standard request response, returning a `Hello World` message.

It is important to consider the following factors:

- If you want to rearrange the order of these middleware components, the way requests are processed and errors are handled will be different.

- **SoC (Separation of concerns)**: Middleware allows for a clear separation of different concerns, enabling the definition of a clear execution context in a pipeline and facilitating a clearer, extensible, and maintainable code base.

- **Extensibility**: You can develop a custom middleware to extend the application's functionality – for example, by adding validation capabilities to requests or modifying responses globally within the application.

Suppose you need custom middleware to validate an API key in request headers. You can create this middleware as follows:

```
public class ApiKeyCheckMiddleware
{
    private readonly RequestDelegate _next;
    private const string API_KEY = "X-API-KEY";
    private const string VALID_API_KEY = "XYZ123";

    public ApiKeyCheckMiddleware(RequestDelegate next)
    {
        _next = next;
    }

    public async Task InvokeAsync(HttpContext context)
    {
        if (!context.Request.Headers
          .TryGetValue(API_KEY,
          out var extractedApiKey) ||
          extractedApiKey != VALID_API_KEY)
        {
            context.Response.StatusCode = 401;
            await context.Response
              .WriteAsync("Unauthorized");
            return;
        }
        await _next(context);
    }
}
```

The preceding code aims to create a customized middleware that checks the existence of an API key that must be provided in the header of a request, where the header key is X-API-KEY and the expected value is, exactly, XYZ123.

When performing validation, if the header and value are not part of the request, then the user receives an unauthorized return message with HTTP status code 401.

In fact, middleware is a powerful feature that allows you to have greater control over the flow of requests and responses in an application developed in ASP.NET Core 9.

Don't worry about the details related to the preceding code examples. We will learn about the structure of a middleware class in the *Implementing custom middleware* section.

Despite the great benefits of applications using middleware, it is important to be aware of good practices; otherwise, what could be a benefit could become a major problem.

Let's look at some best practices:

- **Order matters**: The order in which middleware components are added is crucial as it affects how requests and responses are processed.

- **Keep it simple**: Middleware should do one thing and do it well. Complex logic should be avoided in middleware.

- **Error handling**: Make sure your middleware components handle exceptions and errors in the same way as other classes in your application.

- **Performance**: Be aware of the impact of middleware on performance, especially in high-load scenarios. As it operates in request and response processes, avoid large amounts of processing during these stages to avoid causing problems for users and the application.

- **Reuse existing middleware**: Use built-in middleware whenever possible to reduce the need for custom implementations. As we have already learned, there is some middleware available in ASP.NET Core 9.

Now that we understand the principles, benefits, and best practices of middleware, let's implement our first custom middleware and learn the details of this approach.

## Implementing custom middleware

Custom middleware allows you to encapsulate functionality and reuse it in different parts of your application.

Creating custom middleware in ASP.NET Core 9 involves several steps, such as the following:

- Middleware class definition
- The implementation of the `Invoke` or `InvokeAsync` method
- Middleware registration in the request pipeline

Let's analyze the following code, which represents a customized middleware:

```
public class BeforeAfterRequestMiddleware
{
    private readonly RequestDelegate _next;

    public BeforeAfterRequestMiddleware(RequestDelegate next)
    {
```

```
    _next = next;
    }

    public async Task InvokeAsync(HttpContext context)
    {
        // Logging request information
        Console.WriteLine($"Request:
          {context.Request.Method}
          {context.Request.Path}");

        // Call the next middleware in the pipeline
        await _next(context);

        // Logging response information
        Console.WriteLine($"Response:
          {context.Response.StatusCode}");
    }
}
```

This custom middleware code aims to just write a string to the console at the beginning and in the response of the request.

However, it is important to understand the structure of the preceding code:

- `RequestDelegate`: This is a delegate that represents the next middleware in the pipeline. This delegate is stored in a field called `_next` for use in the context of the class.

- `Constructor`: The class constructor receives an instance of the `RequestDelegate` class as a parameter, representing the next middleware in the execution flow.

- `Invoke` or `InvokeAsync` method: Contains the logic for processing HTTP requests. The difference between the methods is that one is executed asynchronously and the other is not. The `InvokeAsync` method receives an `HttpContext` object as a parameter. The `HttpContext` object allows you to access request and response information. It is a good practice to use the `InvokeAsync` method to improve performance and scalability.

- `await _next(context)`: Execution of the `_next` delegate, which receives the `HttpContext` object as a parameter. In this example, we are just writing a string containing request information before propagating the execution of the next middleware, and then another string is written with response information after executing the middleware.

> **Dependency injection (DI) in middleware**
>
> Custom middleware classes must use the **Explicit Dependencies Principle** (EDP), as we have already learned in previous chapters, where the dependencies of a class are defined in the constructor.
>
> As middleware is built during application initialization, it is not possible to inject services added to a scoped lifetime as is done with each request in a `Controller` class, for example.
>
> So, if you want to use any services available in DI control in a middleware class, add these services to the signature of the `InvokeAsync` method, which can accept additional parameters resolved by DI.

The previous code example, although simple, demonstrates the basic structure of a middleware, which requires a `RequestDelegated` field, a constructor that depends on an instance of `RequestDelegated`, and the implementation of the `Invoke` or `InvokeAsync` method.

For the customized middleware to be used in the application, it is necessary to register it in the ASP.NET Core 9 execution pipeline through the `Program.cs` file:

```
var builder = WebApplication.CreateBuilder(args);
var app = builder.Build();

app.UseMiddleware<BeforeAfterRequestMiddleware>();
app.Run(async context =>
{
    await context.Response.WriteAsync("Hello, World!");
});

app.Run();
```

The preceding code has been shortened to make it easier to read and learn. For the middleware to be registered, the `UseMiddleware` extension method is used, which is a generic method, where we define the previously executed custom middleware as the type.

During the application startup flow, all custom or non-customized middleware is created, forming part of the application lifecycle, and not by request, as is generally done in scoped services. This behavior prevents other dependencies from being added to the constructor of a custom middleware class but allows the addition of dependencies with parameters through the `Invoke` and `InvokeAsync` methods.

> **Obtaining HTTP context objects in middleware**
>
> As an alternative to using DI in the `InvokeAsync` method, it is possible to use the `context.RequestService` property (https://learn.microsoft.com/ en-us/dotnet/api/microsoft.aspnetcore.http.httpcontext. requestservices?view=aspnetcore-9.0), as shown in the following code:
>
> ```
> public async Task InvokeAsync(HttpContext context)
> {
>   var logger = context.RequestServices
>     .GetRequiredService<Ilogger
>     < BeforeAfterRequestMiddleware >>();
>   logger.LogInformation($"Request:{context.Request.Method}
>     {context.Request.Path}");
>   await _next(context);
>   logger.LogInformation($"Response:
>     {context.Response.StatusCode}");
> }
> ```
>
> However, this somewhat decreases dependency visibility in code.

However, ASP.NET Core 9 offers an approach to enabling the use of custom middleware on a per-request basis using factory-based middleware, which we will discuss in the next section.

# Working with factory-based middleware

Another way to create custom middleware is by using the factory-based approach, which offers better performance and flexibility using DI.

This approach is particularly useful when the middleware requires scoped services.

Factory-based middleware uses the `IMiddleware` interface, which allows the middleware to be activated by the **DI container (DIC)**.

The `IMiddleware` interface has only one `InvokeAsync` method that must be implemented in the class. The structure of a customized middleware that uses the factory-based approach is very similar to the traditional approach learned in the previous section.

Let's look at a code example:

```
public class RequestLimitingMiddleware : IMiddleware
{
  private readonly ILogger
    <RequestLimitingMiddleware> _logger;

  public RequestLimitingMiddleware
    (ILogger<RequestLimitingMiddleware> logger)
  {
    _logger = logger;
  }

  public async Task InvokeAsync(HttpContext context,
    RequestDelegate next)
  {
    // Logic to limit the number of requests
    _logger.LogInformation("Processing request");
    await next(context);
  }
}
```

The big difference with the factory-based approach is the definition of a dependency in the class constructor instead of declaring it as a parameter in the `InvokeAsync` method. In the preceding code example, the constructor has a dependency on an `ILogger` interface.

The `InvokeAsync` method must only have two parameters, `HttpContext` and `RequestDelegate`.

Now, let's look at custom middleware registration, using the factory-based approach, by analyzing the `Program.cs` class code:

```
var builder = WebApplication.CreateBuilder(args);
builder.Services.AddScoped<RequestLimitingMiddleware>();

var app = builder.Build();
app.UseMiddleware<RequestLimitingMiddleware>();

app.Run(async context =>
{
    await context.Response.WriteAsync("Hello, World!");
});

app.Run();
```

Middleware registration is done using the `app.UseMiddleware` method, as we have already learned. However, note that the `RequestLimitingMiddleware` class is added to the scoped lifetime through the `builder.Services.AddScoped<RequestLimitingMiddleware>()` code with the lifecycle managed per request.

> **Service lifetimes**
>
> ASP.NET Core 9 offers different types of service lifetimes; you can learn more at `https://learn.microsoft.com/en-us/dotnet/core/extensions/dependency-injection#service-lifetimes`.

As we can see, the factory-based approach allows us to use DIC resources and manage the middleware lifecycle by request.

Whether to use a factory-based or the traditional approach depends, of course, on the application requirements. However, both are powerful solutions that add precious features to our applications.

In the next section, we will create and use some common middleware used in many applications.

# Adding capabilities to applications using middleware

Now that we have knowledge about the features and possibilities of middleware, we will work on some capabilities that will bring greater quality to our web applications.

There is no strict standard directory structure or namespace for creating middleware classes. However, it is good practice to organize classes into well-defined namespaces.

For this example, we will default to creating a folder called `Middlewares` in the root of your application project.

In this section, we will focus on the following middleware:

- Global error handling
- Adding request logging – logging request information
- Rate limiting – defining request limits in your application

The project containing the classes mentioned in the preceding list is available in the book repository, the link to which can be found in the *Technical requirements* section.

Let's create a new application. Open the terminal, and in a folder of your choice, create a project with the following command:

```
dotnet new mvc -n CommonMiddlewares
```

Then, in the root of the directory, create a folder called `Middlewares`.

Now, we will start creating the first middleware: global error handling.

## Global error handling

During the execution flow of an application, errors or exceptions may arise that, if not handled correctly, may cause inconvenience to users.

In this case, we must handle errors in our code to prevent exceptions from causing applications to malfunction.

To achieve this, a good practice is to use a global error-handling middleware that makes it possible to manage the application's exception flow in a centralized manner, even allowing it to extend its functionality by adding logs in different monitoring tools, which is essential for error corrections.

Create a file called `ErrorHandlingMiddleware.cs` in the `Middlewares` folder you created earlier and add the following code:

```
public class ErrorHandlingMiddleware
{
  private readonly RequestDelegate _next;
  public ErrorHandlingMiddleware(RequestDelegate next)
  {
    _next = next;
  }

  public async Task InvokeAsync(HttpContext context)
  {
    try
    {
      await _next(context);
    }
    catch (Exception ex)
    {
      await HandleExceptionAsync(context, ex);
    }
  }
  private Task HandleExceptionAsync(HttpContext context,
    Exception exception)
  {
```

```
    context.Response.ContentType = "application/json";
    context.Response.StatusCode = (int)HttpStatusCode
      .InternalServerError;
    return context.Response.WriteAsync(new ErrorDetails()
    {
      StatusCode = context.Response.StatusCode,
      Message = "Internal Server Error from the custom middleware."
    }.ToString());
  }
}

public class ErrorDetails
{
  public int StatusCode { get; set; }
  public string Message { get; set; }

  public override string ToString()
  {
    return JsonSerializer.Serialize(this);
  }
}
```

We can see in the preceding code the common structure of a middleware. The great functionality of this global error-handling middleware is the use of the try/catch block, in the body of the InvokeAsync method.

The await _next(context) command is executed in a try block so that if there is an exception in the application, it will be handled globally. Exception handling is done through the HandleExceptionAsync method, called in the catch block.

The HandleExceptionAsync method modifies the request response by changing the StatusCode property to Internal Server Error, **HTTP status code 500**, in addition to returning an object in the request body. This object is represented by the ErrorDetails class, which has the StatusCode and Message properties.

Therefore, in addition to guaranteeing the handling of any exception in the application, there is a customized, but common, return that can be used appropriately for handling in a UI, allowing a better experience for the developers and also for the users of the application.

**Problems Details in ASP.NET Core 9**

ASP.NET Core 9 provides built-in support for Problem Details, a standardized format for error responses based on RFC 7807 (https://datatracker.ietf.org/doc/html/rfc7807). By incorporating Trace ID into the response, developers can enhance debugging and error tracking.

A Problem Details response with a Trace ID looks like this:

```json
{
  "type": "https://example.com/probs/server-error",
  "title": "An unexpected error occurred.",
  "status": 500,
  "detail": "The system encountered an issue.",
  "instance": "/example-path",
  "traceId": "00-abcdef1234567890abcdef1234567890-1234567890abcdef-01"
}
```

The ProblemDetails class can be used in conjunction with the Middleware following the following implementation example, changing the HandleExceptionAsync method of the ErrorHandlingMiddleware class:

```csharp
    private static Task HandleExceptionAsync(HttpContext context,
Exception exception)
    {
        var traceId = Activity.Current?.Id ?? context.
TraceIdentifier;

        var problemDetails = new ProblemDetails
        {
            Type = "server-error",
            Title = "An unexpected error occurred.",
            Status = StatusCodes.Status500InternalServerError,
            Detail = "Internal Server Error from the custom
middleware.",
            Instance = context.Request.Path
        };
```

```
        // Include the Trace ID in the Problem Details.
        problemDetails.Extensions["traceId"] = traceId;


        context.Response.ContentType = "application/problem+json";
            context.Response.StatusCode = StatusCodes.
Status500InternalServerError;


        return context.Response.WriteAsJsonAsync(problemDetails);
    }
```

The preceding code is a customization of the Global Error Handler implemented through Middleware. In addition to using the `ProblemDetails` class, code is added to obtain the trace id value:

```
var traceId = Activity.Current?.Id ?? context.TraceIdentifier;
```

Then, the trace ID is added to the extensions of the object ProblemdDetails>:

```
problemDetails.Extensions["traceId"] = traceId;
```

The trace ID is excellent information that should be part of the application Log, facilitating the correlation between error responses to resolve issues.

ASP.NET Core 9 also has alternatives for error handling that you can learn more about at the following URL: `https://learn.microsoft.com/en-us/aspnet/core/web-api/handle-errors?view=aspnetcore-9.0`.

Using global error handling brings an excellent benefit to applications, and, in addition, some log writing strategies could be used in cloud monitoring tools, in the terminal, or even in files, facilitating problem resolution.

The log functionality can be used for other purposes, not just to handle errors. Let's analyze another middleware approach for logging requests.

## Adding request logging

Every web application has a constant flow of communication and processing of requests that generate different types of information, as well as exceptions that must be handled, and we took care of this scenario when creating global error-handling middleware in the previous section.

In addition to handling errors and exceptions, we must log this information to be able to carry out effective troubleshooting. However, in many cases, it is necessary to log information processed during the request and response flow of an application. This approach offers several benefits:

- **Centralized logging**: Centralize logging logic, ensuring all requests are logged consistently in a single location in the pipeline

- **Request tracking**: The ability to trace all requests is useful for monitoring application performance, debugging issues, and understanding user behavior

- **Security and auditing**: By logging requests, you can maintain an audit trail of access to your application, which is essential for security compliance

- **Error diagnosis**: When problems arise, logs can help you diagnose and troubleshoot problems by providing a detailed history of the request activity that led to an error

- **Performance monitoring**: Logging the time it takes to process requests can help identify performance bottlenecks and optimize application performance

- **Flexibility**: The middleware can be configured to log only certain types of requests or responses, providing flexibility in how logging is implemented

Let's look at an example of middleware responsible for logging request data into the application. To do this, create a class called `PerformanceLoggingMiddleware.cs` in the `Middlewares` folder and add the following code:

```
public class PerformanceLoggingMiddleware
{
  private readonly RequestDelegate _next;

  public PerformanceLoggingMiddleware(RequestDelegate next)
  {
    _next = next;
  }

  public async Task InvokeAsync(HttpContext context,
    ILogger<PerformanceLoggingMiddleware> logger)
  {
    var timestamp = Stopwatch.GetTimestamp();
    await _next(context);
    var elapsedMilliseconds = Stopwatch
      .GetElapsedTime(timestamp).TotalMilliseconds;

    logger.LogInformation("Request {Method} {Path}
      took {ElapsedMilliseconds} ms",
      context.Request.Method, context.Request.Path,
      elapsedMilliseconds);
  }
}
```

The preceding code aims to record the execution time of a request. This is an interesting approach to measuring the limits of your application and allowing you to improve the performance of your implementation.

When analyzing the code, we have the following:

- **DI**: The `InvokeAsync` method accepts an `ILogger<PerformanceLoggingMiddleware>` parameter, which is provided by DI

- **Log request metrics**: The `InvokeAsync` method uses the `ILogger` instance to log the HTTP method, request path, and time taken to process the request

- **Collecting the request execution time**: Before executing the request, use the `GetTimestamp()` static method of the `Stopwatch` object to get the initial timestamp

  After executing the request through the `_await _next(context)` request delegation, the `Stop` method of the `Stopwatch` object is used to end the timer.

  A log is then created containing information about the request, such as the method, path, and execution time in milliseconds, obtained from the `Stopwatch` class throughout the `GetElapsedTime(timestamp).TotalMilliseconds` method.

> **The Stopwatch class**
>
> The `Stopwatch` class in .NET is a high-resolution timer provided by the `System.Diagnostics` namespace. It is used to measure elapsed time with great precision, making it ideal for performance measurement and benchmarking tasks. Get more information about the features available in `Stopwatch` through the documentation: `https://learn.microsoft.com/en-us/dotnet/api/system.diagnostics.stopwatch?view=net-9.0`.

As we can see when implementing customized logs such as `PerformanceLoggingMiddleware`, creating customized middleware enhances the functionalities of our applications, helping both the experience of users who consume quality applications and supporting teams in maintenance processes, diagnostics, and also application evolution.

However, ASP.NET Core 9 provides some middleware capable of dealing with several other important aspects of an application's execution flow, such as rate limiting, which we will understand in the next section.

## Rate limiting

The rate-limiting middleware in ASP.NET Core 9 is a powerful feature that is essential for protecting applications from abuse and improving overall performance and reliability. This middleware controls the number of requests a client can make to a server within a specified period of time.

Using the rate-limiting middleware in ASP.NET Core 9 is done by adding the configuration in the `Program.cs` file. The following is a step-by-step guide:

1. Add the required NuGet packages.
2. Register the middleware in the HTTP request pipeline.
3. Add rate-limiting middleware to the pipeline. Rate-limiting middleware is included in `Microsoft.AspNetCore.RateLimiting`.

Let's see an example of implementation in a Razor Pages-type application using the following code:

```
using Microsoft.AspNetCore.Builder;
using Microsoft.AspNetCore.Hosting;
using Microsoft.AspNetCore.Http;
using Microsoft.Extensions.DependencyInjection;
using Microsoft.Extensions.Hosting;
using Microsoft.AspNetCore.RateLimiting;
using System.Threading.RateLimiting;

var builder = WebApplication.CreateBuilder(args);
builder.Services.AddRazorPages();

// Configure rate limiting policies
builder.Services.AddRateLimiter(options =>
{
  options.AddPolicy("fixed", context =>
    RateLimitPartition.GetFixedWindowLimiter(new
    RateLimitPartitionKey(context.Request
    .Headers["X-Forwarded-For"].ToString(),
    PartitionKeyKind.ClientIP), partition =>
      new FixedWindowRateLimiterOptions
      {
        PermitLimit = 5,
        Window = TimeSpan.FromMinutes(1),
        QueueProcessingOrder = QueueProcessingOrder
          .OldestFirst,
          QueueLimit = 2
      }));

  options.AddPolicy("sliding", context =>
    RateLimitPartition.GetSlidingWindowLimiter(new
    RateLimitPartitionKey(context.Request
    .Headers["X-Forwarded-For"].ToString(),
    PartitionKeyKind.ClientIP), partition =>
      new SlidingWindowRateLimiterOptions
      {
        PermitLimit = 5,
        Window = TimeSpan.FromMinutes(1),
          SegmentsPerWindow = 3,
        QueueProcessingOrder = QueueProcessingOrder
          .OldestFirst,
          QueueLimit = 2
      }));
```

```
options.AddPolicy("tokenBucket", context =>
  RateLimitPartition.GetTokenBucketLimiter(new
  RateLimitPartitionKey(context.Request
  .Headers["X-Forwarded-For"].ToString(),
  PartitionKeyKind.ClientIP), partition =>
    new TokenBucketRateLimiterOptions
    {
      TokenLimit = 10,
      TokensPerPeriod = 5,
      ReplenishmentPeriod = TimeSpan.FromSeconds(10),
      QueueProcessingOrder = QueueProcessingOrder
        .OldestFirst,
        QueueLimit = 2
    }));
});

var app = builder.Build();

if (app.Environment.IsDevelopment())
{
    app.UseDeveloperExceptionPage();
}

// Use rate limiting middleware
app.UseRateLimiter();
app.MapRazorPages();
app.Run();
```

Now, let's analyze the important aspects of the preceding code:

- `builder.Services.AddRateLimiter`: Required to define the rate limit policies that will be used in this application. Each policy uses a unique client identifier, adding the `X-Forwarded-For` HTTP header, to enforce limits per client IP address. In the previous code, we configured three policies – namely, the following:

  - **Fixed window**: Limits requests to 5 per minute. Once the limit is reached, no further requests will be allowed until the window is reset.

  - **Sliding window**: Similar to the fixed window policy, but divides the window into segments, allowing for a more distributed request margin per minute.

  - **Token bucket**: Allows you to make up to 10 tokens (requests) available, with 5 new tokens replenished every 10 seconds. If tokens run out, incoming requests will be queued.

- `app.UseRateLimiter()`: This line adds the rate-limiting middleware to the request pipeline, enabling the configured rate-limiting policies to take effect. Unlike the traditional way of adding middleware where the `UseMiddleware<>` method is used, rate limiting has an exclusive extension method. We will learn how to create extension methods to add middleware in the next section.

Rate limiting is an important feature that should be considered when developing ASP.NET Core 9 applications, bringing some benefits such as the following:

- **Overload protection**: Prevents the server from being overloaded by too many requests, ensuring stable performance

- **Fair use**: Ensures that no client can monopolize server resources, promoting equitable access for all users

- **Security:** Mitigates certain types of attacks, such as **Distributed Denial-of-Service (DDoS)** attacks, by limiting the rate at which clients can make requests

- **Improved user experience**: By preventing server overload, rate limiting helps maintain consistent response times and service availability

> **Learning more about rate-limiting middleware**
>
> Rate limiting has several other features that can add to your strategy for using this middleware. See the documentation for more details: `https://learn.microsoft.com/en-us/aspnet/core/performance/rate-limit?view=aspnetcore-9.0`.

In addition to rate-limiting middleware, ASP.NET Core 9 offers different other middleware that are widely used in different types of applications, such as authentication and authorization middleware, discussed in *Chapter 6*. Depending on your application requirements, you can combine the capabilities of middleware to create powerful, high-quality solutions that run in modern environments.

> **ASP.NET Core 9 built-in middleware**
>
> Consult the documentation to analyze the different middleware available on the ASP.NET Core 9 platform at the following URL: `https://learn.microsoft.com/en-us/aspnet/core/fundamentals/middleware/?view=aspnetcore-9.0#built-in-middleware`.

Now that we have created customized middleware and learned how to use the rate-limiting middleware available in ASP.NET Core 9, it is time to learn a good practice for registering middleware using extension methods.

# Creating an extension method for middleware registration

With the exception of middleware built into ASP.NET Core 9, which have their respective extension methods for registration in the HTTP pipeline, each custom middleware must be registered using extension methods, such as `UseMiddleware<>`, already used in several code examples from this chapter.

However, the addition of different middleware to the `Program.cs` file can create complexity in reading and maintaining these resources in the application.

A good practice is to create extension methods in order to centralize the registration of middleware and have the benefit of abstracting the complexity of configuring these mechanisms, in addition to centralizing responsibilities appropriately.

Let's create an extension method to centralize the configurations of the previously created middleware. To do this, in the `Middlewares` folder, create a new class called `CommonMiddlewareExtension.cs`.

Add the following code to this class:

```
using Microsoft.AspNetCore.Builder;
using Microsoft.Extensions.DependencyInjection;
using Microsoft.AspNetCore.RateLimiting;
using System.Threading.RateLimiting;

public static class CommonMiddlewareExtensions
{
  public static IServiceCollection AddCustomRateLimiting
    (this IServiceCollection services)
  {
    services.AddRateLimiter(options =>
    {
      options.AddPolicy("fixed", context =>
        RateLimitPartition.GetFixedWindowLimiter(new
        RateLimitPartitionKey(context.Request
        .Headers["X-Forwarded-For"].ToString(),
        PartitionKeyKind.ClientIP), partition =>
          new FixedWindowRateLimiterOptions
          {
            PermitLimit = 5,
            Window = TimeSpan.FromMinutes(1),
            QueueProcessingOrder = QueueProcessingOrder
              .OldestFirst,
            QueueLimit = 2
          }));
```

```
      options.AddPolicy("sliding", context =>
        RateLimitPartition.GetSlidingWindowLimiter(new
        RateLimitPartitionKey(context.Request
        .Headers["X-Forwarded-For"].ToString(),
        PartitionKeyKind.ClientIP), partition =>
          new SlidingWindowRateLimiterOptions
          {
            PermitLimit = 5,
            Window = TimeSpan.FromMinutes(1),
            SegmentsPerWindow = 3,
            QueueProcessingOrder = QueueProcessingOrder
              .OldestFirst,
            QueueLimit = 2
          }));

    options.AddPolicy("tokenBucket", context =>
        RateLimitPartition.GetTokenBucketLimiter(new
        RateLimitPartitionKey(context.Request
        .Headers["X-Forwarded-For"].ToString(),
        PartitionKeyKind.ClientIP), partition =>
          new TokenBucketRateLimiterOptions
          {
            TokenLimit = 10,
            TokensPerPeriod = 5,
            ReplenishmentPeriod = TimeSpan.FromSeconds(10),
            QueueProcessingOrder = QueueProcessingOrder
              .OldestFirst,
            QueueLimit = 2
          }));
  });
  return services;
}


public static void UseCommonApplicationMiddleware
  (this IApplicationBuilder app)
{
  builder.UseMiddleware<ErrorHandlingMiddleware>();
  builder.UseMiddleware<PerformanceLoggingMiddleware>();
  app.UseRateLimiter();
}
}
```

The preceding code contains all the rate-limiting middleware settings, in addition to the use of global error-handling and request performance measurement middleware.

This extension method class exposes two `AddCustomRateLimiting` methods, responsible for adding the rate-limiting policies, and the `UseCommonApplicationMiddleware` method, responsible for adding the previously created custom middleware and the rate-limiting middleware to the HTTP pipeline.

After creating the class, we will change the `Program.cs` file, which will have the following code:

```
using Microsoft.AspNetCore.Builder;
using Microsoft.AspNetCore.Hosting;
using Microsoft.Extensions.DependencyInjection;
using Microsoft.Extensions.Hosting;

var builder = WebApplication.CreateBuilder(args);
builder.Services.AddRazorPages();

builder.Services.AddCustomRateLimiting();

var app = builder.Build();

if (app.Environment.IsDevelopment())
{
    app.UseDeveloperExceptionPage();
}

// Use custom rate limiting middleware
app.UseCommonApplicationMiddleware();
app.MapRazorPages();
app.Run();
```

As we can see in the highlighted code, the `Program.cs` class uses the previously created extension methods, making it more readable and easier to maintain.

The extension method approach is a good practice for grouping a set of configurations in your application flow in order to correctly separate responsibilities.

Use these features in your web application deployment flow with ASP.NET Core 9 and combine different middleware to create more powerful applications.

In the next chapters of the book, we will cover other different techniques to further add possibilities to your ASP.NET Core 9 applications, such as secure configuration management.

# Summary

In this chapter, we learned how to use the power of middleware to customize the execution flow of ASP. NET Core 9 applications, understanding how the middleware pipeline works. In addition, we learned how to implement custom middleware, work with factory-based middleware, and add capabilities to applications by working with global error handling approaches, information logging, and request limit settings. In the next chapter, we will explore how to manage application configurations securely.

## Get This Book's PDF Version and Exclusive Extras

UNLOCK NOW

Scan the QR code (or go to `packtpub.com/unlock`). Search for this book by name, confirm the edition, and then follow the steps on the page.

*Note: Keep your invoice handly. Purchase made directly from packt don't require one.*

# 9

# Managing Application Settings

In the dynamic world of web applications, the ability to adapt to different environments and requirements is crucial. ASP.NET Core 9 provides a robust configuration system that allows developers to manage settings and behavior effectively. This chapter will explore the importance of application settings, how to manage them using the configuration system, and how to make your applications adaptable at runtime.

In this chapter, we will focus on the following topics:

- Understanding `IConfiguration` concepts and abstractions
- Working with configuration providers
- Learning about the Options pattern
- Working with dynamic configurations and behaviors

ASP.NET Core 9 provides a robust configuration system that allows developers to effectively manage configurations and behaviors. This chapter will explore the importance of application configurations, how to manage them using the configuration system, and how to make your applications adaptive at runtime.

## Technical requirements

To support the learning of this chapter, the following tools must be present in your development environment:

- **Docker**: The Docker engine must be installed on your operating system and have a SQL Server container running. You can find more details about Docker and SQL Server containers in *Chapter 5*.
- **Postman**: This tool will be used to execute requests to APIs of the developed application.
- **Redis Insight**: This tool is used to connect to a Redis server database (https://redis.io/insight/).

You will also need access to an Azure subscription.

The code examples used in this chapter can be found in the book's GitHub repository: `https://github.com/PacktPublishing/ASP.NET-Core-9.0-Essentials/tree/main/Chapter09`

# Understanding IConfiguration concepts and abstractions

In the dynamic world of web applications, the ability to adapt to different environments and requirements is crucial, in addition to security requirements that have become increasingly essential in applications that run on different cloud providers.

Most web applications have some type of configuration managed in files or classes, in order to centralize parameters that are used throughout the application flow. With each change in configurations or even application behaviors, a new version of the software must be generated. Furthermore, when working with remote teams, it is essential to maintain the correct management of configurations and sensitive data and not keep these parameters versioned in the application version control.

ASP.NET Core 9 provides powerful ways to manage application configurations in addition to enabling the use of other features, such as changing application behaviors without the need to generate new versions of the software.

We will start learning about these resources via the fundamentals of configuration management through the `IConfiguration` interface.

## IConfiguration interface

ASP.NET Core 9 has the `IConfiguration` interface, which aims to provide a mechanism for managing application settings and configurations in a unified manner, allowing access to diverse configuration sources such as JSON files, environment variables, and arguments.

Among the main concepts regarding the `IConfiguration` interface, we have the following:

- **Configuration sources**: Support multiple configuration sources, which can be combined and layered. Common sources include JSON files (such as `appsettings.json`), environment variables, command-line arguments, and user secrets.

- **Hierarchical configuration**: Configuration settings are organized in a hierarchical structure. This means that settings can be nested into sections, making complex settings easier to manage.

- **Options pattern**: The Options pattern uses `IConfiguration` to bind configuration settings to strongly typed objects.

In *Chapter 5*, we used the `appsettings.json` file to manage the connection string with the SQL Server database and retrieved the value of this configuration through the `IConfiguration` interface, in the `Program.cs` class. This practice brings several benefits, such as the following:

- **Flexibility**: `IConfiguration` allows you to extract configuration values from multiple sources, offering flexibility in how you manage configurations across different environments (development, test, production)

- **Centralized management**: Centralizes configuration management, making it easier to maintain and update settings without spreading them across the application

- **Environment-specific settings**: Supports environment-specific configuration, allowing you to customize settings based on the environment in which the application is running

- **Strongly typed configuration**: Through the Options pattern, it supports configuration settings linked to strongly typed classes, improving type safety and reducing errors

The following code examples demonstrate a configuration defined in the `appsettings.json` file; this value is then retrieved through the `IConfiguration` interface, in the `Program.cs` file:

- The following is the content of the `appsettings.json` file:

```
{
    "ConnectionStrings": {
      "DefaultConnection": "Server=myServerAddress;
        Database=myDataBase;User Id=myUsername;
        Password=myPassword;"
    }
}
```

- The following is the content of the `Program.cs` file:

```
var builder = WebApplication.CreateBuilder(args);
builder.Services.AddRazorPages();
string connectionString = builder.Configuration
    .GetConnectionString("DefaultConnection");
builder.Services.AddDbContext<MyDbContext>(options =>
  // options.UseSqlServer(connectionString));
  var app = builder.Build();

if (app.Environment.IsDevelopment())
{
    app.UseDeveloperExceptionPage();
}
app.UseStaticFiles();
app.UseRouting();
```

```
app.MapRazorPages();
app.Run();
```

As we can see in the highlighted line of the previous code snippet, the connection string is obtained from the `appsettings.json` file using the `IConfiguration` interface, using the `GetConnectionString` method and informing the configuration name or key.

As the `IConfiguration` lifecycle considers the application lifecycle, all the complexity of obtaining settings through files such as `appsettings.json` or other data sources is abstracted, simply using the methods available in the interface to obtain the desired parameters throughout the ASP. NET Core 9 application.

The `IConfiguration` interface is also available in the **dependency injection container** (DIC), allowing you to reference it in the constructor of any application class that will have its dependencies resolved dynamically.

> **IConfiguration methods**
>
> The `IConfiguration` interface provides several extension methods that offer different ways to obtain configuration data in ASP.NET Core 9 applications. See the following link for more details: `https://learn.microsoft.com/en-us/dotnet/api/microsoft.extensions.configuration.iconfiguration?view=net-9.0`.

The process of obtaining configurations in JSON files is a standard model for use in ASP.NET Core 9 applications. However, there are other ways of managing configurations, and for this possibility, there is the concept of providers, which we will explore in the next section.

# Working with configuration providers

Configuration providers allow configurations to be obtained from various sources, such as JSON files, environment variables, and more.

Through configuration providers, we have greater flexibility and the ability to prepare our applications to run in different environments (such as development, test, or production) in an appropriate way without the need to implement string replacement logic in JSON files, in addition to bringing greater reliability and security.

Next, we will understand how to add other configuration providers to our ASP.NET Core 9 applications.

## Adding configuration providers

Configuration providers are used to read configuration data from various sources. This flexibility allows you to manage your application's configuration settings in a consistent and centralized manner.

This makes it possible to use configuration sources such as databases and even cloud services.

In ASP.NET Core 9, there are already some configuration providers integrated by default, such as the following:

- **JSON configuration provider**: Reads configuration data from JSON files such as `appsettings.json`

- **Environment variable configuration provider**: Reads configuration data from environment variables

- **Command-line configuration provider**: Reads configuration data from command-line arguments

- **Memory configuration provider**: Allows you to add in-memory configuration data, useful for unit testing

During the implementation of example applications in this book, we have constantly used the following method in the `Program.cs` file: `WebApplication.CreateBuilder(args);`.

This method creates an instance of a `Builder` object, which represents a web application and allows us to add features such as services, middleware, and configurations. It creates a web application builder with some default parameters, so there is no need to define the provider configuration to obtain configuration data from the `appsettings.json` file.

> **Default builder settings**
>
> The `CreateBuilder` method defines some standardized parameters for the builder that will be created. You can learn more about these parameters by accessing the following URL: `https://learn.microsoft.com/en-us/aspnet/core/fundamentals/host/generic-host?view=aspnetcore-9.0#default-builder-settings`.

However, observe the following code example from the `Program.cs` file where configuration providers are explicitly added:

```
var builder = WebApplication.CreateBuilder(args);
 // Add configuration from environment variables
builder.Configuration.AddEnvironmentVariables();

 // Add configuration from command-line arguments
builder.Configuration.AddCommandLine(args);
var app = builder.Build();
app.Run();
```

The preceding code uses two extension methods, `AddEnvironmentVariables` and `AddCommandLine`, allowing the application to obtain configurations from different providers. These extension methods are natively part of ASP.NET Core 9 applications. For other types of providers, it may be necessary to add NuGet packages to have access to extension methods for registering providers.

> **Built-in ASP.NET Core 9 configuration providers**
>
> ASP.NET Core 9 offers several types of providers natively, as presented in the documentation: `https://learn.microsoft.com/en-us/aspnet/core/fundamentals/configuration/?view=aspnetcore-9.0#configuration-providers`.

In the *Working with dynamic configurations and behaviors* section, we will use a provider to connect to a cloud resource that allows the management of configurations and behaviors in a dynamic and secure way. For now, let's understand some important fundamentals, such as creating custom providers.

## Creating a custom configuration provider

Creating a custom configuration provider in ASP.NET Core 9 allows you to load configuration data from sources not natively supported by the framework. This can be useful for integrating with custom configuration stores, third-party services, or even proprietary formats.

We already understand configuration management in native provisions in ASP.NET Core 9; now, we will create our first custom provider.

To create a custom provider, you need to create two classes:

- `ConfigurationSource`: The `IConfigurationSource` interface represents a source of configuration data. It is responsible for creating an instance of `IConfigurationProvider`, which will actually load the data. Separating the source and provider interfaces allows for a clear delineation between where configuration data comes from and how it is loaded. Through this approach, we benefit from encapsulating data source configurations and implementing best practices through the **Factory** pattern.

- `ConfigurationProvider`: The `ConfigurationProvider` class is an abstract base class that implements `IConfigurationProvider`. It is responsible for the actual loading and providing of configuration data. This class allows you to define how data is read, cached, and accessed.

We will start creating a custom provider through the class responsible for creating a custom provider instance:

```csharp
using Microsoft.Extensions.Configuration;
public class CustomConfigurationSource :
  IConfigurationSource
{
  public IConfigurationProvider Build
    (IConfigurationBuilder builder)
    {
    return new CustomConfigurationProvider();
  }
}
```

The IConfigurationSource interface has only one method, Build(), which is responsible for returning a custom provider instance.

Despite being simple, this class allows for better separation of responsibilities, with the sole objective of providing an instance of the provider that will have all the necessary mechanisms for interacting with another data source.

Now, let's look at the CustomConfigurationProvider class:

```
using Microsoft.Extensions.Configuration;
using System.Collections.Generic;

public class CustomConfigurationProvider :
   ConfigurationProvider
{
   public override void Load()
   {
      var data = new Dictionary<string, string>
      {
         { "MyCustomSetting:Key1", "Value1" },
         { " MyCustomSetting:Key2", "Value2" }
      };

      Data = data;
   }
}
```

The custom provider implemented in the preceding code has an inheritance from the abstract ConfigurationProvider class, which already has some utility implementations.

For this provider, we are creating two configurations that will be managed by an object of type Dictionary<string, string>, allowing us to create configurations based on key and value in memory.

The logic for managing provided information must be implemented by overriding the Load method, inherited from the ConfigurationProvider class.

At the end of the Load method, it is necessary to set the value of the Data property, also inherited from the ConfigurationProvider class. The data type of the Data property is Dictionary<string, string?>; that is, representing a key-value pair. Settings are persisted or serialized in string format. However, even with this feature, it is possible to create strongly typed configurations. We will cover this approach in the *Learning the Options pattern* section.

Of course, this is a simple and didactic example. However, we can easily connect the custom provider to a SQL Server database, a storage account, or any other persistence resource. In the book's code repository, the link to which is in the *Technical requirements* section, you can analyze another version of a custom provider where the data is persisted in a database. However, the implementation principles are the same as those demonstrated in the previous code snippets.

For the new provider to be used, simply add the following code to the `Program.cs` file:

```
builder.Configuration.Add(new CustomConfigurationSource());
```

You can also use the extension method creation technique learned in *Chapter 8*.

To obtain the settings through the new provider, simply use `Configuration` property methods, such as the `GetValue<T>` method, and rename the desired configuration, as demonstrated in the following code:

```
string key1 = _configuration.GetValue<string>
    ("MyCustomSetting:Key1");
string key2 = _configuration.GetValue<string>
    ("MyCustomSetting:Key2");
```

As we can see, the creation of a custom provider does not change the development model already available in ASP.NET Core 9, bringing greater flexibility and possibilities.

Providers are an excellent abstraction for configuration management. However, ASP.NET Core 9 provides other types, such as the Options pattern, which we will discuss in the next section, making the configuration management model in our applications even more powerful.

# Learning the Options pattern

ASP.NET Core 9 offers a good way to handle application configurations through the use of the Options pattern. This pattern provides a robust mechanism for managing and accessing configuration settings in a strongly typed manner, improving the maintainability and testability of your code and organizing configuration settings into classes. In this section, we will understand what the Options pattern is and how to implement it.

## What is the Options pattern?

Every application must interact with some type of configuration, and in the previous chapters, we used the `IConfiguration` interface to obtain continuous information in the `appsettings.json` file. However, this is not the only way to interact with configurations in ASP.NET Core 9, which offers an implementation of the Options pattern.

The Options pattern is a design pattern that uses classes to represent groups of related configurations, allowing you to link configuration sections from various configuration sources (such as JSON files, environment variables, and so on) to these classes, allowing access to configuration settings, type-safe configuration, leveraging IntelliSense, and compile-time checking.

In ASP.NET Core 9, the Options pattern has the following class hierarchy:

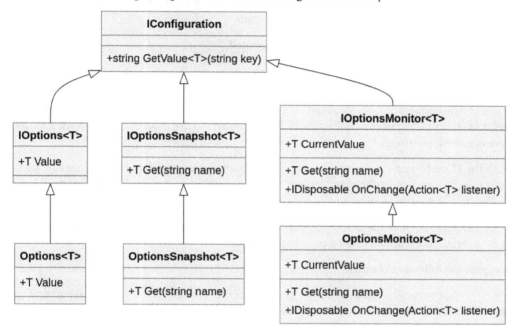

Figure 9.1 – Main Options pattern abstraction in ASP.NET Core 9

As we can see in *Figure 9.1*, there are several interfaces for abstracting the Options pattern, in addition to their respective implementations. Let's briefly understand the purpose of each of the interfaces represented in *Figure 9.1*:

- `IOptions<T>`: The basic interface used to retrieve configured options. `IOptions<T>` types are registered as singletons. Then, when starting the application, the configurations are loaded into memory and made available throughout the application using **dependency injection** (**DI**). However, if any changes are made to the application so that they can be reflected, the application must be restarted.

- `IOptionsSnapshot<T>`: A variation of `IOptions<T>` that provides a mechanism that updates configurations with each request. This interface allows application settings to be updated in real time. The lifecycle of this class is scoped; that is, the configurations are loaded with each request.

- $IOptionsMonitor<T>$: An interface that allows you to monitor option changes and provides a way to receive notifications when options are updated. The lifecycle of this interface is singleton, available when the application is initialized.

- Classes that do not have the "$I$" prefix represent the concrete implementation of each interface.

The Options pattern offers an excellent option for manipulating configurations without the need to call strings but by creating strongly typed configurations.

Let's understand how the Options pattern is implemented.

## Implementing the Options pattern

As we learned throughout the book's chapters, it is a good practice to centrally manage configuration information, and in most of the code available in this book, we use basic configurations, such as a database connection string.

Although the $IConfiguration$ interface provides us with mechanisms for obtaining configurations, in some cases, this can affect the management and responsibilities of each class, which must know exactly the strings it wants to obtain from the configuration file.

There are practices such as the use of constants; however, working with strongly typed classes to aggregate a set of information can be a powerful resource.

Let's imagine the following context:

Imagine an e-commerce application, where we have different services and resources such as payment and shipping. These resources have a set of distinct settings. In this example, we would have approximately the following configurations:

- $PaymentGatewayURL$: URL of the gateway responsible for processing the payment

- $APIKey$: API key for using the payment gateway

- $Timeout$: Timeout configuration

- $DefaultCarrier$: Default carrier for delivering orders

- $FreeShippingThreshold$: Free shipping threshold setting

When developing the e-commerce application, for each configuration, it would be necessary to use the $IConfiguration$ class to obtain data from the $appsettings.json$ file, for example. Let's look at the following code:

```
// Accessing settings directly using IConfiguration
string paymentGatewayURL =
  _configuration["PaymentGatewayURL"];
string apiKey = _configuration["APIKey"];
int timeout = _configuration.GetValue<int>("Timeout");
```

```
string defaultCarrier = _configuration["DefaultCarrier"];
decimal freeShippingThreshold =
  _configuration.GetValue<decimal>
  ("FreeShippingThreshold");
```

The preceding settings would be available in the `appsettings.json` file as follows:

```
{
    "PaymentGatewayURL": "https://payment.aspnetcore9.com",
    "APIKey": "your-api-key",
    "Timeout": 30
    "DefaultCarrier": "UPS",
    "FreeShippingThreshold": 30.00
}
```

The implementation of the settings recovery code demonstrated is correct. However, in more complex scenarios, it may be difficult to manage different types of configurations; there may be code duplications, which makes maintenance difficult, and if there is a typing error in the configuration key, for example, this problem will only be detected at runtime.

Fortunately, through the abstraction of the Options pattern in ASP.NET Core 9, we have the possibility of grouping configurations in a simple way.

Based on the preceding example, we basically have two types of information:

- `PaymentSettings`
- `PaymentGatewayURL`
- `APIKey`
- `Timeout`
- `ShipmentSettings`
- `DefaultCarrier`
- `FreeShippingThreshold`

This way, we could group the configurations into two distinct classes, as shown in *Figure 9.2*:

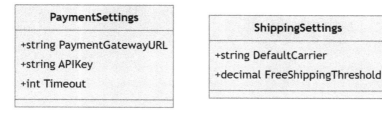

Figure 9.2 – Grouping configurations

The preceding classes only have the properties that will reference the respective configurations in a grouped manner. With this, we will have the following code defining `PaymentSettings` and `ShipingmentSettings` classes:

```
public class PaymentSettings
{
    public string PaymentGatewayURL { get; set; }
    public string APIKey { get; set; }
    public int Timeout { get; set; }
}

public class Shippingettings
{
    public string DefaultCarrier { get; set; }
    public decimal FreeShippingThreshold { get; set; }
}
```

The classes represented in the preceding code only aim to abstract a set of configurations, not having any types of implemented behaviors, but there may be methods if necessary.

However, the classes that will be used in the Options pattern must follow the following rules:

- Being non-abstract
- Having public read-and-write properties
- Fields are disregarded during binding

For this example, we will just keep the properties. Additionally, we will change the `appsettings.json` file, which will have the following code:

```
{
    "PaymentSettings": {
    "PaymentGatewayURL":
        "https://payment.aspnetcore9.com",
    "APIKey": "your-api-key",
    "Timeout": 30
    },
    "ShippingSettings": {
    "DefaultCarrier": "UPS",
    "FreeShippingThreshold": 30.00
    }
}
```

We can see in the preceding code that the settings are grouped by PaymentSettings and ShippingSettings, which are exactly the names of the classes, and respectively, the properties also have the same names.

The Options pattern uses this convention to bind the settings with the class that will abstract this information in the application.

Now, let's look at the Program.cs file with the changes made to use the Options pattern:

```
using Microsoft.Extensions.Configuration;
using Microsoft.Extensions.DependencyInjection;
using Microsoft.Extensions.Hosting;

var builder = WebApplication.CreateBuilder(args);

builder.Services.Configure<PaymentSettings>
    (builder.Configuration.GetSection("PaymentSettings"));
builder.Services.Configure<ShippingSettings>
    (builder.Configuration.GetSection("ShippingSettings"));

builder.Services.AddRazorPages();
builder.Services.AddSingleton<EcommerceService>();

var app = builder.Build();
if (app.Environment.IsDevelopment())
{
    app.UseDeveloperExceptionPage();
}
app.UseStaticFiles();
app.UseRouting();
app.MapRazorPages();
app.Run();
```

As you can see in the highlighted code lines in the preceding code block, the GetSection method is used from the IConfiguration interface, accessed through the Configuration extension method. The GetSection method is a generic implementation, where the type entered determines the return type. The name of the section is entered as a parameter, which, in this case, is the desired configuration group.

> **Extension methods**
>
> In the preceding code example, to facilitate understanding, we are registering the configuration classes using the Options pattern directly in the Program.cs file. However, it is good practice to create an extension method for registering classes that use the Options pattern.

When executing these methods, the settings will be loaded into a `PaymentSettings` or `ShipmentSettings` object and these will be instantiated as a singleton and available in every application through the DIC.

The following is an example of code where the configurations depend on a given service class:

```
public class OrderService
{
    private readonly PaymentSettings _paymentSettings;
    private readonly IPaymentGateway _paymentGateway;

    public OrderService(IOptions<PaymentSettings>
      paymentSettings, IPaymentGateway paymentGateway)
    {
        _paymentettings = paymentSettings.Value;
        _paymentGateway = paymentGateway;
    }

    public async Task<IOrder> Pay(decimal ammount)
    {
        var order = _paymentGateway(ammount,
        _paymentSettings.ApiKey,
        _paymentSettings.PaymentGatewayURL);
    // ..
    }
}
```

As we noted in the `OrderService` implementation, we just injected an `IOptions` interface for the `PaymentSettings` type. With this, the dependency is resolved by the ASP.NET Core 9 DIC.

Adopting the Options pattern offers several benefits, such as allowing the organization of configuration settings, grouping them into dedicated classes, and the use of strongly typed configuration.

In addition to improving maintenance and implementation quality, errors can also be detected during compilation time. You can also benefit from using unit tests, which is an excellent practice.

The Options pattern in ASP.NET Core 9 is a powerful and flexible way to manage configuration settings, supporting environment-specific configurations and making it easier to manage configurations for different deployment environments.

Now that we have learned how to use the Options pattern to properly deal with application configurations, it is time to understand how to manage these configurations securely in a cloud environment, in addition to learning how to dynamically manipulate behaviors in our applications.

# Working with dynamic configurations and behaviors

In the ever-evolving landscape of web applications, maintaining flexibility and responsiveness is crucial. As developers, we must ensure that our applications can adapt to changes quickly and securely. Dynamic configurations and behavior management are key strategies that allow us to achieve this flexibility. By managing configurations dynamically, we can update them without redeploying our applications. Additionally, by implementing application behavior management using techniques such as **feature toggles**, we can control resource availability in real time, giving us the ability to effortlessly test, deploy, or roll back features.

> **Feature toggles**
>
> Feature toggles or feature flags are a software development technique used to enable or disable specific functionality in a software application at runtime, facilitating **continuous integration and delivery (CI/CD)** by allowing code changes to be merged into the main code base without immediately exposing new functionality to all users. This technique helps in mitigating risks, conducting A/B testing, performing canary releases, and rolling back features without redeploying the code.
>
> Access the following article to learn more about the technique: `https://martinfowler.com/articles/feature-toggles.html`

Let's delve into the details of dynamic configuration management and implement a practical example.

## Working with dynamic settings

Dynamic settings refer to the ability to modify application configurations at runtime without the need for redeployment. This capability is essential for maintaining application uptime, ensuring quick responses to changes in requirements, and enhancing security by allowing rapid adjustments to sensitive configurations.

Modern applications must have dynamic configuration management mechanisms to guarantee the quality of the solution, in addition to benefits such as the following:

- **Zero downtime**: Update configurations without redeploying the application, ensuring continuous availability. This is an important feature that allows us to bring reliability and a better experience to users.

- **Security**: Quickly update security settings and credentials in response to threats.

- **Flexibility**: Adjust settings in real time to accommodate changing business requirements.

- **Simplified deployments**: Reduce the complexity and risk associated with application deployments by decoupling configuration changes from code changes. In scenarios with many environments, such as development, testing, and production, the application will have different configurations based on the resources of each environment. Having the ability to abstract the management of application configurations improves quality, segregates responsibilities, and maintains continuous delivery flow.

Several options are available to dynamically manage configurations in ASP.NET Core 9, including configuration files, environment variables, and cloud-based services such as **Azure App Configuration**. Azure App Configuration stands out for its robust features and seamless integration with other Azure services.

Azure App Configuration is a service that provides a centralized way to manage configuration settings and feature flags. It allows applications to dynamically adjust their behavior without redeployment.

---

**Azure App Configuration**

Azure App Configuration is a powerful feature available in Microsoft Azure that allows us to manage configurations and feature toggles securely, supporting the deployment of cloud-native applications.

For more details about Azure App Configuration, I suggest reading the rich documentation about the resource: `https://learn.microsoft.com/en-us/azure/azure-app-configuration/`.

---

We won't cover all the details of setting up and using Azure App Configuration in this book. For now, we will use the main resources to exemplify the use of dynamic configurations in our applications.

Let's create an application that interacts with Azure App Configuration and uses some patterns already learned in this chapter, such as the Options pattern.

### Setting up Azure App Configuration

Azure App Configuration is a cloud-based service that provides a centralized repository for application configurations, enabling dynamic configuration management.

Let's create an Azure App Configuration resource before creating an application. You will need access to an Azure subscription, as described in the *Technical requirements* section.

With access to the Azure subscription, follow these steps to create an Azure App Configuration resource:

1.  Navigate to the Azure portal (`https://portal.azure.com`), and in the search field, in the top bar, type `App Configuration` and click on the icon, as highlighted in *Figure 9.3*:

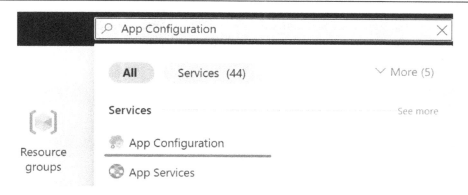

Figure 9.3 – Accessing the App Configuration service

2.  On the next screen, click on the **+ Create** option to add the new resource, as shown in *Figure 9.4*:

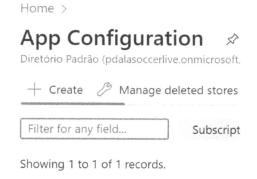

Figure 9.4 – Creating a new App Configuration resource

3.  On the next screen, we must configure the parameters of the new resource. We will keep the default settings. Use the following parameter suggestions as a reference:

    - **Resource group**: rg-aspnetcore8. Be sure to click the **Create new** button below the **Resource group** field to create the new resource group.

    - **Location**: **East US 2**

    - **Resource name**: <Your Last Name>-configuration

    - **Pricing tier**: **Standard**

    - Leave the **Create replicas** option unchecked.

4.  Click on the **Review + Create** button then the **Create** button, and wait for the resource to be created.

5.    When you finish creating the new resource, click the **Go to resource** button, as shown in *Figure 9.5*, or access the **App Configuration** list, as described in *step 1*, and click on the created resource:

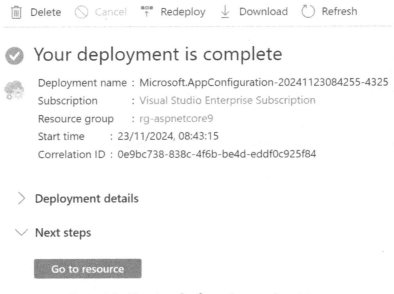

Figure 9.5 – New App Configuration creation status

Now that we have the configuration management resource created, it's time to create and configure our application to interact with Azure App Configuration.

### Creating and connecting an application in Azure App Configuration

For this example, an ASP.NET Core 9 MVC application will be created and connected to the Azure App Configuration service created previously.

Follow these steps:

1.    Open the terminal, and in a folder of your choice, create a directory named DynamicConfiguration:

```
mkdir DynamicConfiguration
```

2.    Now, access the directory with the following command:

```
cd DynamicConfiguration
```

3.    Run the following command to create the application:

```
dotnet new mvc -n DynamicConfiguration -o .
```

The previous command creates an MVC application with the name `DynamicConfiguration`, defined with the `-n` parameter and in the current directory, determined by the `-o` `.` parameter.

With the application created, we will simply prepare it to integrate with Azure App Configuration. To do this, run the following command in the application directory to open Visual Studio Code:

```
code .
```

Now, in the root of the project, create an `Options` folder and then create a file called `GlobalOptions.cs`. This file must contain the following code:

```
namespace DynamicConfiguration.Options;
public class GlobalOptions
{
    public string Title { get; set; }
}
```

The `GlobalOptions` class has only one property called `Title` that will be obtained through Azure App Configuration.

When the application starts, it loads the settings as we learned previously, using files such as `appsettings.json` and environment variables, among other providers that can be configured. However, for our classes, the details of obtaining the configurations are abstracted by ASP.NET Core 9, and, in this case, whatever the provider, when using the Options pattern, we will have the correct separation of responsibility, maintainability, flexibility, and extensibility.

Let's change the code of the `HomeController` class, in the `Controllers` folder, and add the settings previously created using the Options pattern. The `HomeController` class code will look like the following:

```
public class HomeController : Controller
{
    private readonly ILogger<HomeController> _logger;
    private readonly GlobalOptions _globalOptions;

    public HomeController(ILogger<HomeController> logger,
        IOptionsSnapshot<GlobalOptions> globalOptions)
    {
        _logger = logger;
        _globalOptions = globalOptions.Value;
    }

    public IActionResult Index()
    {
        ViewData["Title"] = _globalOptions.Title;
        return View();
```

```
    }

    public IActionResult Privacy()
    {
        return View();
    }

    [ResponseCache(Duration = 0,
      Location = ResponseCacheLocation.None,
      NoStore = true)]
    public IActionResult Error()
    {
        return View(new ErrorViewModel {
            RequestId = Activity.Current?.Id ??
            HttpContext.TraceIdentifier });
    }
}
```

Simple changes were made to the class. Let's understand each of them:

- **GlobalOptions field**: A new field was created for the class that is of type GlobalOptions, created previously

- **Change in the constructor**: Configurations will be injected through the ASP.NET Core 9 DIC, and that is why we added a parameter of type IOptionsSnapshot<GlobalSettings>. The purpose of using the IOptionsSnapshot<> interface is to allow you to obtain configurations dynamically, as we learned in the *What is the Options pattern?* section. If another interface is used, such as IOptions<>, the parameters will be loaded, but not dynamically.

- **Changing the Index action**: We change the Index action where we set the value of the Title property in the ViewData dictionary with the value of the configuration of the Title property of the _globalOptions object. The ViewData["Title"] dictionary is used in the Views/Home/Index.cshtml file to display the page title.

Now, let's change the code on the Views/Home/Index.cshtml page to display the title in the body of the page:

```
<div class="text-center">
<h1 class="display-4">Welcome @ViewData["Title"]</h1>
<p>Learn about <a
  href="https://learn.microsoft.com/aspnet/core">
  building Web apps with ASP.NET Core</a>.</p>
</div>
```

As can be seen in the highlighted code, we are only rendering the value contained in the `ViewData["Title"]` dictionary.

The application is prepared to render data obtained through configuration. Now, it's time to connect the application to Azure App Configuration.

First, open the terminal in the application directory and run the following command to add the NuGet package that contains the necessary SDK:

```
dotnet add package Microsoft.Azure.AppConfiguration.AspNetCore
```

Now, you will need to get the connection string containing the resource from Azure App Configuration. Let's execute the following steps:

1.  Access the Azure portal (`https://portal.azure.com`).
2.  In the search field, in the top bar of the portal, type `App Configuration` and click on the option.
3.  Then, in the list of configuration resources, click on the previously created resource with the name `<Your Last Name>-configuration`.
4.  In the side menu, look for the **Access settings** option and copy the connection string as shown in *Figure 9.6*:

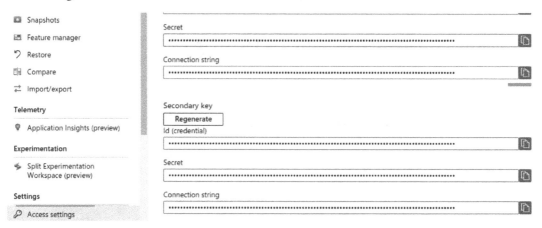

Figure 9.6 – Getting the connection string from App Configuration

5.  Now, run the following command in the terminal, in the application directory. The command uses a secret manager to store a secret named `ConnectionStrings:AppConfig`, which stores the connection string for your App Configuration store. Replace the `<your_connection_string>` placeholder with your App Configuration store's connection string. This is a good practice to prevent sensitive data, such as connection strings that are credentials or have passwords, from being persisted in version control, bringing vulnerabilities to your application:

```
dotnet user-secrets init
dotnet user-secrets set ConnectionStrings:AppConfig "<your_
connection_string>"
```

With the definition of the secret that contains the App Configuration connection string, we will change the `Program.cs` file to add the necessary services and middleware. Let's look at the changed `Program.cs` code:

```
using Microsoft.Extensions.Configuration
  .AzureAppConfiguration;
var builder = WebApplication.CreateBuilder(args);
Builder.Services.AddAzureAppConfiguration();
var connectionString = builder.Configuration
  .GetConnectionString("AppConfig");
builder.Configuration.AddAzureAppConfiguration(options =>
  {
    options.Connect(connectionString)
    .Select("DynamicConfiguration:*", LabelFilter.Null)
    .ConfigureRefresh(refreshOptions =>
    refreshOptions.Register("DynamicConfiguration:
      Sentinel", refreshAll: true));
  });
builder.Services.Configure<GlobalOptions>
  (builder.Configuration
  .GetSection("DynamicConfiguration:GlobalOptions"));
builder.Services.AddControllersWithViews();

var app = builder.Build();
if (!app.Environment.IsDevelopment())
{
  app.UseExceptionHandler("/Home/Error");
  app.UseHsts();
}
// Middleware to refresh configuration
app.UseAzureAppConfiguration();
app.UseHttpsRedirection();
app.UseStaticFiles();
```

```
app.UseRouting();
app.UseAuthorization();
app.MapControllerRoute(
name: "default",
pattern: "{controller=Home}/{action=Index}/{id?}");
app.Run();
```

The App Configuration SDK has excellent abstraction and is simple to integrate into the application. Let's understand the changes made to the preceding code:

- `builder.Services.AddAzureAppConfiguration()`: This method registers the necessary services for Azure App Configuration to work within your ASP.NET Core 9 application.

- `builder.Configuration.GetConnectionString("AppConfig")`: This line of code gets the Azure Application Configuration connection string, previously obtained from the Azure portal and added to the application via a secret. Note that getting the connection string is identical to getting it from the `appsettings.json` file. The big difference in managing configurations through secrets is that they are only kept on the local machine.

- `builder.Configuration.AddAzureAppConfiguration`: This extension method adds Azure App Configuration as a configuration provider to your application.

- `options.Connect(connectionString)`: Connects to the Azure application configuration instance using the previously obtained connection string.

- `.Select("Dynamic Configuration:*", LabelFilter.Null)`: Specifies that all keys with the `DynamicConfiguration:` prefix should be selected. The `LabelFilter.Null` parameter indicates that only unlabeled configurations are retrieved.

- `.ConfigureRefresh`: The `ConfigureRefresh` method registers keys that you want to monitor for changes in your application configuration store.

- `refreshOptions.Register("Dynamic Configuration", updateAll: true)`: Registers a sentinel key (`DynamicConfiguration:Sentinel`) that triggers an update. When the value of this key changes, all settings will be updated (`refreshAll: true`).

- `builder.Services.Configure<GlobalOptions>(builder.Configuration. GetSection("DynamicConfiguration: GlobalOptions"))`: This line of code binds the configuration created in Azure App Configuration and the `GlobalOptions` class created previously. With this, it will be possible to obtain the configuration through the DIC using the Options pattern.

- `UseAzureAppConfiguration`: Allows your application to use the application configuration middleware to update configuration automatically.

In summary, the previous configurations, added to the `Program.cs` file, allow the application to connect to Azure App Configuration via the connection string.

The App Configuration SDK works with the concept of pooling. In this case, when obtaining the configurations, a cache is made in the application's memory, to avoid constant requests to the Azure service and optimize the application's functioning.

By default, the time the application queries Azure App Configuration for updates is 30 seconds. It is possible to specify the refresh call time using the `refreshOptions.SetCacheExpiration` method. A `Sentinel` parameter was also configured, responsible for determining whether there were changes to the settings.

It is important as it prevents the SDK from analyzing each configuration individually, and if `Sentinel` has been changed, all configurations will be updated.

Now that we've learned how Azure App Configuration settings work, let's create configuration keys in the Azure portal:

1.  In the Azure portal (`https://portal.azure.com`), in the App Configuration resource created previously, select the **Configuration explorer** option, as shown in *Figure 9.7*:

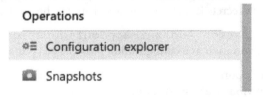

Figure 9.7 – Accessing the Configuration explorer option of Azure App Configuration

2.  Then, click on the **Create | Key-value** option, as shown in *Figure 9.8*:

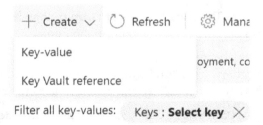

Figure 9.8 – Adding a new configuration on Azure App Configuration

A form will be displayed where we will enter the following parameters:

- **Key**: `DynamicConfiguration:Sentinel`
- **Value**: 1

3.  Leave the rest of the parameters at their defaults.
4.  Click **Apply**.

5.  Repeat *step 2* and add another key with the following configuration:

    -   **Key**: `DynamicConfiguration:GlobalOptions:Title`

    -   **Value**: `ASP.NET Core 9`

    Note the `DynamicConfiguration:GlobalOptions:Title` key. This key represents a hierarchy following the pattern `<Group Settings>:<Section>`. In this case, it is the name of the previously created settings class, configuration, or desired property of the configuration class format.

---

**Labels in Azure App Configuration**

The `Label` parameter in Azure Application Configuration is used to differentiate configuration settings based on different contexts or environments.

Labels allow you to separate configurations for different environments (for example, development, staging, production).

This approach brings benefits, such as the following:

• **Flexibility**: Easily switch between different sets of configurations

• **Isolation**: Keep settings for different environments or scenarios isolated and organized

• **Testing**: Safely test new configurations without affecting other environments

Settings that do not have a `Label` parameter will be treated as default settings.

To learn more about labels, visit the following URL: `https://learn.microsoft.com/en-us/azure/azure-app-configuration/howto-labels-aspnet-core`.

---

Now that the application is integrated with Azure App Configuration, open the terminal and access the application directory. Then, run the following command:

```
dotnet run
```

Now, access the application URL available on your terminal via the following URL: `http://localhost:<port>`. In the example shown in *Figure 9.9*, the URL is `http://localhost:5295`. We can also see in *Figure 9.9* a welcome message with the value defined in the App Configuration resource:

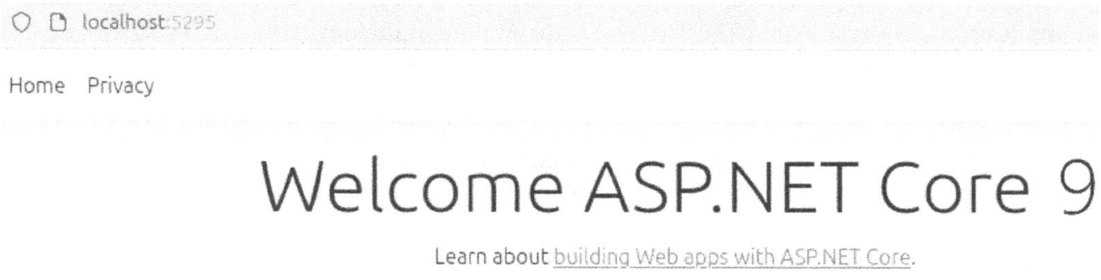

Figure 9.9 – Application getting settings from Azure App Configuration

As we can see, the configurations are being loaded directly from the Azure resource.

With the application still running, access the Azure portal (http://portal.azure.com) and the Azure App Configuration resource.

Then, access the **Configuration explorer** option. We will change the settings.

To do this, in the settings display grid, click on the three dots (**...**) as shown in *Figure 9.10* and click **Edit**:

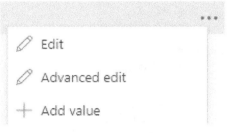

Figure 9.10 – Editing configurations

Provide the following settings:

- DynamicConfiguration:GlobalOptions:Title: **ASP.NET Core 9 With Dynamic config**

- DynamicConfiguration:Sentinel:**2**

Wait a few seconds, access the application again, and refresh the page. The page body message was changed, as shown in *Figure 9.11*:

Figure 9.11 – Application obtaining configurations dynamically

Despite being a simple implementation example, using a config server is a good practice in cloud-native applications, as suggested in The Twelve-Factor App methodology (https://12factor.net), and ASP.NET Core 9 provides several extensibility mechanisms, such as the one we use when integrating with Azure's App Configuration feature.

This approach in large application scenarios in production environments can bring several benefits by offering an immediate response to certain changes.

> **The Twelve-Factor App methodology**
>
> The Twelve-Factor App methodology is a methodology used as a reference in creating **SaaS** (**Software as a Service**) application and has 12 factors, technology agnostic, that offer best practices for developing cloud-native solutions. One of the factors is related to configuration management, related to what we learned in this chapter, and you can learn more about this factor through the following URL: `https://12factor.net/config`.

Managing configurations on a server such as Azure App Configuration brings several benefits, the most important being security. With the easy integration with ASP.NET Core 9 applications, we can allow our applications to change settings dynamically and even segregate them by environment. This approach is very important in a CI/CD process. We will talk more about CI/CD in *Chapter 10*.

Another approach that can be used to bring greater capacity to our applications in addition to improving user experience, among other benefits, is real-time behavior management, which we will learn about in the next section.

## Connecting an ASP.NET Core 9 application to Azure App Configuration

Surely at some point, you have already used a mechanism that dynamically changes the behavior of an application. Imagine a scenario where you install, for example, a messaging app that allows users to send videos, photos, and audio.

These media are automatically downloaded when you receive messages, which requires data consumption on your smartphone. In general, the first action we would take would be to disable the automatic media download option. This setting is found in a settings menu; however, this setting completely changes, in real time, the way the application will behave.

The aforementioned example is a simple concept of changing the behavior of applications in real time. Likewise, at some point, web applications may have their behavior dynamically managed, and their use brings several benefits, such as the following:

- **Controlled releases**: Gradually release features to a subset of users to monitor performance and user feedback
- **A/B testing**: Conduct experiments by rotating features for different groups of users to determine the best approach
- **Instant rollbacks**: Quickly disable a feature if it causes problems, without redeploying the application

The technique that allows changing the behavior of applications in real time is called feature toggles or feature flags.

Feature toggles, also known as feature flags, are a software development technique that allows you to enable or disable features in an application at runtime without deploying new code, bringing flexibility for better risk management and improving the deployment process, enabling teams to release resources to specific users or environments, and improving overall development and operational efficiency.

In terms of coding, a feature toggle can be represented as shown in *Figure 9.12*:

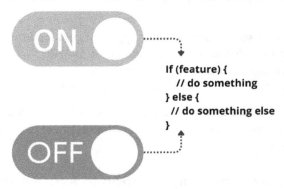

Figure 9.12 – Representation of the feature toggle concept

As we can see in *Figure 9.12*, the feature toggle is basically a decision point in the application's source code. This decision point checks whether a certain value, called a toggle, is activated. To check if a toggle is activated, we can obtain this value through a configuration file, environment variables, and even on a remote server, which is the most recommended way.

> **Single Responsibility Principle**
>
> Implementing feature toggles in ASP.NET Core 9 should follow best practices to make your code cleaner, easier to maintain, and more scalable. When using feature toggles, it is bad practice to lump multiple behaviors into a single class, such as handling different features or switching between old and new logic within a service. This approach can lead to code that is difficult to understand and modify. A good practice is to follow the **Single Responsibility Principle (SRP)**, which means that each class should handle only one responsibility or feature. By keeping each class focused on one task, you reduce complexity and make your application easier to maintain and extend.
>
> Additionally, using factory methods with DI in ASP.NET Core 9 allows you to easily swap out different implementations based on feature toggles without breaking the SRP. If you need to add a new feature, you can simply create a new class for that feature, isolating the existing logic. To learn more about the SRP, access the following URL: https://learn.microsoft.com/en-us/dotnet/architecture/modern-web-apps-azure/architectural-principles#single-responsibility.

All the details surrounding the use of the feature toggle technique and its respective benefits not only for development teams but also for management and complexity aspects go beyond the scope of this book.

We already have a basic knowledge of using this technique, and now, it's time to use it in an ASP.NET Core 9 application.

## Managing feature toggles with Azure App Configuration

In the previous topic, we used the Azure App Configuration feature for configuration management; however, this service also includes feature flags, which you can use to enable or disable a feature. Through the UI in the Azure portal, we can create and manage the feature flags of our applications.

Let's make some changes to the DynamicConfiguration project code, created previously, and add feature toggles:

1.  Open the terminal and go to the application directory. Then, run the following commands:

    ```
    dotnet add package Microsoft.Azure.AppConfiguration.AspNetCore
    dotnet add package Microsoft.FeatureManagement.AspNetCore
    ```

2.  These packages are necessary to incorporate the SDK for managing toggles in the application.

3.  Open the application in Visual Studio Code, then we will edit the Program.cs file, which will have the following updated code:

    ```
    using DynamicConfiguration.Options;
    using Microsoft.Extensions.Configuration
      .AzureAppConfiguration;
    using Microsoft.FeatureManagement;
    var builder = WebApplication.CreateBuilder(args);
    builder.Services.AddAzureAppConfiguration();
    builder.Services.AddFeatureManagement();
    var connectionString = builder.Configuration
      .GetConnectionString("AppConfig");
    builder.Configuration
      .AddAzureAppConfiguration(options =>
    {
      options.Connect(connectionString)
      .Select("DynamicConfiguration:*", LabelFilter.Null)
      .ConfigureRefresh(refreshOptions => refreshOptions
      .Register("DynamicConfiguration:Sentinel",
        refreshAll: true))
      .UseFeatureFlags(featureFlagsOptions =>
      {
        featureFlagsOptions.CacheExpirationInterval =
        TimeSpan.FromSeconds(5);
    ```

```
    });
  });
builder.Services.Configure<GlobalOptions>
  (builder.Configuration.GetSection(
    "DynamicConfiguration:GlobalOptions"));
builder.Services.AddControllersWithViews();
var app = builder.Build();
if (!app.Environment.IsDevelopment())
{
  app.UseExceptionHandler("/Home/Error");
  app.UseHsts();
}

// Middleware to refresh configuration
app.UseAzureAppConfiguration();
app.UseHttpsRedirection();
app.UseStaticFiles();
app.UseRouting();
app.UseAuthorization();
app.MapControllerRoute(
name: "default",
pattern: "{controller=Home}/{action=Index}/{id?}");
app.Run();
```

Basically, we make three changes to the `Program.cs` file:

- `using Microsoft.FeatureManagement`: Adding the namespaces necessary to add the SDK's toggle management features.

- `builder.Services.AddFeatureManagement()`: Adding services to the application's DIC.

- `.UseFeatureFlags`: We changed the connection settings with Azure App Configuration, informing us that the toggle management feature will be used. Additionally, a 5-second cache was defined using the `featureFlagsOptions.CacheExpirationInterval` standard.

As part of the Azure App Configuration SDK, we can work with toggles directly in the code of controllers or services, using the `IFeatureManager` interface, the `FeatureGate` attribute, or a **tag helper** directly in views. For this example, we will use a tag helper.

**Using IFeatureManagement and the FeatureGate attribute**

In some cases, we can analyze whether a toggle is activated or not through the `IFeatureManagement` interface, which is injected into a class and provides us with methods to test the values, such as the following:

```
public class MyController : Controller
{
  private readonly IFeatureManager _featureManager;
  public MyController(IFeatureManager featureManager)
  {
    _featureManager = featureManager;
  }
  private async Task MyMethod()
  {
    if (await    _featureManager
      .IsEnableAsync("FeatureToggleName"))
    {
      Console.WriteLine("New Approach");
    }
    else
    {
      Console.WriteLine("Legacy Approach");
    }
  }
}
```

In the same way, it is possible to annotate an action or controller with the `FeatureGate` attribute:

```
using Microsoft.FeatureManagement.Mvc;
[FeatureGate("FeatureToggleName)]
public class MyController : Controller
{
  // ....
}
```

This way, it is possible to benefit from the use of toggle management with different implementations but the same concept.

Let's change the application to use a tag helper, which will use the feature toggle. Follow the next steps:

1.  In Visual Studio Code, edit the `Views/_ViewImports.cshtml` file and add the following code to the file, below the existing code:

    ```
    @addTagHelper *, Microsoft.FeatureManagement
      .AspNetCore
    ```

    This code adds a tag helper from the Azure App Configuration SDK.

2.  Then, open the `Views/Home/Index.cstml` file and use the following code:

    ```
    <div class="text-center">
    <h1 class="display-4">Welcome @ViewData["Title"]</h1>
    <p>Learn about <a
      href="https://learn.microsoft.com/aspnet/core">
      building Web apps with ASP.NET Core</a>.</p>
    </div>
    <feature name="NewFeature">
    <div style="background-color: silver;
      border: dotted 1px #000000">
    <h3>New Feature using Toggles and
      the Azure App Configuration</h3>
    </div>
    </feature>
    ```

    Note the use of the feature tag, which will basically obtain information on whether a toggle is enabled. If yes, the new `div` tag will be displayed on the screen.

    Now that everything is configured in the application, let's add the feature toggle in Azure App Configuration.

3.  Open the Azure portal (`https://portal.azure.com`) and access the App Configuration resource created in the previous section.

4.  Then, click on the **Feature manager** menu, **Create | Feature flag**, as shown in *Figure 9.13*:

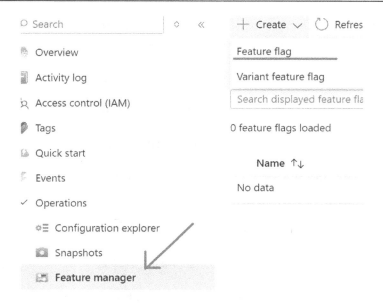

Figure 9.13 – Adding a new feature flag

5.  On the next screen, set the **New feature flag** field to the NewFeature value and leave the rest at their default values.

6.  Click on the **Apply** button.

    A new feature flag will be created and disabled, as shown in *Figure 9.14*:

Figure 9.14 – Application using a disabled feature flag

We did this configuration on purpose. Now, run the application again using the dotnet run command, executed through the terminal in the application directory and you'll see there is no changes on the application. The reason the new Div tag was not displayed is that we created the toggle as Enabled= false.

7.  Keep the application running, access the Azure portal again, and enable the toggle by clicking on the **Enabled** column in the grid, as shown in *Figure 9.15*:

| Label ↑↓ | Enabled ↑↓ | Feature filter(s) ↑↓ |
|---|---|---|
| *(No label)* | ⬤▬ | None |

Figure 9.15 – Enabling the feature flag

8.  Access the application again, and we can see in *Figure 9.16* that a new HTML element has been added to the page:

Welcome ASP.NET Core 9 With Dynamic config

Learn about building Web apps with ASP.NET Core.

New Feature using Toggles and the Azure App Configuration

Figure 9.16 – Application behavior changed at runtime

By understanding and implementing dynamic configurations and feature toggles, we can create robust, flexible, and responsive ASP.NET Core 9 applications.

In this chapter, we have used Azure App Configuration as a feature flag manager. However, ASP. NET Core 9 has integrations with several other types of toggle management servers using the same techniques learned in this chapter.

The combination of configuration management techniques and feature flags is very powerful for different application contexts, mainly interacting with cloud resources in a scenario of continuous delivery of value through automated mechanisms.

We will discuss how to host our applications in cloud environments using automated processes in the next chapter.

## Summary

In this chapter, we delved into good practices for managing application configurations by understanding the concepts and abstractions of the IConfiguration interface. We also worked with concepts related to the ASP.NET Core 9 configuration provider, along with the implementation of the Options pattern. Finally, we worked with changing application configurations and behavior in real time using Microsoft Azure's Azure App Configurator to implement the concept of feature flags or feature toggles. Working with cloud resources is an important premise for Software Engineers and in the next chapter, we will explore how to deploy applications in a Cloud environment.

## Get This Book's PDF Version and Exclusive Extras

Scan the QR code (or go to packtpub.com/unlock). Search for this book by name, confirm the edition, and then follow the steps on the page.

*Note: Keep your invoice handly. Purchase made directly from packt don't require one.*

# Part 4:
# Hosting, Deploying, and Preparing to the Cloud

Modern applications are dynamic, and as software engineers, our work doesn't end after synchronizing the latest code developed. In a scenario where the market is constantly changing, it is necessary for applications to be dynamic enough to meet constant market demands. Therefore, development teams must adapt to the new topics surrounding the modern development model. ASP.NET Core 9 is prepared to provide high-quality solutions, suitable for cloud environments. In this part, we will learn about aspects involving the continuous delivery of solutions through the understanding and implementation of application publishing flows in a cloud environment with the support of automated pipelines such as **Continuous Integration** (**CI**) and **Continuous Delivery** (**CD**), processes associated with the DevOps culture. We will understand what a cloud-native mindset is and how to direct our solutions to a constantly changing market.

This part has the following chapters:

- *Chapter 10, Deploying and Hosting Applications*
- *Chapter 11, Cloud-Native Development with ASP.NET Core 9*

# 10
# Deploying and Hosting Applications

After following a good development process, implementing good practices, and covering all the functionalities required for an application, it's necessary to publish it in an environment. For this to be done successfully, it's important to understand various concepts, practices, and application packaging models that go beyond the source material. In this chapter, we'll discuss different approaches to hosting and deploying applications, as well as understand concepts related to **continuous integration and continuous deployment (CI/CD)** and containers.

ASP.NET Core 9 provides a robust configuration system that allows developers to manage configurations and behaviors effectively. This chapter will explore the importance of application configurations, how to manage them using the configuration system, and how to make your applications adaptive at runtime.

In this chapter, we'll cover the following topics:

- Preparing to publish your application and host locally
- Publishing the solution in a cloud environment
- Understanding the Docker principles and how to pack the application in a container
- Understanding the DevOps approach with CI/CD

## Technical requirements

To complete this chapter, the following tools must be present in your development environment:

- **An Azure subscription**: In this chapter, we'll be creating resources in Microsoft Azure. To do this, if you haven't already, you will need to have an Azure subscription so that you can access the platform. You can sign up for a subscription with limited credits to learn about the concepts presented in this chapter at `https://azure.microsoft.com/en-us/free`.

- **A Docker Hub account**: You will need to create an account on the Docker Hub website at `https://hub.docker.com`.

- **The Azure Tools extension**: You will need to install the Azure Tools extension for Visual Studio Code from `https://marketplace.visualstudio.com/items?itemName=ms-vscode.vscode-node-azure-pack`. Once it's been installed, log in with your Azure credentials.

The code examples for this chapter can be found in this book's GitHub repository: `https://github.com/PacktPublishing/ASP.NET-Core-9.0-Essentials/tree/main/Chapter10`.

# Preparing to publish your application and host locally

Publishing an application is a natural process in the software development life cycle. After development and testing, the next step is to make the application available to users. This involves creating a deployable version of the application and configuring it in an environment where it can be accessed and used.

Let's understand the details of publishing applications while following various strategies, from manual to automated ones, using CI/CD. But before we do this, let's understand some of the fundamentals, such as the importance of the publishing process.

## The importance of the publishing process

The publishing process transforms your application from source code into a deployable format. This process ensures that all dependencies, configurations, and compiled code are packaged together, making it easier to deploy and run the application in different environments.

The publishing process in ASP.NET Core 9 involves three steps:

1. Restoring the package.
2. Compiling the application.
3. Generating a publishable package.

The publication package that's generated may vary, depending on the type of application that's developed. It may contain different files, such as the following:

- The application's DLL files
- Third-party dependencies and libraries
- Static files (for example, JavaScript, CSS, and images)
- Configuration files (for example, `appsettings.json`)
- Executables for standalone deployments

To understand how this process works, follow the instructions provided in the *Technical requirements* section to download the example application from this book's GitHub repository. This will be used as the basis for this chapter.

Now, let's understand how to generate publishing packages.

## Generating a publishing package

We've been working with the .NET platform CLI tool extensively throughout this book to create and run applications. The CLI tool also has a specific command for generating publishing packages for ASP.NET Core 9 projects.

The `publish` command provides various options that allow us to configure the publication package's output, as listed in *Table 10.1*:

| Option | Description | Example |
|--------|-------------|---------|
| `<PROJECT>` | Specifies the project file to operate on. Defaults to the current directory if not specified. | `dotnet publish project_name.csproj` |
| `-c, --configuration` | Defines the build configuration (**Debug** or **Release**). Defaults to **Debug**. | `dotnet publish -c Release` |
| `-f, --framework` | Specifies the target framework – for example, `net8.0`. | `dotnet publish -f net8.0` |
| `--runtime` | Publishes the application for a specific runtime (for example, `win-x64`, `linux-x64`, or `osx-x64`). | `dotnet publish -runtime linux-x64` |
| `-o, --output` | Specifies the output directory for the published files. | `dotnet publish -o ./publish` |
| `--self-contained` | Publishes the application as a self-contained deployment, including the .NET runtime. | `dotnet publish -self-contained` |
| `--no-restore` | Disables the ability to restore project dependencies during the publish operation. Assumes restoration has already been done. It's useful during CI/CD pipelines. | `dotnet publish -no-restore` |
| `--manifest` | Specifies one or more target manifests to calculate the set of packages to include in the published output. | `dotnet publish -manifest ProjectManyfest.xml` |

| Option | Description | Example |
|---|---|---|
| `--version-suffix` | Sets the $(VersionSuffix) property value to use when building the project. Useful for prerelease versions. | `dotnet publish -version-suffix beta1` |

Table 10.1 – dotnet publish CLI tool options

The use of each option will depend on each scenario. In our context, we'll use the `<PROJECT>`, `-c`, `-o`, and, when necessary, `--no-restore` options.

Now, let's generate a publishing package for the **UrlShortener** application. To do this, open your terminal or bash, access the previously downloaded application directory, and execute the following command:

```
dotnet publish UrlShortener.csproj -c Release -o ./published
```

The preceding command will generate the `publish` package in the `published` folder. However, it's important to understand the `-c` parameter in more detail:

- The `-c` option specifies the build configuration, and there are typically two main configurations: **Debug** and **Release**:

  - The **Debug** configuration includes additional debug information and is optimized for debugging. When running the project locally with the `dotnet run` command, the default configuration is **Debug**, which allows the debugging process to be carried out.

  - The **Release** configuration is optimized for performance and does not include debug information. It's typically used to deploy the application to production environments.

When accessing the `published` folder, we have to simulate the directory/file structure:

```
publish/
├── appsettings.Development.json
├── appsettings.json
├── Azure.Core.dll
├── Azure.Identity.dll
├── Microsoft.Bcl.AsyncInterfaces.dll
├── Microsoft.Data.SqlClient.dll
├── Microsoft.EntityFrameworkCore.Abstractions.dll
├── Microsoft.EntityFrameworkCore.dll
├── Microsoft.EntityFrameworkCore.Relational.dll
├── Microsoft.EntityFrameworkCore.SqlServer.dll
```

```
├── Microsoft.Identity.Client.dll
├── Microsoft.Identity.Client.Extensions.Msal.dll
├── Microsoft.IdentityModel.Abstractions.dll
├── Microsoft.IdentityModel.JsonWebTokens.dll
├── Microsoft.IdentityModel.Logging.dll
├── Microsoft.IdentityModel.Protocols.dll
├── Microsoft.IdentityModel.Protocols.OpenIdConnect.dll
├── Microsoft.IdentityModel.Tokens.dll
├── Microsoft.SqlServer.Server.dll
├── Microsoft.Win32.SystemEvents.dll
├── runtimes/
│   ├── (runtime-specific files and directories)
├── System.Configuration.ConfigurationManager.dll
├── System.Drawing.Common.dll
├── System.IdentityModel.Tokens.Jwt.dll
├── System.Memory.Data.dll
├── System.Runtime.Caching.dll
├── System.Security.Cryptography.ProtectedData.dll
├── System.Security.Permissions.dll
├── System.Windows.Extensions.dll
├── UrlShortener
├── web.config
└──wwwroot/
    ├── (static files like css, js, images)
```

As we can see, there are several .dll files, which are the dependencies that the application uses, in addition to static files such as wwwroot and configuration files.

The contents of this folder are exactly what should be published in an environment, be it locally or via a cloud provider.

By accessing the published directory through the terminal and executing the following command, it's possible to run the application:

```
dotnet UrlShorterner.dll
```

The UrlShorterner.dll file is the executable for an ASP.NET Core 9 application. It's possible to run the application through the .dll file on your development machine since the .NET SDK is installed. The SDK must not be installed on servers that will run the applications. For this, you only need to install **.NET Runtime**.

**.NET Runtime**

.NET Runtime is a software framework developed by Microsoft that provides a managed execution environment for running .NET applications. It includes the components needed to run .NET programs, manage memory, handle exceptions, and collect garbage. .NET Runtime is typically installed on servers and machines that run specific .NET applications. Unlike the .NET SDK, .NET Runtime has features for running applications rather than building and developing them. To learn more about .NET Runtime, go to `https://learn.microsoft.com/en-us/dotnet/core/introduction`.

The .NET platform and ASP.NET Core 9 are portable, which means they can be run on different operating systems that have the SDK or .NET Runtime installed. *Table 10.2* shows the application servers that can be used in each of the most important operating systems:

| Operating System | Prerequisites |
| --- | --- |
| Linux | • .NET SDK/Runtime, Kestrel<br>• Optional: Nginx/Apache, Hosting bundle |
| macOS | • .NET SDK/Runtime, Kestrel<br>• Optional: Nginx/Apache |
| Windows | • .NET SDK/Runtime, Kestrel<br>• Optional: IIS, NGINX, HTTP.sys, ASP.NET Core Hosting bundle |

Table 10.2 – Web server options for ASP.NET Core 9 applications

Generating publication packages using the CLI tool is straightforward. We'll follow this process while automating via CI/CD, something we'll cover in the *Understanding the DevOps approach with CI/CD* section.

Now that we've learned how to generate publishing packages, it's time to learn how to publish them in a cloud environment.

## Publishing the solution in a cloud environment

The advantage of developing modern applications with ASP.NET Core 9 goes beyond the ability to use implementation best practices – it also encompasses the need to deliver high-quality solutions to application users.

So far, we've learned about the importance of using various features of the .NET platform, such as using the .NET CLI to compile applications and install support tools such as Entity Framework Core. We've also learned about the process of generating publishable packages that can be run both locally and in any other environment that uses .NET Runtime.

At the time of writing, it's impossible not to work in a cloud environment. This offers us benefits such as elasticity, availability, security, and many other features that simplify the process of deploying, maintaining, and evolving applications through the continuous process of delivering value.

To learn how to publish the solution in a cloud environment, we'll use Azure as our cloud provider.

Moving an ASP.NET Core 9 application to Azure allows developers to benefit from the dynamic capabilities provided by such a cloud provider while focusing on the application context and business objectives. Azure, through its diverse resources and services, allows applications to handle varied workloads, remain accessible to users, and stay protected against security threats.

Based on the **UrlShortener** application that we worked on previously and in conjunction with the process of generating publishable packages, we'll implement the benefits of Azure and publish this application in a cloud environment.

## Creating Azure app services and database resources

The Azure environment provides different types of resources for publishing applications, at different service levels and with varying publishing approaches.

For this application, we'll use a resource called **App Service**, a **Platform-as-a-Service (PaaS)** offering provided by Azure that allows us to focus on our applications. App Service provides a great application server while also supplying us with a URL to access the published application.

You must have prepared your environment based on the information provided in the *Technical requirements* section.

> **Application services and PaaS**
>
> Azure App Service is a fully managed PaaS that allows developers to build, deploy, and scale web applications, mobile backends, and RESTful APIs in the programming language of their choice, without the need for infrastructure management. App Service provides a prepared server, providing the runtime needed to run your applications. The PaaS approach is a cloud computing model that provides a complete development and deployment environment in the cloud, freeing developers from the need to deal with infrastructure. For more details, see the Azure App Service documentation: `https://docs.microsoft.com/en-us/azure/app-service/`.

Our goal will not be to exhaust all resource options available in the Azure environment since a separate book dedicated to this subject would be needed.

Instead, we'll focus on publishing the **UrlShortener** application while using Azure App Service as the web host.

Follow these steps to publish the application:

1. Access the Azure portal (`https://portal.azure.com`).

2. On the main screen, click on the **Create a resource** button, as shown in *Figure 10.1*:

Figure 10.1 – Creating a new Azure resource

3. Then, select **Create** under the **Web App** resource, as shown in *Figure 10.2*:

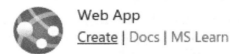

Figure 10.2 – Creating a new Web App resource

4. On the **Basics creation** screen of the new **Web App** resource, fill in the information provided in *Table 10.3*:

| Parameter | Value | Description |
|---|---|---|
| **Subscription** | Select your subscription. | A subscription is necessary to onboard the resources and related costs. |
| **Resource Group** | Here, the value is `rg-aspnet-core8`. If this resource group doesn't exist, click on **Create new link** below the **Resource Group** field and create it. | The resource is a logical group of resources in Azure. |
| **Name** | `urlshortener.<your last name>.` | This parameter will be the URL of your application. Please keep it unique. |

| Parameter | Value | Description |
|---|---|---|
| **Publish** | **Code**. | App Service has different ways to host and publish applications. In this case, we're using the **Code** option because we'll publish the generated package. |
| **Runtime stack** | **.NET 9 (LTS)**. | This parameter defines the type of application that will be hosted on App Service. It supports .NET, Node.js, Java, PHP, and Python. |
| **Operational System** | Linux. | Linux is a good option for many use cases. However, for this exercise, you can select Windows as well. The definition of the operating system depends on the requirements of the application. |
| **Region** | EastUS 2 | The region where App Service will be hosted. We're using **East US 2** because the database we'll be creating is not available in the East US region. |
| **Linux Pan** | Leave as-is. | We'll be creating a new service plan to host the application. The service plan is an important component of App Service. Depending on the pricing plan, the service plan can host more than one application. |
| **Pricing plan** | Basic B1. | The **Basic B1** option is enough for this example. Keep in mind that if you select a different Pricing plan, you can be charged higher costs. |
| **Zone redundancy** | Disabled. | This parameter is used in production environments where applications require a high-availability configuration. |

Table 10.3 – Basic parameters of the new Web App resource

5.   Click on the **Next: Database >** button.

6.   Select the **Create a database** option and fill in the parameters as per *Figure 10.3*:

# Create Web App ...

Basics    **Database**    Deployment    Networking    Monitor + secure    Tags    Review + create

Once database is enabled, a new VNet and related networking resources will be created automatically. Learn More ↗

Create a Database                  ☑

**Database**

Engine * ⓘ                 | SQLAzure (recommended)              ⌄ |

Server name *              | urlshortener-db-server-lastname    ✓ |

Database name *            | UrlShortenerDB                     ✓ |

Figure 10.3 – Database server configuration

At this stage, we're configuring a database, which is necessary for the **URLShortener** application. We'll use the Azure SQL Server resource since it provides a server where you can host different databases. For this example, we're using just one database. However, if desired, other databases can be added later.

7.  Now, click on the **Monitor + Secure** tab and set the **Enable Application Insights** option to **No**.

    This option aims to create a monitoring resource for the application. This is a best practice, especially for production resources. Therefore, at this stage, the objective is to publish the application; there's no need for monitoring, something that can be added later.

8.  Next, click **Review and Create**. Then, click **Create** and wait for the resource to be created.

9.  On the review screen, in the **Database** section, you'll see username and password information, as shown in *Figure 10.4*. Copy those details and keep them handy; we'll need the password later to configure the database:

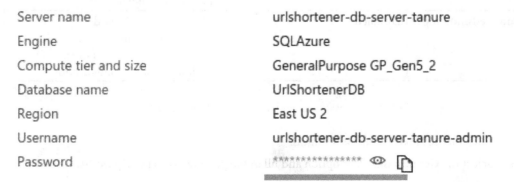

| Server name | urlshortener-db-server-tanure |
| Engine | SQLAzure |
| Compute tier and size | GeneralPurpose GP_Gen5_2 |
| Database name | UrlShortenerDB |
| Region | East US 2 |
| Username | urlshortener-db-server-tanure-admin |
| Password | ***************** 👁 📋 |

Figure 10.4 – Database credentials

10. Finally, click **Create** and wait for the resource to be created.

11. Once the resource has been created, click the **Go to resource** button, as shown in *Figure 10.5*:

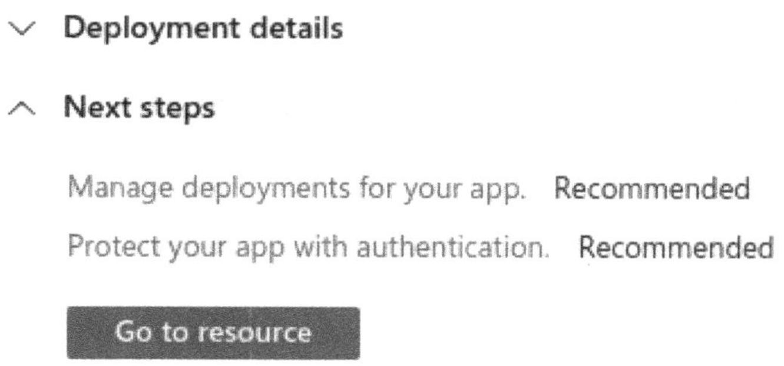

∨  **Deployment details**

∧  **Next steps**

Manage deployments for your app.   Recommended

Protect your app with authentication.   Recommended

Go to resource

Figure 10.5: Resource created screen

You will be redirected to the previously created **App Service** settings summary screen.

As shown in *Figure 10.6*, you'll be able to see the **Default domain** URL that's been made available so that you can access the application:

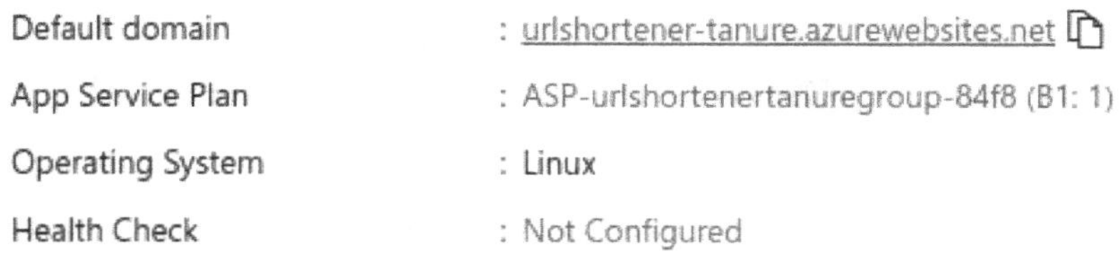

Default domain                          : urlshortener-tanure.azurewebsites.net

App Service Plan                        : ASP-urlshortenertanuregroup-84f8 (B1: 1)

Operating System                        : Linux

Health Check                            : Not Configured

Figure 10.6 – Default domain URL of the created application services

The **Default domain** URL is automatically created by Azure, according to the parameters defined when creating the application services and can be customized with a custom domain. We'll keep the URL available and in operation. Upon clicking on the URL, you'll be redirected to a page containing information similar to what's shown in *Figure 10.7*:

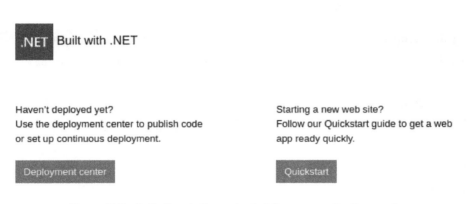

Figure 10.7 – Default website content of the new application services

At this point, the server is up and running, but we must publish the application on Azure. However, before publishing the application, let's configure the database.

## Configuring Azure SQL Server

While creating our application services, other resources were created, such as the database server and the database.

We need to configure the database so that we have the table we used in the application to persist the URLs.

We'll use the Entity Framework Core tool to update the database in the same way we did it locally. However, the database service that's automatically created by Azure is publicly inaccessible for security reasons.

To do this, we must make some configuration changes in advance so that we can manipulate the database. Follow these steps:

1. Go to the previously created resource group – that is, **rg-aspnetcore8**. You will be able to see a list of created resources.

2. Search for the **UrlshortenerDB** resource and access it.

3. Then, in the **Settings** menu group, click **Connection Strings**.

4. The connection string should look like this:

```
Server=tcp:urlshortener-db-server-tanure.database.windows.
net,1433;Initial Catalog=UrlshortenerDB;Persist Security
Info=False;User ID=urlshortener-db-server-tanure-admin;Pass-
word={your_password}; MultipleActiveResultSets=False;En-
crypt=True;TrustServerCertificate=False;Connection Timeout=30;
```

5. Note the `Password={your_password}` parameter. Replace this parameter with the password that you copied when you were creating your application services.

6. Copy the connection string from the **ADO.NET (SQL Authentication)** field.

7. Now, open the `appsettings.json` file of the **URLShortener** application and change the `DefaultConnection` property to the connection string you copied previously. The result will look like this:

```
"Logging": {
  "LogLevel": {
    "Default": "Information",
    "Microsoft.AspNetCore": "Warning"
  }
},
"ConnectionStrings": {
  "DefaultConnection":
    "Server=tcp:urlshortener-db-server-tanure.database.windows.
net,1433;Initial Catalog=UrlshortenerDB;Persist Security
Info=False;User ID=urlshortener-db-server-tanure-admin;Password=
XL6l61uv9t4$K4Q6;MultipleActiveResultSets=False;Encrypt=True;Tru
stServerCertificate=False;Connection Timeout=30;"
  },
  "AllowedHosts": "*"
}
```

8. Save the `appsettings.json` file.

9. Now, let's configure access to the database server. To do this, go back to the **rg-aspnetcore8** resource group and click on the **urlshortener-db-server<your last name>** resource.

10. From the main menu, go to **Security | Networking** and click on the **Add your client IPv4 address** option, as shown in *Figure 10.8*:

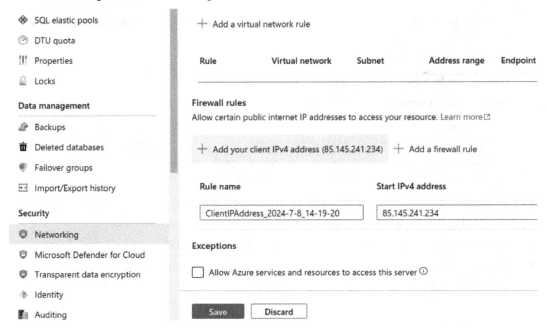

Figure 10.8 – Adding a firewall rule to access the private database of an IPv4 address

This configuration will create a rule so that the database is only accessible via its current IP. Keep in mind that if your IP changes, you will have to perform these steps again to add the new IP.

11. Finally, click **Save**.

With this, we've configured the application for the connection string of the database hosted in Azure and added a firewall rule so that the database can be accessed through our current IP.

Now, we need to update the database. To do this, access your operating system's terminal and navigate to the **URLShortener** project directory. Then, run the following command:

```
dotnet ef database update
```

Wait for the process to complete. To check whether the table was created correctly, in the Azure portal (`https://portal.azure.com`), access the **rg-aspnetcore9** resource group, then access the **UrlShortenerDB** resource. Click on the **Query Editor** menu and access the database with the credentials that were provided when you were creating the application service.

As shown in *Figure 10.9*, the new table has been created:

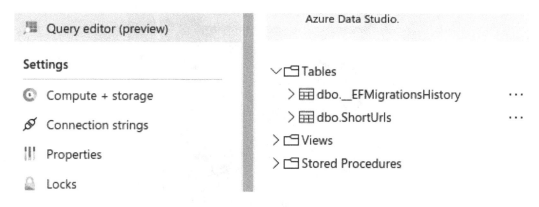

Figure 10.9 – The database tables that were created using Entity Framework Core migrations

This is one of the benefits of using migrations through Entity Framework Core. By doing this, it's possible to apply changes to a local database or server and maintain compliance with the application code.

Now that the database has been configured, it's time to publish the application. We'll do this through Visual Studio Code.

## Publishing an application with Visual Studio Code

With all the prerequisites for hosting the application in Azure configured, it's time to publish the application.

The process of publishing via Visual Studio Code or even with Visual Studio is quite straightforward.

In the *Technical requirements* section, it was suggested that you install and configure the Azure Tools extension (https://marketplace.visualstudio.com/items?itemName=ms-vscode.vscode-node-azure-pack). This extension makes the manual publishing process easier.

Follow these steps to publish the application version in the application services we created previously:

1.  Access the **UrlShortener** application directory and run the following command:

    ```
    code .
    ```

2.  Then, click on the Azure Tools extension icon in Visual Studio Code, as shown in *Figure 10.10*:

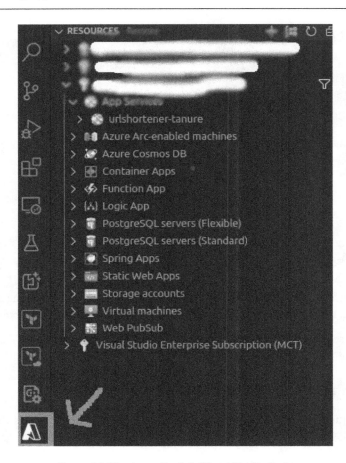

Figure 10.10 – Azure Tools in Visual Studio Code

A list of subscriptions that are available to your user will be displayed. By expanding the subscription, we'll be able to see the App Service resource and the resource that's been created for the **UrlShortener** application.

3.  Now, right-click on the **urlshortener-<your last name>** application and select the **Deploy to Web App...** option, as shown in *Figure 10.11*:

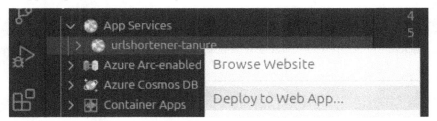

Figure 10.11 – Deploying a web app using the Azure Tools extensions in Visual Studio Code

4. You'll be asked for some configuration details so that you can deploy. Just confirm the options that are provided and wait for the deployment process to complete.

5. After the publication process is complete, a notification similar to the one shown in *Figure 10.12* will be displayed:

Figure 10.12 – A notification stating that application deployment has been completed

6. You can navigate to the published website by clicking the **Browse Website** button. You'll see a result similar to the one shown in *Figure 10.13*:

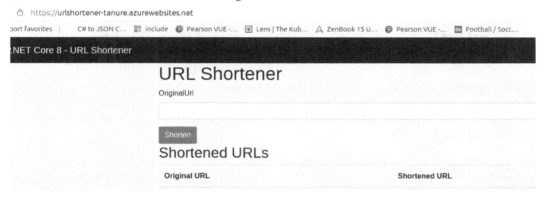

Figure 10.13 – The URL Shortener application running on Azure

Now, you can use the application that contains the short URL functionality directly in your Azure environment publicly.

The Azure Tools extension automates the process of publishing new application versions by running the following processes in the background:

- Restoring packages
- Compiling the application
- Generating a publishing package
- Compressing the publishing package in `.zip` format
- Connecting to the Azure environment
- Deploying the ZIP file containing the publication package
- Extracting the ZIP file

These steps are performed every time you choose to deploy using the Azure Tools extension. We'll learn about another way to publish packages in a C/ICD model in the *Understanding DevOps approach with CI/CD* section of this chapter.

Hosting solutions in cloud environments is a necessary activity today and several resources can help us with this task.

The definition of each hosting resource and service layer will depend on the application requirements, as well as the team's level of knowledge. There are cases where we can use strategies that allow us to host our applications in different environments, in a way that's agnostic to the specific resources of cloud providers.

To achieve this, a strategy that's often used in cloud-native applications is the containers strategy. We'll learn about this in the next section.

# Understanding the Docker principles and how to package the application in a container

Nowadays, using a container strategy has become essential, especially for cloud-native applications. Containers provide a consistent environment for development, testing, and deployment, ensuring applications run smoothly regardless of where they're deployed. When using containers, we practically have everything needed for the application to run in a given environment, with no need to install additional packages or runtimes.

With this, we have consistency, which is crucial for cloud environments such as Azure or any other cloud provider as they offer robust services to manage and scale containerized applications. As an analogy, the container strategy helps combat the behavior that generates the statement *"It works on my machine."*

This phrase is true since the development environment has everything necessary to run an application. However, being agile in delivering value and having no dependencies for running applications, regardless of the environment, is one of the great advantages of containers. Before we create a container, let's understand what they are.

## Understanding what a container is

A container is a self-contained executable software package that includes everything needed to run a piece of software. Containers are isolated from each other and the host system, providing a consistent runtime environment. This isolation ensures that the application behaves the same regardless of the environment in which it runs.

Containers provide a type of virtualization that's different from what's provided by traditional **virtual machines (VMs)**.

---

**VMs**

VMs are software emulations of physical computers. Each VM runs a complete operating system, including its own kernel, and simulates all the hardware that the operating system requires. VMs run on a hypervisor, which manages multiple VMs on a single physical host.

*Figure 10.14* shows some of the differences between containers and VMs:

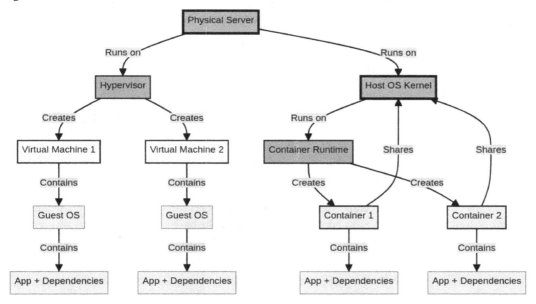

Figure 10.14 – Differences between containers and VMs

As we can see, containers don't depend on a complete operating system for their execution, only on a runtime that shares a machine's resources, such as networking and processing. However, they are executed independently and in isolation.

Containers offer several benefits:

- **Portability**: Containers encapsulate all dependencies, making it easy to move applications between different environments without compatibility issues occurring.

- **Consistency**: They ensure that applications run consistently across development, testing, and production environments.

- **Scalability**: They can easily be scaled up or down to handle varying loads, making them ideal for cloud environments.

- **Efficiency**: Containers share the kernel and host system resources efficiently, resulting in lower overhead compared to traditional VMs.

To be able to run a container, it's necessary to use a runtime to manage it, as is the case with ASP.NET Core 9 applications. The most famous container runtime is **Docker**. We'll understand its fundamentals in the next section.

## Understanding Docker fundamentals

Docker is an open source platform that automates the process of deploying, scaling, and managing containerized applications, providing a simple and powerful way to build, ship, and operate containers.

Docker provides three components for managing containers:

- **Docker Engine**: The runtime that manages containers
- **Docker CLI**: The command-line interface used to interact with Docker
- **Docker Hub**: A cloud-based registry service for sharing and storing Docker images, similar to how we have GitHub for managing source code repositories

Through these tools, Docker provides mechanisms that allow us to manipulate the components that involve the container development strategy. In this case, containers have the following components:

- **Images**: An image can be compared to a photo of a current version of your application, including everything needed to run your application. Images are the basis of containers and are created using a **Dockerfile**, which contains a set of instructions for building the image.

- **Containers**: A container is a running instance of an image. We can relate an image to a class and a container to an instance of this class. Containers are created from images and run on Docker Engine. Each container is isolated from the others and has its own filesystem, CPU, memory, and process space.

- **Dockerfile**: A Dockerfile is a text document that contains a series of instructions on how to build a Docker image. It specifies the base image to use, the application code, dependencies, and any commands required to configure the environment.

- **Container registry**: The container registry is a repository for storing and distributing images. Docker Hub is a popular public registry, though there are private registries such as Azure Container Registry available.

The relationship between Docker components and their container structure is shown in *Figure 10.15*:

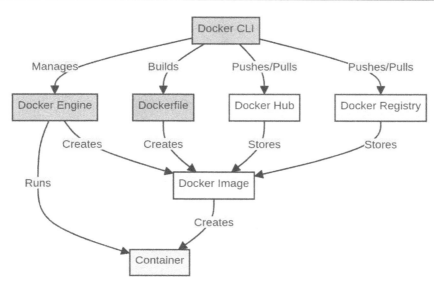

Figure 10.15 – The relationship between Docker and its container components

As mentioned previously, Docker is the most used container solution, but there are other types of runtimes available that implement the same concepts presented here.

*Table 10.4* explains some of the container runtimes that are available on the market:

| Runtime | Description | Website |
|---|---|---|
| **containerd** | The core runtime used by Docker and Kubernetes. It focuses on simplicity and portability. | `https://containerd.io/` |
| **CRI-O** | A lightweight runtime for Kubernetes that implements the Kubernetes **Container Runtime Interface** (**CRI**). | `https://cri-o.io/` |
| **runc** | A CLI tool for spawning and running containers according to the OCI specification. | `https://github.com/opencontainers/runc` |
| **Podman** | A daemonless container engine that's compatible with Docker. | `https://podman.io/` |
| **LXC** | A traditional container runtime that provides a VM-like experience. | `https://linuxcontainers.org/` |
| **Kata Containers** | This runtime combines the security of VMs with the speed of containers by running lightweight VMs. | `https://katacontainers.io/` |
| **Rancher** | Rancher Desktop provides container and Kubernetes management. | `https://rancherdesktop.io/` |

Table 10.4 – Container runtime options

As we can see, there are several options for running containers in environments and the use of each solution will depend on the requirements of each application and organization. However, it's worth remembering that containers include images, other containers, a Dockerfile, and a container registry, all of which are used by runtimes.

At this point, we can package the **UrlShortener** application in a container.

## Packing the UrlShortener application

Docker Engine provides us with different types of resources and commands to manage containers. We'll focus on the packaging process for the **UrlShortener** application and use the main features of a container, which include images, containers, and a container registry.

Before proceeding, make sure you've installed Docker Engine, as per the *Technical requirements* section.

Our packaging process will take place through the following flow:

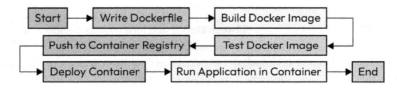

Figure 10.16 – Container creation flow

In Visual Studio Code, be sure to open the **UrlShortener** application and perform the following steps:

1.  In the root of the directory, create a file called Dockerfile. This file has no extension.

2.  Add the following content to the file:

```
FROM mcr.microsoft.com/dotnet/aspnet:8.0 AS base
WORKDIR /app
EXPOSE 8080

FROM mcr.microsoft.com/dotnet/sdk:8.0 AS build
WORKDIR /src
COPY ["UrlShortener.csproj", "MyApp/"]
RUN dotnet restore "MyApp/UrlShortener.csproj"
COPY . ./MyApp
WORKDIR "/src/MyApp"
RUN dotnet build "UrlShortener.csproj" -c Release
  -o /app/build

FROM build AS publish
RUN dotnet publish "UrlShortener.csproj" -c Release
```

```
    -o /app/publish

FROM base AS final
WORKDIR /app
COPY --from=publish /app/publish .
ENTRYPOINT ["dotnet", "UrlShortener.dll"]
```

3.  Save the file.

The preceding code is a bit long and seems complicated, so let's understand each line of our `Dockerfile`:

*   **Base image and initial configuration**: At this stage, we're configuring a base image that contains the default configurations for running an ASP.NET Core 9 application.

*   `FROM mcr.microsoft.com/dotnet/aspnet:8.0 AS base`: This line specifies the base image of the final container, which uses the ASP.NET Core version 8.0 runtime image from the **Microsoft Container Registry** (**MCR**). All Docker images start with a reference to a base image. The `AS base` tag names this stage `base`.

*   `WORKDIR /app`: This line sets the working directory within the container to `/app`. All subsequent commands will be executed in this directory.

*   `EXPOSE 8080`: This line tells Docker that the container will listen on port `8080` at runtime. This is used for documentation purposes, as well as for configuring port mapping when running the container.

*   **Build stage**: The build stage will be an image that's responsible for compiling the application. It will use an image that already has the .NET SDK installed as a base.

*   `FROM mcr.microsoft.com/dotnet/sdk:8.0 AS build`: This line uses the .NET SDK image version 8.0 from MCR to build the application. The `AS build` tag names this stage `build`.

*   `WORKDIR /src`: Sets the working directory to `/src`.

*   `COPY ["UrlShortener.csproj", "MyApp/"]`: Copies the `UrlShortener.csproj` project file to the `MyApp/` directory in the container.

*   `RUN dotnet restore "MyApp/UrlShortener.csproj"`: Restores the project dependencies specified in the `UrlShortener.csproj` file.

*   `COPY . ./MyApp`: Copies all the files from the current directory on the host to the `MyApp` directory in the container.

*   `WORKDIR "/src/MyApp"`: Sets the working directory to `/src/MyApp`.

- `RUN dotnet build "UrlShortener.csproj" -c Release -o /app/build`: Builds the project in `Release` configuration and outputs the build results to the `/app/build` directory.

- **Publish stage**: At this stage, the publication package is generated.

- `FROM build AS publish`: This line uses the build stage as the base for the publish stage.

- `RUN dotnet publish "UrlShortener.csproj" -c Release -o /app/publish`: This line publishes the project, which means it compiles the application, copies all the necessary files, and produces a deployable version of the application in the `/app/publish` directory.

- **Final stage**: The final stage takes the package that was generated by the previous configuration and runs it on an image containing the settings from the base image.

- `FROM base AS final`: Uses the base stage as the base for the final image.

- `WORKDIR /app`: Sets the working directory to `/app`.

- `COPY --from=publish /app/publish .`: Copies the contents of the `/app/publish` directory from the publish stage to the current directory (`/app`) in the final stage.

- `ENTRYPOINT ["dotnet", "UrlShortener.dll"]`: Sets the entry point for the container so that it can run the `dotnet UrlShortener.dll` command, which starts the ASP.NET Core application.

As explained previously, the code available in the `Dockerfile` file uses various stages to generate an image of the application.

The Docker build stage is a phase of the Docker multi-stage build process where the application is compiled, dependencies are restored, and all the required files are prepared for deployment. In a multi-stage build, each stage can use a different base image and environment to perform specific tasks.

The build stage typically uses a development image or SDK to compile and build the application, producing output artifacts that can be used in subsequent stages. This approach helps you create a clean, optimized final image that only contains the runtime dependencies and the application itself, without build tools or intermediate files.

---

**Docker multi-stage build**

Docker's multi-stage build process allows you to generate optimized images and uses container technology to compile and generate publishable applications. To learn more about this, go to `https://docs.docker.com/build/building/multi-stage/`.

When observing the flow of the multi-stage approach, we can automate the process of generating a Docker image by going through the package creation steps that we learned about previously. It's possible to generate a Docker image without using the multi-stage process. In this case, it's necessary to compile and generate the application package manually and, later, just copy the generated package into the image. This results in a `Dockerfile` file that looks similar to the following:

```
FROM mcr.microsoft.com/dotnet/aspnet:8.0 AS base
WORKDIR /app
EXPOSE 8080
COPY ./published .
ENTRYPOINT ["dotnet", "UrlShortener.dll"]
```

By doing this, the `Dockerfile` file will certainly be simpler. However, before generating the image, it's necessary to execute the `docker build` and `docker publish` commands so that we can generate the application package that will be copied to the image.

Now that we understand the principles of generating a `Dockerfile` file, it's time to generate an image.

## Generating a container image

To generate a Docker image, you need to run the `docker build` command. This command will execute the code described in the `Dockerfile` file.

To do this, open your terminal and, in the **UrlShortener** application directory, execute the following command:

```
docker build -t urlshortener:1.0 .
```

The preceding command compiles the image, which will be tagged, using the `-t` parameter, with the name `urlshortener:1.0`. The image tag works as the name of the image to be generated as is in `<name_lower_case>[:<version>]` form.

The version is optional. If it isn't entered, Docker will use the latest version. However, it's good practice to define a version for the image.

After defining the image tag, the context where the compilation process will be executed is informed of this. The context is defined by the `.` parameter, which indicates the local directory that contains the `Dockerfile` file. It's important to keep in mind that the `build` command needs to know where the `Dockerfile` file is located so that it can be executed correctly.

Once the image generation process has run, run the following command to see the list of images on your computer:

```
docker images
```

After executing the preceding command, you'll be able to view the list of images in your local container registry, as shown in *Figure 10.17*:

```
REPOSITORY                            TAG         IMAGE ID       CREATED       SIZE
localhost/urlshortener                1.0         a463c13ac1d7   4 hours ago   245 MB
mcr.microsoft.com/dotnet/sdk          8.0         08854ef383c0   6 days ago    863 MB
mcr.microsoft.com/dotnet/aspnet       8.0         3565a28fb0fd   6 days ago    221 MB
```

Figure 10.17 – List of Docker images in the local container registry

In this example, there are three images:

- `localhost/urlshortener:1.0`: This is the previously generated image that contains the application. The `localhost/` prefix before the image's name represents the owner of the image – in this case, the local registry.

- `mcr.microsoft.com/dotnet/sdk:8.0` and `mcr.microsoft.com/dotnet/aspnet:8.0`: These images represent the .NET SDK and .NET Runtime for compiling and running the application in a container, respectively. These images are automatically downloaded from Docker Hub. Note the `mcr.microsoft.com/dotnet` prefix, which refers to the owner of the images.

Additionally, *Figure 10.17* shows the size of the images in MB. The application image is smaller than the other two. Containers must be optimized as they could affect the performance and startup of the application.

Container images should be considered immutable – that is, each version is unique. This means that if there's any change in the application, we must generate a new image with a different tag. It's a best practice to follow this convention as it allows you to have control over the containers running on a server.

With the image generated, it's time to run a container and test its operation.

## Running a Docker container

To run the Docker container from the previously generated image, run the following command:

```
docker run -d -p 8899:8080 localhost/urlshortener:1.0
```

Let's take a closer look at this command:

- It runs a new container from the `localhost/urlshortener:1.0` image.

- It runs the container in detached mode (`-d`), allowing it to run in the background.

- It maps port `8899` on the host to port `8080` inside the container (`-p 8899:8080`). This makes the application run on port `8080` inside the container that's accessible via port `8899` on the host machine.

The output of the successfully executed command will be a key that represents the container's ID. To check whether the container is running, run the following command:

```
docker ps
```

An output similar to the one shown in *Figure 10.18* will be displayed:

Figure 10.18 – Running containers

Now, open a browser of your choice and go to `http://localhost:8899`.

---

**Connection string**

If the application's connection string has been configured for the database in Azure and you get a connection error when you access the application through the container, make sure you add your IP address, as presented in the *Configuring Azure SQL Server* section. You can also change the connection string by using environment variables in conjunction with the `docker run` command, as follows:

```
docker run -d -p 8899:8080 -e ConnectionStrings__
DefaultConnection="Server=.;Database=UrlShortenerDB;user id=sa;
password=P4sword123;Encrypt=False;" localhost/urlshortener:1.0
```

The preceding command contains the `-e <EnvironmentVariable>=<value>` parameter.

---

We can run the `docker run` command several times for the same image while changing the host port on which the container will run. For example, the following commands will run two new containers of the same application on ports `9900` and `9910`:

```
docker run -d -p 9900:8080 localhost/urlshortener:1.0
docker run -d -p 9910:8080 localhost/urlshortener:1.0
```

Currently, three different containers contain the same application running in your local environment.

To finish running the containers, execute the following command:

```
docker stop <container ID>
```

You can obtain the container ID from the list of running containers by running the `docker ps` command.

Understanding Docker principles and how to package your ASP.NET Core 9 application in a container is very important for the modern software development model. Containers offer consistency, portability, and efficiency, making them ideal for cloud-native applications.

As we've learned, the use of containers is related to components such as images, which are generated according to the runtime and the published application. Later, the image that's been used is made available through a public or private container registry. Finally, we can run different instances of an application that's been published in a container registry through the use of an image, thus generating an executed application called a container.

Next, we'll learn how to automate the process of publishing applications in a cloud environment.

## Understanding the DevOps approach with CI/CD

It's common to talk about the DevOps culture in depth. Despite the term being a combination of two specific areas – that is, **development** (**Dev**) and **operations** (**Ops**) – this approach goes far beyond these two teams.

The DevOps culture connects processes, people, and tools, all of which work together to generate value and provide continuous learning in the face of constant market needs:

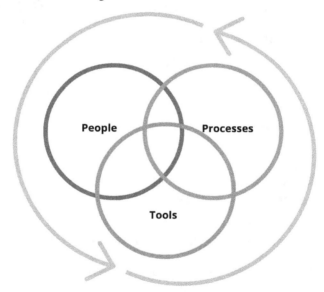

Figure 10.19 – The DevOps culture cycle

*Figure 10.19* represents this continuous flow of collaboration in different aspects involving the DevOps culture.

Among the practices suggested in the DevOps culture, we have the CI/CD process, making development teams agile, eliminating dependencies, minimizing errors, and enabling continuous evolution and learning in teams.

CI and CD processes are commonly called pipelines because they represent a set of sequential instructions that allow new pipes or tasks to be added and reorganized in this flow.

Before we look at the pipeline development model, let's understand the fundamentals of CI and CD.

## CI

CI is a development practice where developers regularly merge their code changes into a central repository, after which there are automated builds and testing.

Development teams are distributed remotely and require a central repository, usually based on Git. When new code is developed and changed, it's synchronized or integrated into the local repository.

This process occurs asynchronously – that is, each developer synchronizes their code version at a different time to other developers. Then, the CI pipeline is executed, where the main objective is to detect integration problems in advance and then frequently integrate code changes and check them through automated tests.

*Figure 10.20* shows a basic CI pipeline scenario:

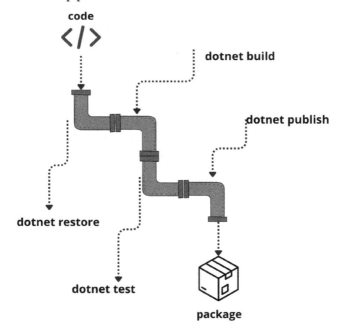

Figure 10.20 – The CI pipeline flow

As we can see, *Figure 10.20* presents a flow that we're already used to executing manually. Automating these processes brings several benefits:

- **Early error detection**: By integrating code changes frequently, CI helps us identify and resolve errors and integration issues early in the development process.

- **Improved code quality**: Automated tests are run on each integration, ensuring that code changes don't break existing functionality and maintain code quality.

- **Faster feedback cycle**: Developers receive immediate feedback on their code changes, allowing them to fix issues immediately and iterate quickly.

- **Improved collaboration**: CI promotes collaboration between team members by integrating code changes from different developers into a shared repository, ensuring everyone is working with the latest code base.

Another great benefit of the CI process is the practice of performing a code review, which allows team members to analyze the code to be integrated and carry out reviews of good practices and whether unit tests have been written, for example.

The code review approach generates constant learning. However, despite being done manually, it's extremely powerful for the evolution of teams and has support from CI so that no revisions are made to code that presents compilation errors or test failures. It's a constant flow of learning, allowing teams to be proactive before they publish any version of an application to production environments.

> **Code review**
>
> A code review is a human review process in which one or more developers review code written by another developer. To learn more about this approach, take a look at the following GitHub article: `https://github.com/resources/articles/software-development/how-to-improve-code-with-code-reviews`.

The CI pipeline is of great importance in the development flow as its main objective is to prepare an application package that follows the quality requirements defined by the development and business teams. As output, it delivers this package to the CD process, which executes the procedures for implementing this in one or more environments.

## CD

CD is the next step after CI and automates the process of deploying applications to production environments.

The CD pipeline simulates what happens in CI, making it possible to add automated tests, among other processes, before the automatic deployment procedures are executed for new versions of applications in different environments, such as development, testing, and production.

*Figure 10.21* shows the CD pipeline. It's very similar to the one for CI, but it consists of different tasks and processes:

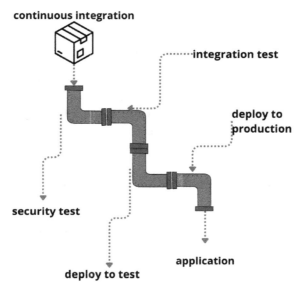

Figure 10.21 – The CD pipeline flow

While the CI pipeline generates a valid package based on the quality flow of the development process, the CD pipeline's main objective is to obtain the package that's been generated through the CI pipeline and distribute it in an on-premises or cloud environment.

The CD pipeline brings the following benefits:

- **Accelerated delivery**: CD enables faster delivery of new features and bug fixes, reducing time to market and improving customer satisfaction.

- **Reduced deployment risk**: By deploying small, incremental changes, CD minimizes the risk associated with large, infrequent deployments.

- **Consistent deployments**: Automated deployment processes ensure deployments are consistent and repeatable, reducing human error.

- **Improved reliability**: Continuous monitoring and automated rollback mechanisms increase the reliability of the deployment process.

Although the CD pipeline is an automated process, which means it's capable of publishing new versions of an application in different environments automatically, it's possible to establish approval flows where those responsible for each environment can choose whether they approve a deployment. The act of approval triggers the automatic deployment flow or cancels it, depending on the need.

The approvals gate approach brings compliance benefits and allows teams to have full control of the deployment flow in certain environments.

> **Review deployments**
>
> Depending on the delivery flow of each organization, there's a need to review deployments, especially in production environments. This approach generates an automated communication process between the CD pipeline and reviewers. Tools such as GitHub, Azure DevOps, and GitLab, among others, have mechanisms that allow you to configure this approval flow. You can learn more about the deployment review process through GitHub Actions at `https://docs.github.com/en/actions/managing-workflow-runs/reviewing-deployments`.

CI and CD are great approaches to automating processes so that our applications can be delivered to different environments constantly and with quality in mind. This is something that allows us to deliver new versions of applications several times on the same day, at the same time, and it helps us quickly provide corrections and rollbacks in those environments, if necessary.

In the next section, we'll implement a CI/CD flow using GitHub Actions and learn how to automatically publish a Docker image in a container registry.

## Automating with GitHub Actions

To demonstrate CI/CD in action, we'll use GitHub Actions to automate the process of generating and publishing a Docker image from the **UrlShortener** application. Make sure you've installed everything mentioned in the *Technical requirements* section so that you can take advantage of the steps described here.

To automate the process of including CI/CD, we'll have to do the following:

1. Configure secrets in the GitHub repository.
2. Create GitHub Actions.
3. Activate GitHub Actions with each push event that's sent to the repository.
4. Build a Docker image.
5. Publish the created image to Docker Hub.
6. Run the previously created Docker image on the local machine.

Before you start automating, you must understand the basics of GitHub Actions.

### Understanding the fundamentals of GitHub Actions

GitHub Actions is an automation tool that's built into GitHub that lets you create, manage, and run workflows directly in your repository.

Actions, as it's commonly known, can be triggered by various events, such as code submission, pull request creation, or time triggers.

GitHub Actions can be created using the **YML/YAML** file structure located in the `.github/workflows` directory of this book's GitHub repository. The basic structure of a workflow is represented at a high level in *Figure 10.22*:

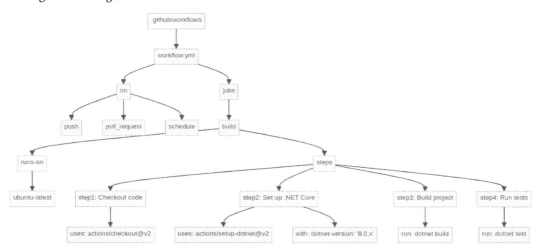

Figure 10.22 – The basic structure of GitHub Actions

---

YAML files

A **YAML Ain't Markup Language** (**YAML**) file is a human-readable data standard that's commonly used for configuration files and exchanging data between programming languages with different data structures. YAML files use indentation to denote structure, making them easy to read and write. It's often used in scenarios where configuration needs to be human-readable and easily parsed by machines, such as in CI/CD pipelines, cloud provisioning files, and application configuration settings. In the context of GitHub Actions, YAML files define workflows that automate processes such as building, testing, and deploying applications. To learn more, visit `https://docs.github.com/en/actions/using-workflows/workflow-syntax-for-github-actions`.

*Figure 10.22* shows the main components that are part of the structure of GitHub Actions. Let's take a closer look:

- **workflow.yml**: A YAML file that defines the workflow.
- **on**: This specifies the events that trigger the workflow. Examples include `push`, `pull_request`, and `schedule`.
- **jobs**: Defines a set of jobs to be executed within the workflow.
- **build job**: A job named `build` running on `ubuntu-latest`. Here, `ubuntu-latest` is a type of agent or machine that will execute all the steps of a job. This machine is made available by GitHub itself.

  This flow contains a series of steps:

  - **Checkout code**: Uses the `actions/checkout@v2` action.
  - **Set up .NET Core**: Uses the `actions/setup-dotnet@v2` action with .NET version `'8.0.x'`.
  - **Build project**: Runs the `dotnet build` command.
  - **Run tests**: Runs the `dotnet test` command.

> **GitHub-hosted runners**
>
> On GitHub, agents are called runners and are available for Windows, Linux, and macOS.
>
> Runners are a fundamental component for running GitHub Actions and are provisioned during a CI or CD pipeline.
>
> To learn more about runners, visit `https://docs.github.com/en/actions/using-github-hosted-runners/about-github-hosted-runners/about-github-hosted-runners`.

With GitHub Actions, we have a multitude of possibilities for automating processes that aren't restricted to CI/CD contexts.

Now that we know how GitHub Actions works, let's start by configuring our repository and creating our first actions.

### Preparing a GitHub repository

To automate the process of creating and publishing a Docker image through GitHub Actions, it's important to understand how the pipeline we'll create works, as shown in *Figure 10.23*:

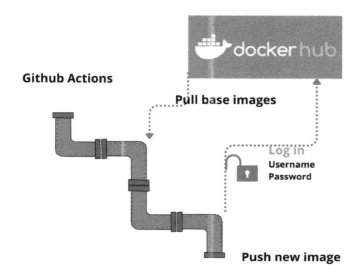

Figure 10.23 – Example of the GitHub Actions flow integrated with Docker Hub

Previously, we learned about the fundamentals of the container strategy when using Docker and used Docker's build multi-stage approach to implement it.

This multi-stage approach has all the necessary steps to generate an application package and, in the end, generate an image that's ready to be used.

As shown in *Figure 10.23*, during the pipeline flow, some calls to Docker Hub are necessary. This is the public container registry that we used when we packaged the **URLShortener** application. However, we can generate a local image without the need to communicate with Docker Hub.

To be able to publish a Docker image to a public or private container registry, authentication must be performed.

In the case of Docker Hub, this authentication takes place using a username and password. Since this information is sensitive, we shouldn't add it directly to a GitHub Actions YAML file, especially if the repository is public.

The best practice is to manage these credentials securely using Secrets. So, follow these steps to add the necessary secrets:

1.  Access your **ASP.NET-8.0-Core-Essentials** repository via your GitHub user. This should have been prepared as per the *Technical requirements* section.

2.  Then, access the **Settings** tab.

3.  From the side menu, access **Secrets and variables | Actions**.

4.  In the center of the screen, click the **New repository secret** button.

5. Set the **Name** field to DOCKER_HUB_USERNAME.

6. In the **Secret** field, add your Docker Hub user.

7. Click on the **Add Secret** button.

8. Again, click on the **New repository secret** button.

9. Set the **Name** field to DOCKER_HUB_PASSWORD.

10. Set the **Secret** field with your password.

11. Click on the **Add Secret** button.

Secrets will be accessed securely while we're running GitHub Actions. Now, let's create the CI/CD pipeline.

### Creating the CI/CD pipeline

So far, we've learned how to manage Docker Hub credentials securely, something we'll need to do so that we can authenticate through the pipeline and submit the newly generated image.

Still in the GitHub repository, access the **Actions** tab. As shown in *Figure 10.24*, there are several readymade pipeline templates that suit different types of applications and are a great starting point for creating a pipeline:

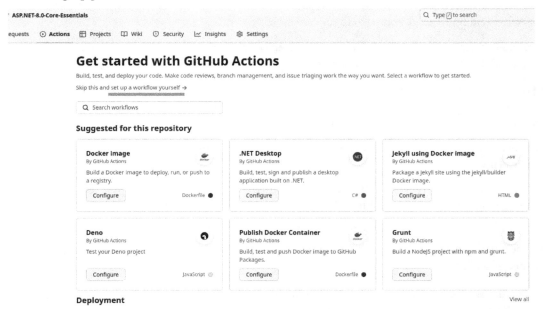

Figure 10.24 – GitHub Actions templates screen

For this example, we'll click on the **set up a workflow yourself** link, as highlighted in *Figure 10.24*.

You'll see an editor and a list of **Featured Actions**, as well as the file's name, as shown in *Figure 10.25*:

Figure 10.25 – GitHub Actions editor

*Figure 10.25* shows three important areas of the GitHub Actions editor:

- **A**: This is where you can define the filename. Note the suggested directory structure. We'll set the filename to `cicd-pipeline.yml`.

- **B**: This is where we'll add the pipeline code.

- **C**: The pipeline consists of tasks, called actions. These actions are abstractions for executing tasks related to a certain technology. The technical community shares different types of custom actions that we can use.

Add the following code to the pipeline editor:

```
name: CI/CD Pipeline
on:
  push:
    branches:
      - main

jobs:
  build-and-deploy:
    name: Build and deploy
    runs-on: ubuntu-latest
```

```
    steps:
    - name: Checkout code
      uses: actions/checkout@v4.1.7

    - name: Build and publish Docker image
      run: |
        docker build -t ${{ secrets.DOCKER_HUB_USERNAME }}
          /urlshortener:latest .
        echo ${{ secrets.DOCKER_HUB_PASSWORD }} |
          docker login -u ${{ secrets
          .DOCKER_HUB_USERNAME }} --password-stdin
        docker push ${{ secrets.DOCKER_HUB_USERNAME }}
          /urlshortener:latest
      working-directory: ./Chapter-10/UrlShortener
```

The hierarchical structure of YAML files is created using spaces. Therefore, nested elements define the hierarchy. If these spaces aren't respected, the file won't be valid. Let's consider using two spaces for each item in the hierarchy, as shown in the following example:

```
on:
<space><space>push:
<space><space><space><space>branches:
<space><space><space><space><space><space>-main
```

Let's take a closer look at this pipeline code:

- on: This defines how the action will be executed. In this case, every time there is an update or push in the main branch, this action will be triggered, executing the CI pipeline.

- Jobs: Jobs are processes that are executed sequentially. There might be jobs for build, test, generate-package, and more. Using Jobs allows us to have well-defined steps and dependencies between steps, thus creating the pipeline flow.

- build-and-deploy: This is the definition for a job named build-and-deloy. The name parameter produces a more user-friendly description during pipeline execution, but the job's name can be referenced in the pipeline flow.

- Steps: Steps are the tasks or actions that are performed in each Job. For this example, only two tasks need to be performed.

- `uses: actions/checkout@v4.1.7`: This is a native GitHub action that aims to clone the repository. The `checkout` action is necessary since runners are created on demand and don't have the application's source code.

- `name: Build and publish Docker image`: Here, we're executing an inline action where we define a script to build and publish the Docker image.

- `docker build -t ${{ secrets.DOCKER_HUB_USERNAME }} / urlshortener:latest .`: This script builds the Docker image. Note the use of the secret containing the Docker Hub username. This is necessary so that we can tag the image with its owner – that is, the Docker Hub username. We're using the `latest` label here to facilitate understanding.

- `echo ${{ secrets.DOCKER_HUB_PASSWORD }} | docker login -u ${{ secrets.DOCKER_HUB_USERNAME }} --password-stdin`: This command is executed in a Linux bash shell, which allows us to combine commands and execute other commands by obtaining input and output from previously executed commands. In this case, we're writing the secret that contains the Docker Hub user's password and sending the output as a parameter to the `docker login` command. This way, the secret won't be exposed in the pipeline execution log. The `docker login` command is required for publishing new versions of images.

- `working-directory: ./Chapter-10/UrlShortener`: The directory containing the `Dockerfile` file.

- `docker push`: The `docker push` command submits the previously generated image to Docker Hub.

With this, the pipeline has been configured and contains both the CI and CD pipelines, where a new version of the Docker image is published at the end of the pipeline. At this point, it's time to run the created GitHub action.

### Running the CI/CD pipeline

In the pipeline editor, click the **Commit Changes** button. You'll be taken to a new page where you must click **Commit Changes** once more. This is necessary since we're creating a new file in the repository.

When you commit these changes, the pipeline will be triggered automatically.

Click on the **Actions** tab; you'll see the pipeline's execution, as shown in *Figure 10.26*:

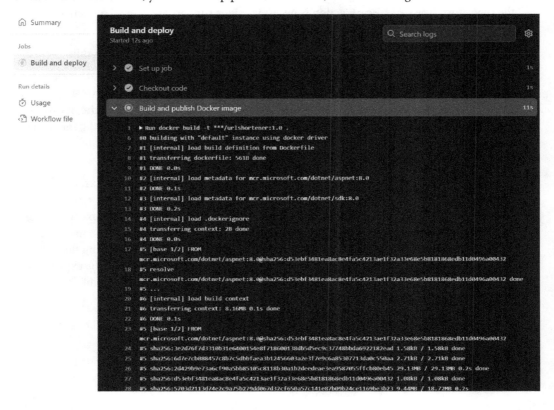

Figure 10.26 – Running the GitHub action

After running the pipeline, the new image will be generated in Docker Hub, as shown in *Figure 10.27*:

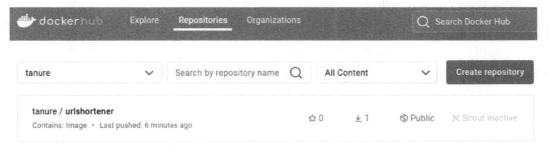

Figure 10.27 – Container image published on Docker Hub by GitHub Actions

To test the new image on your local machine, run the following command:

```
docker run -d -p 7777:8080 -e ConnectionStrings__
DefaultConnection="<Your Connection String>" <your username>/
urlshortener:latest
```

The new image will be downloaded, which means your application can be run on your local machine at `http://localhost:7777`.

As we've learned, GitHub Actions can automate tasks in environments for the purpose of CD. This brings agility and consistency and allows teams to act quickly in the face of the constant changes demanded by the market.

At this point, any changes that are made to your repository and submitted to GitHub will automatically generate a new version of the container for your Docker Hub user.

GitHub Actions has several applications and, together with solutions developed in ASP.NET Core 9, it's a powerful tool for creating high-quality applications.

In this section, we learned about the fundamentals of working in a continuous flow of value delivery. We'll explore how to attain a cloud-native application development mindset in the next chapter.

## Summary

In this chapter, we learned how to publish ASP.NET Core 9 applications and generate a publishing package using the `dotnet` CLI tool. Furthermore, we learned how to publish an application in an Azure cloud environment and explored the fundamentals of Docker's container strategy. Using the knowledge we'd acquired, we were able to learn how value delivery flows through DevOps practices such as CI and CD and benefits from automated processes via GitHub Actions. All the knowledge we've acquired in this chapter forms the basis for the next chapter, where we'll learn about cloud-native development with ASP.NET Core 9.

## Get This Book's PDF Version and Exclusive Extras

UNLOCK NOW

Scan the QR code (or go to packtpub.com/unlock). Search for this book by name, confirm the edition, and then follow the steps on the page.

*Note: Keep your invoice handly. Purchase made directly from packt don't require one.*

# 11

# Cloud-Native Development with ASP.NET Core 9

Modern applications are designed to operate in cloud environments and take advantage of the various features provided, such as agility, scalability, availability, and resilience. ASP.NET Core 9 provides us with a set of powerful tools that allow us to develop high-quality solutions. However, it is important to be aware of the patterns and best practices related to the cloud-native development model.

In this chapter, we will learn about important aspects related to applications hosted in cloud environments, exploring patterns, best practices, the mindset required for cloud-native application development, the principles of the twelve-factor app, and architectural design principles so that you can get the most out of your cloud environment.

In this chapter, we will focus on the following topics:

- Creating a cloud-native mindset
- Working with cloud-native tools
- The principles of the twelve-factor app
- Understanding cloud architecture principles

## Technical requirements

The code examples used in this chapter can be found in the book's GitHub repository: `https://github.com/PacktPublishing/ASP.NET-Core-9.0-Essentials/tree/main/Chapter11`.

In order for you to take advantage of all the examples proposed in this chapter, it is important that you fork the book repository. Forking is a feature available on GitHub that copies a repository so that it can be managed by a Git user. You can learn how to fork a repository using the following URL: `https://docs.github.com/en/pull-requests/collaborating-with-pull-requests/working-with-forks/fork-a-repo`.

# Creating a cloud-native mindset

Every year brings new innovations in cloud computing: there are always new features that bring new possibilities and companies that want new ways to deliver value to users in an increasingly demanding market.

In previous chapters, we learned about various tools, patterns, and best practices and interacted with cloud resources. But even in a scenario where applications are built with best practices and standards in mind, are they able to benefit from all the features that a cloud environment can provide?

Even today, there are many organizations that run applications in private environments (on-premises), which brings several benefits. Consequently, applications developed in these environments have limited scalability and deal with high costs for purchasing servers and qualified professionals to maintain them.. In this solution model, computing resources are limited, but at the same time, it brings benefits of greater control, compliance, and security for companies.

The cloud appears is an alternative to this model that enhances computing power for organizations, but at the same time, several other challenges arise, including in the development model and process.

To use the cloud model, we need to understand how it works, its service layers, the necessary investments, and how we can adapt our applications to a cloud-native model.

Let's start by looking at the service layers offered in cloud environments.

## Understanding the service layers in a cloud environment

Maybe you've already heard about **CapEx** and **OpEx** and how important these two words are in the corporate world:

- **Capital expenditure (CapEx)**: CapEx is not a term exclusive to the IT area but is a financial term related to expenses or investments in assets. The calculation is simple: if there is a need for more servers to support user demand, CAPex comes into play and is related to the cost of investment in servers, physical location for installing the servers, electricity, UPS, and so on.

- **Operating expenditure (OpEx)**: OpEx refers to the ongoing costs of running daily operations. This includes expenses for services, utilities, rent, software licensing, and other operational activities such as staff salaries.

Observing these concepts, every organization needs to reflect on its investments, costs, and professionals to remain competitive.

When moving to an approach involving cloud computing, the transition from CapEx to OpEx takes place. This change has several implications:

- **Reduced upfront costs**: Adopting cloud services reduces the need for large upfront investments in physical hardware and infrastructure. Instead, organizations pay for the cloud services they use.

- **Scalable costs**: Cloud services offer a pay-as-you-go model, allowing organizations to scale their usage and expenses according to demand.

- **Operational flexibility**: Ability to quickly adapt to changes in business needs without dependence on investments in hardware.

- **Maintenance and updates**: Cloud providers such as Azure provide infrastructure maintenance, updates, and security services, reducing the operational burden on an organization's IT team and allowing them to focus on strategic initiatives.

However, having services running in the cloud does not mean that there will be less cost as there is a pay-as-you-go model. As with any tool or strategy, if not used correctly, the cloud can cause major problems for organizations.

Cloud providers such as Azure take care of the entire infrastructure for providing computing services; however, there is shared management with the organizations that use the services. This service model is very important to understand.

In the cloud computing model, organizations focus their efforts on their products and services, benefiting from shared management with cloud providers. Organizations basically have three options to choose from when deciding what service model they want:

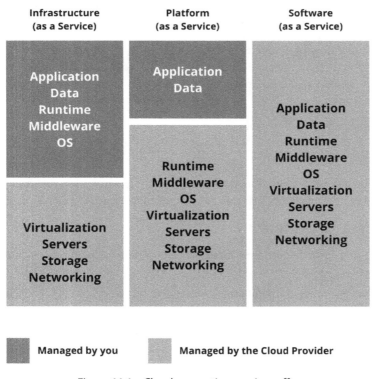

Figure 11.1 – Cloud computing services offer

As shown in *Figure 11.1*, we have the following types of service layers:

- **Infrastructure as a Service (IaaS)**: Provides virtualized computing resources, where the company dynamically provisions virtual machines, storage, and networking. It is a common adoption model in on-premises migration strategies to the cloud.

- **Platform as a Service (PaaS)**: Provides a platform that abstracts infrastructure, allowing organizations and development teams to focus on solutions and data. We used a PaaS resource in *Chapter 10* when publishing an Azure App Service application.

- **Software as a Service (SaaS)**: Provides software applications on a subscription basis, such as streaming applications and Microsoft 365 applications.

Cloud services are essential components of cloud-native development, helping to define migration strategies, cost optimization, scalability, resiliency, security, and deployment.

So that we can understand how we should adapt our tools and development processes and benefit from the power of cloud computing, it is important to start with best practices.

## Cloud-native development best practices

Microsoft provides extensive documentation and powerful services in Azure, where it is possible to host applications using different technologies and, of course, solutions developed in ASP.NET Core 9.

In addition to documenting the resources available in Azure, it is very important that development teams know about the **Cloud Adoption Framework (CAF)** and the **Well-Architected Framework (WAF)**. These two resources have different use cases and help teams deal with various challenges posed by cloud environments.

Let's briefly learn about each of these features.

### The CAF

Microsoft's CAF has an excellent collection of documentation, implementation guidance, best practices, and tools designed to help organizations plan and execute their cloud adoption strategy.

The CAF basically consists of seven phases:

1. **Strategy**: Define business outcomes, establish a cloud adoption plan, and prioritize workloads for migration.

2. **Plan**: Assess your current digital estate, create a cloud adoption plan, and identify gaps in required skills and resources.

3. **Ready**: Prepare the environment for cloud adoption by configuring a landing zone that includes governance, security, and management tools.

4. **Migrate**: Migrate workloads to the cloud, using tools and methodologies to ensure a smooth transition.

5.  **Innovate**: Develop new cloud-native applications or modernize existing applications to make the most of cloud capabilities.

6.  **Govern**: Implement governance best practices to ensure compliance, manage risk, and establish security controls.

7.  **Manage**: Operate and manage the cloud environment, using monitoring and management tools to ensure performance, reliability, and cost efficiency.

---

**CAF**

CAF has extensive documentation and resources that should be part of a software engineer's daily life. To learn more, visit `https://learn.microsoft.com/en-us/azure/cloud-adoption-framework/`.

---

The CAF aims to help organizations adopt a cloud-native mindset, emphasizing the importance of planning, governance, and continuous improvement, ensuring that cloud adoption aligns with business objectives.

The CAF is an excellent source of knowledge, and generally, the focus is not exactly on one application (or workload, as they are commonly called) but on structuring the entire environment in general. However, it can be used as an excellent source of knowledge and planning for new workloads, as it involves business teams, development, infrastructure, and the entire continuous delivery flow.

In addition to the CAF, there is another very important resource that must be taken into consideration when defining application architectural models for your cloud environment.

### The WAF

The WAF is a set of capabilities offered by Microsoft that contains best practices, principles, and architectural guidance for designing, building, and operating secure, high-performance, resilient, and efficient infrastructures for your cloud applications. The WAF is subdivided into five pillars:

1.  **Operational excellence**: This pillar focuses on operational processes that keep applications running smoothly and efficiently. This includes monitoring, automation, and incident response.

2.  **Security**: This pillar ensures that applications and data are protected from threats. It covers identity management, infrastructure protection, data encryption, and threat detection.

3.  **Reliability**: This pillar ensures that applications can recover from failures and continue to function as expected. This includes disaster recovery strategies, fault tolerance, and data backup.

4.  **Performance efficiency**: This pillar ensures that applications use resources efficiently and can scale to meet demand. It covers capacity planning, resource optimization, and performance monitoring.

5.  **Cost optimization**: This pillar focuses on effectively managing costs while delivering optimal performance and value. This includes cost monitoring, usage analysis, and implementing cost reduction strategies.

> **Learn more about the WAF**
>
> The WAF not only provides great documentation containing strategies and best practices in relation to each of the five pillars, but it also provides tools, such as **Assessment**, where it is possible to analyze your existing cloud workloads to improve them, checklists, and many other resources. To learn more about the WAF, visit `https://learn.microsoft.com/en-us/azure/well-architected/`.

Each of the pillars presented previously supports a cloud-native mindset, providing clear and practical guidelines for each workload. This allows teams to not only analyze solutions from different perspectives but also make the best of the cloud environment through high-quality solutions that meet organizational objectives, such as cost optimization.

## Going beyond code development

To achieve a cloud-native solutions mindset, as software engineers, we must be prepared to go beyond the boundaries of code development.

The DevOps culture brings a collaboration model that is not just restricted to different teams communicating effectively but extends to sharing knowledge, standards, and best practices.

Operations teams have adapted to the code development model by using technology such as Infrastructure as Code, GitHub repositories, and even pipelines.

Likewise, it is important that we learn concepts related to networking, infrastructure, security, and data. This will make all the difference in the architectural design and development of solutions that make the best of cloud environments and will help create a cloud-native mindset.

Now that we have an insight into the challenges associated with cloud computing, it's time to learn about cloud-native tools.

# Working with cloud-native tools

In an increasingly competitive market, being agile and delivering solutions quickly has become synonymous with success.

The cloud-native approach is associated with agility and speed, allowing teams to create solutions, and adding layers of services and functionalities with loose coupling, resilience, management, and observability.

However, we must understand the relationship between agility and speed when it comes to developing cloud-native applications. Being agile is not being fast, and being fast does not necessarily mean being agile. That completely changes the way we think about a solution.

Let's say your team received a request to create an API that aims to provide data on products available for sale in an online store, as shown in *Figure 11.2*:

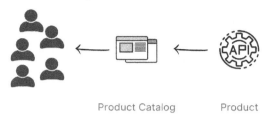

Product Catalog    Product

Figure 11.2 – Online store consuming a Product API

In the example shown in *Figure 11.12*, the Product API would be an application in ASP.NET Core 9, containing good layer and package separation practices – let's say it's hosted in Microsoft Azure. From an application perspective, all expected API features have most likely been implemented according to functional and non-functional requirements. It is also expected that the quality process has been carried out satisfactorily, as shown in *Figure 11.3*:

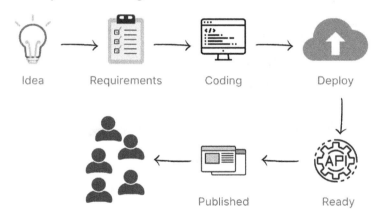

Idea       Requirements       Coding       Deploy

Published       Ready

Figure 11.3 – Development and publishing flow

*Figure 11.3* shows a common scenario of a software development process, involving task management, requirements, coding, deployment, and application maintenance.

The main objective is to quickly meet market needs, that is, reducing the lead time for delivering value.

The shorter the lead time, the better. For teams and organizations to be able to strike a good balance between agility and speed, it is very important to understand the factors in each of the process steps shown in *Figure 11.3*.

An application developed and delivered in an environment is not necessarily a cloud-native solution. As software engineers, we must go beyond the artifact generated after compiling a code, and, prepare applications to be able to take full advantage of cloud environments and handle growing user demand., we must be prepared to act in different areas of knowledge.

Therefore, cloud-native solutions must be based on factors such as the following:

- Infrastructure
- Modern design
- DevOps
- Support services
- Containers and orchestrators
- Microservices

These factors can be represented graphically as follows:

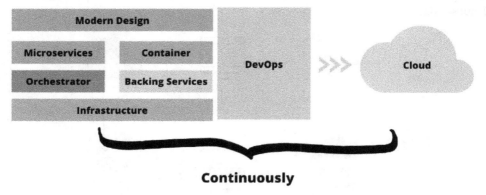

Figure 11.4 – Cloud-native factors

These factors form the basis for the development of cloud-native solutions and must be worked on continuously, since changes, both in service requirements and market needs, are constant.

Another important factor that we can notice in *Figure 11.4* is that there is no relationship between the factors and a specific cloud provider, such as Azure, AWS, or GCP. On the contrary, the cloud-native model is a vendor-agnostic paradigm, and therefore, contrary to what generally happens with hyped-up technologies, there are a range of adoption patterns, definitions, and good practices, maintained by the **Cloud Native Computing Foundation (CNCF)**.

# Getting to know CNCF

CNCF is a consortium created in 2015 within the scope of the Linux Foundation. It involves more than 400 companies that aim to create a common language between technologies, standards, and best practices, independent of the supplier. CNCF aims to build sustainable solution ecosystems for cloud-native software by bringing together communities of developers, end users, and vendors.

CNCF promotes cloud-native technologies, supporting and maintaining projects that enable the adoption of practices such as containerization, microservices, and dynamic orchestration, promoting open standards and best practices, and allowing cloud-native applications to work in an interoperable manner. Additionally, CNCF supports innovation by nurturing a community of contributors and maintaining a neutral ground for the development of cutting-edge cloud-native tools and projects.

One of the important resources of CNCF is the technology landscape, which is a visual representation and interactive guide that maps the cloud-native ecosystem in a categorized way, displaying a wide range of tools, projects, and technologies that are part of or related to the mission of CNCF.

> **The CNCF landscape**
>
> The CNCF landscape is an excellent resource for organizations and professionals, helping you to understand the technology and tool options available, their relationships, and their roles in the cloud-native ecosystem. To learn more about the CNCF landscape, visit the following URL: `https://landscape.cncf.io`.

To understand how we could use CNCF to our advantage, let's look at a development scenario for an ASP.NET Core 9 solution hosted on Microsoft Azure.

# Working with CNCF

Imagine the following scenario:

*You are developing a web application using ASP.NET Core 9 and the application is hosted in Azure. You want to ensure that your application is developed using cloud-native principles and that it leverages the best tools available for deployment, monitoring, and management.*

Let's see how the use of CNCF can support us in the architectural definition and development of the application in the scenario:

- **Containerization strategy**: Based on the knowledge acquired in the previous chapter, you choose to use Docker and containerize your ASP.NET Core 9 application. To recap, Docker, a project formed by CNCF, allows you to package your application and its dependencies in a container, ensuring consistency in different environments.

- These are the benefits:

  - Ensures application consistency across development, testing, and production environments

  - Simplifies dependency management and isolation

- **Container orchestration**: For this application to be hosted, you decide to use Kubernetes, which is another CNCF graduate project, for container orchestration. **Azure Kubernetes Service (AKS)** provides a managed Kubernetes environment in Azure, making it easy to deploy, manage, and scale your containerized applications. AKS uses the same standards defined by the CNCF in relation to Kubernetes but abstracts the complexity of creating a cluster and offers several other services.

  - These are the benefits:

    - Manages the container lifecycle, scaling, and load balancing

    - Ensures high availability and resilience

- **Automation**: You decide to use CI/CD tools such as Jenkins or GitHub Actions to automate your build, test, and deployment processes. These tools ensure that your code changes are continually integrated and deployed, improving your development workflow.

  - These are the benefits:

    - Automates the deployment process, ensuring consistency and reducing the risk of human error

    - Accelerates the development cycle, enabling continuous integration and deployment

- **Monitoring and logging**: Completing development, performing continuous integration, and achieving continuous deployment are just the first steps to working on a project as a cloud-native solutions software engineer. It's important to incorporate observability tools such as **Prometheus** and **Grafana**, both incubating CNCF projects, to monitor the performance and health of your application. Prometheus collects metrics and Grafana visualizes them, providing insights into your application's behavior. Azure Monitor is also an observability tool featured in the CNCF landscape. Furthermore, other types of tools such as **OpenTelemetry**, also incubated by CNCF, would be a great option for applications to have a vendor-agnostic collector, which reduces the dependence on proprietary libraries in applications.

  - These are the benefits:

    - Provides real-time monitoring and alerts for your application

    - Helps you quickly diagnose and resolve performance issues

Leveraging CNCF and its landscape provides numerous tools and best practices for developing, deploying, and managing cloud-native applications. By adopting these tools, a software engineer working on an ASP.NET Core 9 application hosted in Azure can ensure that their application is scalable, resilient, and maintainable. Containerization with Docker, orchestration with Kubernetes, observability with Prometheus and Grafana, and automated CI/CD pipelines with Jenkins or GitHub Actions are just a few examples of how CNCF projects can enhance your cloud-native development workflow.

However, the scenario mentioned previously provides an Azure-agnostic solution model, making it possible to be hosted on different cloud providers, as each of the tools mentioned follows the standards established by CNCF for cloud-provider-agnostic solutions.

It is very important to regularly visit the CNCF website to be aware of news and changes in cloud models and analyze the tools available in the CNCF landscape for the needs of your solutions. These resources will help you create increasingly powerful solutions that adapt to the different needs of your organization and the market.

We know that CNCF is an important resource that sets the standard for cloud-native solutions and should be added to any software engineer's toolbox. Additionally, there are other principles that, in a practical way, guide us in the process of developing cloud-native solutions. ASP.NET Core 9 can help us implement these principles, such as the **twelve-factor app methodology**. We will discuss these principles in the next section.

# The twelve-factor app principles

The twelve-factor app methodology (`https://12factor.net`) is a set of best practices designed to help developers build modern, scalable, and maintainable cloud-native applications. It was created by Heroku developers to provide a framework for developing applications that can be deployed and managed in the cloud.

---

**Heroku**

According to the website's own definition, Heroku is a cloud platform that allows companies to create, deliver, monitor, and scale applications.

Heroku is a cloud PaaS offering, founded in 2007, that allows developers to build, run, and operate applications entirely in the cloud in a simplified way. To learn more, visit `https://www.heroku.com/home`.

---

The twelve-factor app methodology, as the name suggests, has twelve factors or principles:

1.  **Code base**: Use a code base tracked in version control.
2.  **Dependencies**: Explicitly declare and isolate dependencies.
3.  **Config**: Store the configuration in the environment.
4.  **Backing services**: Treat supporting services as attached resources.

5. **Build, release, run**: Strictly separate the build and run stages.

6. **Processes**: Run the application as one or more stateless processes.

7. **Port binding**: Export services via port binding.

8. **Concurrency**: Expansion through the process model.

9. **Disposability**: Maximize robustness with fast startup and smooth shutdown.

10. **Dev/prod parity**: Keep development, staging, and production as similar as possible.

11. **Logs**: Treat logs as streams of events.

12. **Administrative processes**: Perform administrative/management tasks as single processes.

Let's get into more detail about each of the factors mentioned.

## Code base

During the solution development cycle, you should maintain the source code in a remote repository, such as a Git-based repository.

The code base factor entails that there should be a code base for each application context, allowing the correct separation of responsibilities and improving code management.

*Figure 11.5* illustrates the management of the different contexts of an application, such as configurations, source code, and infrastructure scripts. Each of these contexts can be distributed in different environments, at different times in the development flow.

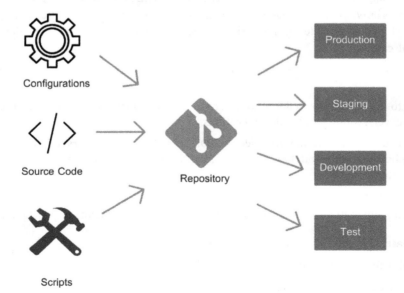

Figure 11.5 – Code base management

Despite being a principle considered natural during the application development flow, its importance goes beyond source code management on remote servers. Development teams must take ownership of the end-to-end solution, defining source code management processes such as the use of branches, development standards, code review, quality processes, and documentation.

In cloud environments, it is common to have one repository for managing application code and another repository specifically for storing infrastructure code. The contextualization and separation of contexts in repositories allow for constant collaboration and management between the development and operations teams.

The code base principle is the basis for all other principles. Next, we will learn about dependencies.

## Dependencies

Dependencies are part of application development, as we have already seen in some examples in the book when using NuGet packages. Using packages brings benefits such as reusability and, together with package management mechanisms, allows for easy package updates. Most programming languages currently provide extensibility mechanisms based on package management.

The dependencies principle defines that dependencies must be managed in a manifest file and a package management tool must be used.

For example, ASP.NET Core 9 applications have the NuGet package manager, and all dependencies are managed through the `<ProjectName>.csproj` file, which contains the references and versions of the packages used in the application.

Through this feature, we can benefit from the interoperability of the .NET platform, and in conjunction with the .NET CLI tool, we are able to obtain dependencies in a simple way, executing the `dotnet restore` command and allowing us to build and generate deployment packages without running the risk of human error.

Using package management avoids managing dependency files manually.

Just as dependencies are necessary in an application, configurations are important. Let's understand how the config factor helps in configuration management.

## Config

All applications have some type of configuration file, which can include sensitive information such as encryption keys and connection strings. Keeping settings in configuration files is an excellent practice and avoids having to change the source code if there is a configuration change.

In the cloud, applications generally have different environments to ensure that with each update, the quality of the solution remains high. Furthermore, production environments have access restrictions for security reasons; application configurations in production environments should not be accessible.

The config factor says that configurations must be kept separate from code, making it easier to manage different environments. *Figure 11.6* illustrates the approach proposed by the config factor:

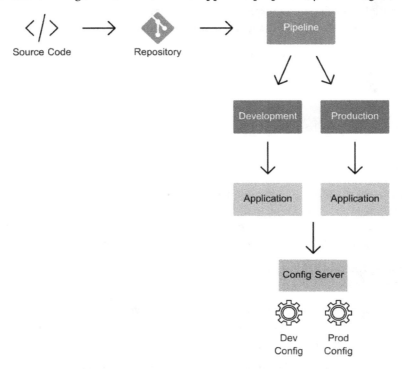

Figure 11.6 – Configuration server and environments

As we can see in *Figure 11.6*, the development flow uses an automation pipeline, CI, and CD, and when the artifact is obtained, it will be published in different environments.

The application then obtains its respective configurations based on the execution environment.

In *Chapter 10*, we learned how to manage application configurations and behaviors using Azure App Configuration. This way, we can abstract the management of developers' configurations and define access to sensitive configurations, and the application can be dynamically deployed in different environments.

Configurations are very important in the context of any application, as are the integrations that are made. The next factor suggests a best practice that directly influences the architectural definitions of a solution.

# Backing services

Most applications have some dependency on external resources or, in this case, backing services. These resources can be databases, email servers, and storage servers, among other services.

Applications must be prepared to isolate such dependencies and, at the same time, be able to use these services independently of the execution environment, without any changes to the code. Backing services must be exposed through a URL and respective credentials, depending on the resource. Resources must be maintained and made available in isolation and applications must reference them. Let's look at *Figure 11.7*:

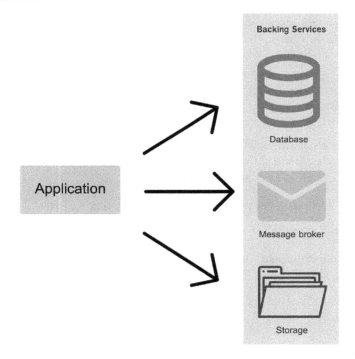

Figure 11.7 – Interaction between an application and backing services

As we can see in *Figure 11.7*, the application's architectural model proposes isolation between services that are consumed externally, such as database, message broker, and storage services. When reflecting on architectural approaches at the source code level, the use of **hexagonal architecture** or **Onion Architecture** can help in this context of service isolation.

**Hexagonal architecture and Onion Architecture**

Hexagonal architecture (or ports-and-adapters architecture) is a design pattern that aims to create a clear separation between core business logic and external elements, such as user interfaces, databases, and other services. In this architecture, the core application logic is in the center, surrounded by several ports, which define interfaces for different functionalities. Adapters are the specific implementation of the interfaces for interacting with some external resource.

The Onion Architecture, also a design pattern, emphasizes the separation of concerns within an application. It places the core domain in the center, surrounded by layers that contain infrastructure and presentation concerns. The innermost layer represents the domain model and business logic, which are independent of external concerns. Surrounding this core are layers for application services, followed by infrastructure and user interfaces in the outermost layer. Dependencies flow inward, which means that external layers can depend on internal layers, but not vice versa.

To learn more about the hexagonal architecture and the Onion Architecture, visit `https://alistair.cockburn.us/hexagonal-architecture/` and `https://jeffreypalermo.com/blog/the-onion-architecture-part-1/`.

The backing services factor, if analyzed further, allows us to reflect on other architectural aspects that are important in a cloud environment, such as resilience and availability. As applications depend on other services, certain questions arise, such as these:

- *How should the application behave if the database or cache is not working?*
- *What if the email service is not working?*

The answers to these questions allow us to expand our horizons beyond source code, moving us toward cloud-native thinking.

The isolation proposed by the backing services factor allows automation approaches to be used in the value delivery flow.

## Build, release, run

In *Chapter 10*, we learned about the importance of DevOps and automated processes, in the *Understanding the DevOps approach with CI/CD* section.

Automation is exactly the concept defined by the build, release, run factor.

The CI process is associated with the moment of building the artifact, where processes such as downloading dependencies and building and executing quality and security flows are carried out, in addition to making the artifact available to be consumed by another process, such as CD.

*Figure 11.8* demonstrates the CI process:

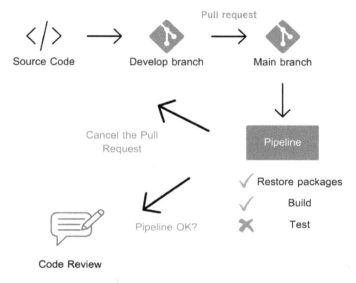

Figure 11.8 – CI and the pull-request approach

In addition to the CI process, we have CD, whose objective is to deploy the artifact in different environments.

*Figure 11.9* demonstrates the CD process:

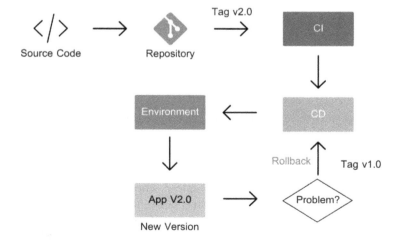

Figure 11.9 – CD with the rollback approach

As seen in *Figure 11.9*, the use of automated processes brings great benefits to the CD flow. CD is executed after CI, and if there is any inconsistency in any environment, or even in the production environment, rollback processes can be executed quickly to publish the latest stable version of the application again. Furthermore, other techniques can be used in this process, such as feature toggles, as discussed in *Chapter 10*.

The next factor is very important for cloud-native environments.

## Processes

The processes factor defines that an application should be executed in an environment, independently and without the state. If state storage is required, it must be stored through external support services. Stateless processes are easily sized and replaced without losing the state, improving reliability and scalability.

*Figure 11.10* shows a high-level view of an application running in different processes and interacting with a database-based state persistence model.

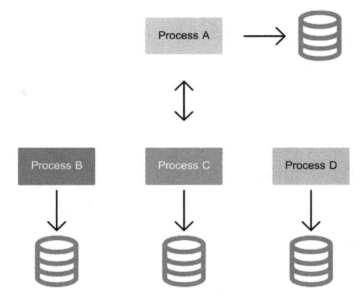

Figure 11.10 – Managing application states with a database

Web APIs developed in ASP.NET Core are an example of stateless applications, where there is no state management through sessions in memory. Each request has the context of the information that needs to be processed by the API, as we learned in *Chapter 6*, where we implement authentication and authorization. For each request, the user information is sent in the request header as a token. Then, the API, using ASP.NET Core 9 middleware, contextualizes the request with the user's information, allowing, or not, an action to be performed. Each request is independent, and the state is obtained during the request cycle of the request.

This is an important feature that allows applications to be ableto scale dynamically , such as the execution of multiple instances of the same application in a Docker container.

See the example shown in *Figure 11.11*:

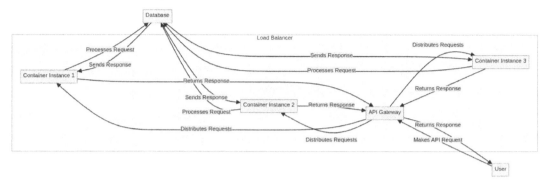

Figure 11.11 – Stateless application

The diagram presented in *Figure 11.11* illustrates how an application performs several stateless processes (using container instances) to deal with requests. The following is a brief description of each component of the diagram:

- **User**: The user makes an API request.

- **API Gateway**: The API gateway receives the request and acts as a load balancer.

- **Load Balancer**: The load balancer distributes API requests to various instances of the container application.

- **Container Instances**: Several container instances process requests independently.

- **Database**: Each container instance interacts with a shared database to process the request and recover or store the necessary data.

- **Response Flow**: After requesting the request, each container instance sends the response back through the API gateway, which returns the final response to the user.

In addition to the processes factor, it is essential to understand the concept of port binding.

## Port binding

Like the previous factor, here, each application should be mapped and made available at a specific address and via a specific port.

If each server has an address and URL, each server can be responsible for responding to multiple applications at the same time. To differentiate which application will respond to a particular request, you must map the port. Thus, **Service A** can be hosted on a server through port 4040, **Service B** through port 3030, and **Service C** through port 8080, as in *Figure 11.12*:

Figure 11.12 – Port binding

When performing the applications developed in this book using the `dotnet run` command, we observed that a URL is provided in the format `http:// localhost:<port>`. The door may vary from environment to environment, and the application may define which door will be executed.

This pattern even applies when adopting the container strategy using Docker, where we map the host and container doors, as shown in *Figure 11.13*:

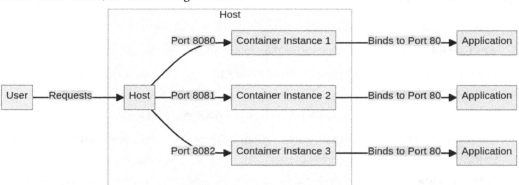

Figure 11.13 – Port binding for containers

In *Figure 11.13*, there are three instances of the same application, responding to different ports through the host. Despite being the same application, each container is performed in an isolated process. Having different instances of a container is a common scenario in applications that require scalability for the needs of competing requests from users, which is the theme of the next factor.

## Concurrency

The cloud environment allows applications to deal with different needs in a dynamic way. The characteristic of elasticity not only enables software engineers to keep their applications working properly according to user needs but also allows insights that help optimize applications.

Each application hosted in an environment needs resources to run, whether memory, CPU, or storage. These metrics are of paramount importance to define the limits of the applications and determine when it is necessary to scale.

Generally speaking, the use of techniques with cargo and monitoring tests should be a constant part of this continuous application flow, directing decisions that are based on concrete data.

If there is a need for scalability, we must define whether the strategy will be horizontal or vertical, as shown in the following example:

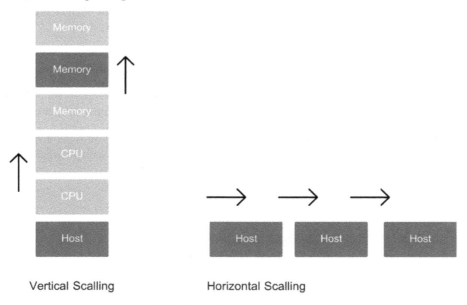

Figure 11.14 – Vertical and horizontal scalability

Basically, there are two types of scalability:

- **Vertical scalability**: This is applied when adding more features to a server, such as memory, CPU, or storage, to support application processing.

- **Horizontal scalability**: Horizontal scalability involves the creation of new instances of servers, such as clusters. In this approach, processing is staggered between servers to support load demand through a load balancer. Horizontal scalability is a strategy widely used by orchestrators such as Kubernetes to create different instances of an application container to support constant user requests.

In addition to the points mentioned, each application, in its context, may depend on different types of simultaneous processing, which can be divided into background processes. Perhaps your application includes the asynchronous processing of an HTTP request and at the same time information is generated that must be processed in the background because it is a long-term execution. Therefore, its architecture can provide a web application for HTTP processing and another application that works with a worker, capable of processing long-term requests in the background. In conjunction with this strategy, the web application and the processes in the background, following the characteristics of the twelve-factor application, can be scaled vertically and/or horizontally.

In the next section, we will understand disposability.

## Disposability

The principle of disposability emphasizes the importance of maximizing the robustness of an application, including fast startup and graceful closure, allowing the application to deal with rapid changes of scale, deployment, and code with no impact on user experience or system stability.

Fast startup times enable quick outages and recoveries, while graceful shutdowns ensure that ongoing requests are completed and resources are released correctly before application interruption.

In *Chapter 10*, when learning about the principles of Docker, we used a multi-stage build, with the aim of generating an optimized container image, which supports the rapid boot of the container if necessary.

Moreover, the principle of disposability helps maintain system resilience and reliability, allowing applications to better resist hardware failures, producing dynamic cloud environments where instances can be created and destroyed frequently.

See *Figure 11.15*:

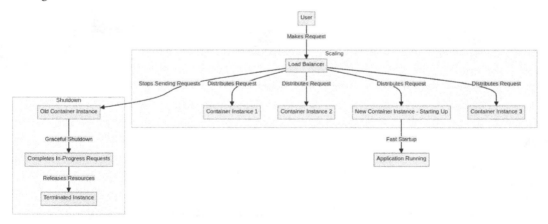

Figure 11.15 – Disposability example

The diagram presented shows how applications should deal with quick startup and graceful startup processes to maintain robustness and reliability in a native cloud environment.

In the following points, we can see the details of each item mentioned in the diagram:

- **User**: The user makes a request for load balancing.

- **Load Balancer**: The load balancer distributes input requests to the available container instances.

- **Scaling**:

  - **New Container Instance - Starting Up**: Upon scaleout, a new container instance is created. The application starts up quickly, making the instance ready to handle requests in minimal time.

  - The load balancer begins to distribute requests to this new instance once it is ready.

- **Shutdown**:

  - **Old Container Instance**: When scaling in or deploying a new version, the load balancer stops sending new requests to the old container instance.

  - **Graceful Shutdown**: The old instance completes any in-progress requests before shutting down, ensuring no request is abruptly terminated.

  - **Terminated Instance**: After completing all requests and releasing resources, the old instance is terminated.

In ASP.NET Core 9, you can implement graceful shutdown by setting up the hosting and handling of cancellation tokens to ensure that continuous requests are completed before application shutdown.

Let's look at an example of code in a `Program.cs` file:

```
using Microsoft.AspNetCore.Builder;
using Microsoft.Extensions.Hosting;
using Microsoft.Extensions.Logging;

var builder = WebApplication.CreateBuilder(args);
builder.Services.AddControllers();
var app = builder.Build();
app.UseRouting();
app.UseEndpoints(endpoints =>
{
    endpoints.MapControllers();
});

var host = app.Services
  .GetService<IHostApplicationLifetime>();
// Handle graceful shutdown
```

```
host.ApplicationStopping.Register(() =>
{
    var logger = app.Services
      .GetService<ILogger<Program>>();
    logger.LogInformation("Application is shutting down...");
    // Add more cleanup tasks here
});

app.Run();
```

In the previous code, the `app.Services.GetService<IHostApplicationLifetime>()` service was configured to deal with application stop events.

The `host.ApplicationStopping.Register` method allows you to register a callback that will be invoked when the application is stops.

In a registered call return, you can perform the necessary cleaning tasks, such as registration shutdown events, release of resources, and filling in ongoing tasks.

By following this approach, you can ensure that your app is gracefully stopped, keeping robustness and reliability. In addition, it is also important that we have consistency at the level of applications and environments, as we will understand when looking at the next factor, dev/prod parity.

## Dev/prod parity

For years one of the most quoted phrases by developers was:

*It works on my machine!*

In a way, this statement is true. Applications may behave differently in different execution environments. There are numerous variables that can contribute to malfunctions, such as the amount of CPU, memory, storage, or even access permissions to resources and dependencies.

To minimize problems related to the environment, there must be as much compatibility as possible between each server.

That's why it's important for teams to work with technologies for creating infrastructure as code, such as Terraform and Bicep, which, in addition to providing agility, improve management, governance, compliance, and security.

*Figure 11.16* demonstrates this concept:

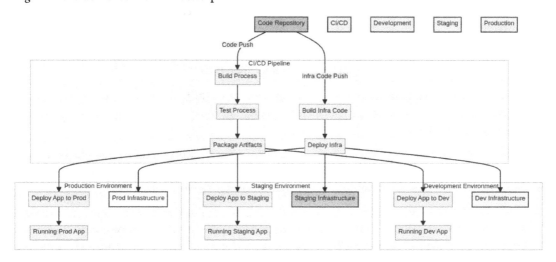

Figure 11.16 – Dev/prod parity

*Figure 11.16* demonstrates a flow in a development process that involves the delivery of applications in an automated manner and the automation of the creation of infrastructure environments through an IaC approach, ensuring that all environments are similar.

In addition to infrastructure, as we have already learned, the container strategy also allows containerized applications to run in different types of environments.

Now let's talk about the logs factor, which goes beyond just recording application events in a file.

## Logs

For a long time, logs were treated purely as records of events during the application execution flow, being recorded, in most cases, in text files, which were only accessed when there was a need to correct issues.

However, in a cloud environment, writing logs to files can pose some challenges for teams working on applications that are constantly changing.

The logs factor determines that this type of information should be treated as streams of events, not managed by files but maintained by specific monitoring-related environments, such as **Elasticsearch**, **Logstash**, **Azure Monitor**, and **Datadog**, or open source solutions such as **Prometheus** and **Grafana**.

Thus, each flow of events generated through applications can provide important information about the execution flow of a given request, generate trend graphs, or even monitor in real time how the application behaves in relation to demand.

The data generated by log collection plays a fundamental role in decision-making, allowing teams to act proactively, optimize resources, define limits for automatic scaling, and, of course, support issue corrections.

There are several solutions on the market that support the event streaming management model, including paid and open source solutions. Many of these solutions are referenced in the CNCF landscape.

When implementing the logs factor in our applications, we must take into account that telemetry and log information must be collected in a transparent manner; however, managing this information is not part of the application context.

Therefore, each logging and metrics solution has different collection methods, which creates a dependency on SDKs in the applications that are necessary to connect to the collection tools. This dependency can be a disadvantage if there is any need to change the log instrumentation tool.

It is important to isolate mechanisms and dependencies. To help with this task, there are options such as **OpenTelemetry**, which offers a vendor-independent approach and allows collaboration and delivery of logs and metrics to be distributed across several monitoring services, avoiding greater coupling between applications, as shown in *Figure 11.17*:

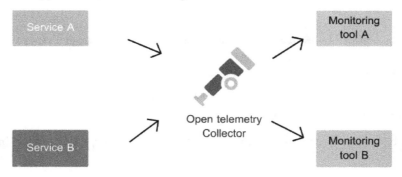

Figure 11.17 – Isolating a log collector mechanism with OpenTelemetry

> **Learn more about OpenTelemetry**
>
> OpenTelemetry is an open source observability framework for cloud-native software maintained by CNCF that provides a standardized way to collect, process, and export telemetry data such as traces, metrics, and logs from applications. OpenTelemetry provides some SDKs that abstract the collection of data from the application and distribute them into different log management tools. For more details, visit `https://opentelemetry.io/docs/`.

Log collection is an important and strategic task in cloud-native applications and, as mentioned previously, allows teams to gain insights into the execution flow of application processes and supports bug fixes in applications. Associated with the logs strategy, strategies for sending alerts for nonconformities, exceptions, and the misbehavior of applications can be included, giving teams the possibility to act proactively.

Logs are also essential in architecture strategies based on events and microservices where there is the distributed processing of information. Through logs, it is possible to map the entire execution flow, if there is a need for auditing, optimization, and bug fixing.

We can see that when working with cloud-native solutions, we isolate responsibilities, ensuring that each part of a solution is decoupled, giving teams flexibility, improved maintenance, and better security, among other aspects. The admin process factor also plays into this.

## Admin process

When talking about the twelve factors, we most often mention the contextualization of the application domain, ensuring that it is built and delivered independently, with as little coupling as possible.

However, even in this scenario, the complexity of the application implies interactions with administrative tasks, such as performing database migrations.

Although the database is part of the solution that makes up the application, tasks such as migrations and scripts for seeding basic information, among other types of administrative tasks, are not the responsibility of the application.

The admin process factor suggests that administrative tasks must be carried out in isolation from applications, in a single process, and that it must be possible to monitor such changes.

Processes such as CI/CD run outside the scope of the application. Thus, during the execution of a pipeline and CI, the execution of tasks, such as generating database migration scripts, for example, can be performed, and these scripts are shared with CD pipelines, which may have different tasks required to apply the changes, as shown in *Figure 11.18*:

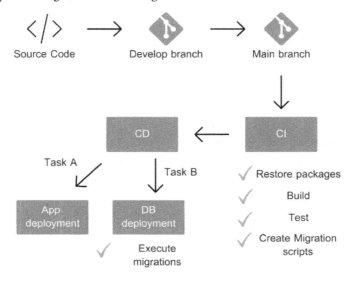

Figure 11.18 – Example of the admin process implementation

*Figure 11.18* demonstrates a pipeline flow whereby, through the CD process, two distinct tasks are executed so that the application can be prepared for its correct execution in an environment.

Performing one-time administrative processes helps maintain the application state and ensures that any changes made during these tasks are immediately reflected in the live environment, reducing discrepancies and potential errors.

The admin process factor plays an important role in the application life cycle, as do the other factors proposed in the twelve-factor app methodology.

## The importance of the twelve-factor app methodology

As we discussed in previous topics, the principles described in the twelve-factor app methodology were designed to help developers create modern, scalable, and maintainable applications, reinforcing the cloud-native mindset necessary for applications that deliver constant value.

Some of the principles are already present in the software engineer's daily life; others open our minds to different perspectives and possibilities. However, we can note that the 12 principles are connected and, furthermore, are closely aligned with the main characteristics of cloud-native computing, such as microservices architecture, containerization, and CI/CD.

Using the methodology proposed by the twelve-factor app methodology, together with the other approaches presented in this chapter, such as the CAF, WAF, and projects available at CNCF, is a great model of best practices for any software engineer.

The concepts and capabilities provided by ASP.NET Core 9 easily allow such principles to be implemented.

In the next section, we will learn about concepts related to cloud architecture.

# Understanding cloud architecture principles

Modern cloud architectures are the foundation of scalable, resilient, and highly available applications. In this chapter, we have learned about several principles and tools necessary for software engineers to combine the development of solutions in ASP.NET Core 9 and fully leverage the benefits of cloud environments such as Microsoft Azure.

The availability of resources in a cloud environment is not enough to deliver the quality and experience needed by users in such a demanding market today.

Each stage of the development flow helps organizations provide applications and services that meet users' needs, in addition to enhancing companies' return on investment and, of course, making users increasingly loyal to the solutions developed.

In this context, we must go beyond the boundaries of source code and layered definitions, and think about strategies that allow applications to deal with users' demands and needs. Therefore, it is important to adapt to the architectural concepts available in cloud-native applications.

Let's understand some of these architectural principles and how they can enhance applications developed in ASP.NET Core 9.

## Working with modern design architecture

As software engineers, we are used to dealing with the implementation of code that is based on best practices and architectural styles such as Clean Code, hexagonal architecture, and design patterns, among other approaches.

By developing using a cloud-native approach, we not only add great possibilities to applications but also add other challenges, such as those mentioned in this chapter.

Software engineers must go beyond writing code and explore a world of different variables and approaches, such as DevOps, infrastructure, network, resilience, availability, agility, security, cost, and other aspects.

Organizations have shifted their focus to emphasize not only the importance of user interfaces such as forms and screens in business contexts and strategies but also the critical need for processing large volumes of data, providing services such as APIs, implementing artificial intelligence, and facilitating seamless integrations between diverse systems.

Dealing with large demands for data requests, ingestion, and analysis is an important feature for organizations to consider.

As a result, some modern architectural styles allow organizations to get the best out of cloud environments and at the same time bring great robustness to the business.

Imagine what an online store application would be like during a promotional event such as Black Friday that did not have the ability to adapt to user demands and deal with growing purchase requests to a payment gateway. If there were a bug in that virtual store application's payment flow, what would be the company's loss if the system was inactive for five minutes?

Certainly, the consequences would be bad. Therefore, there is a need to have the ability to deal with asynchronous processing and work with event-based architectural styles.

## Event-driven architectures

Event-driven architectures allow applications to process information asynchronously, enabling real-time reactions based on events or state changes. They also enable better consistency for the processing of important business flows, such as payment processing for an online store. Another powerful feature of event-driven architecture is the ability to decouple components, generating independence and improving the maintenance and evolution of applications. ASP.NET Core 9 can be integrated with event-driven systems to create scalable and resilient applications. Let's look at the example illustrated in *Figure 11.19*:

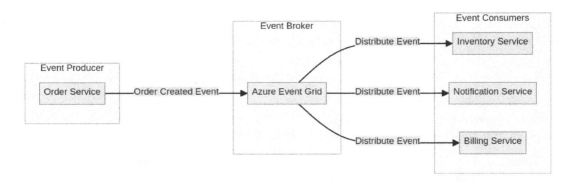

Figure 11.19 – Event-driven architecture example

In this example, the following flow is executed as an event-driven architecture implementation approach:

- **Event Producer**:

  - **Order Service**: The order service acts as the event producer. When an order is created, it publishes an order-created event.

- **Event Broker**:

  - **Azure Event Grid**: Azure Event Grid acts as the event broker. It receives the event from the order service and distributes it to the subscribed consumers.

- **Event Consumers**:

  - **Inventory Service**: The inventory service consumes the order-created event and updates the inventory accordingly.

  - **Notification Service**: The notification service consumes the event to send a notification to the user about the order creation.

  - **Billing Service**: The billing service consumes the event to process the billing for the order.

The example of architecture, combined with other techniques such as scalability, further improves the quality of solutions.

Some event-driven architecture strategies must be considered according to the application requirements, such as these:

- **Event source**: The event source works like a trace, capturing all state changes as they are executed sequentially. This approach favors the complete traceability of the entire execution chain, in addition to providing replay of executed events. ASP.NET Core 9 easily integrates with technologies such as Azure Event Hubs and Apache Kafka to implement event sourcing, as in the example shown in *Figure 11.20*:

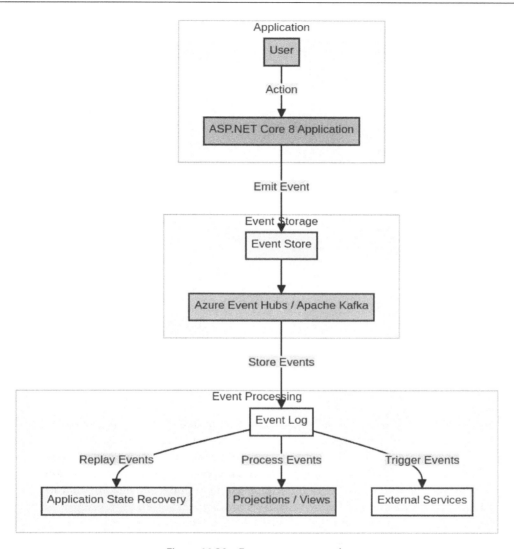

Figure 11.20 – Event source example

- **Command Query Responsibility Segregation (CQRS)**: CQRS separates the read and write operations of an application. This approach is very powerful in contexts where the flow of persistence or writing of information, called commands (writes), is independent of the flow of queries (reads) . *Figure 11.21* illustrates the use of CQRS:

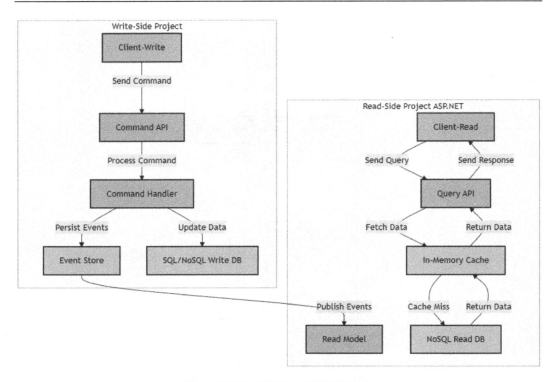

Figure 11.21 – CQRS in ASP.NET Core 9

- **Message brokers**: Message brokers facilitate communication between decoupled services by sending and receiving messages. They ensure that messages are delivered reliably and allow services to scale independently. A great example of this approach is payment processing in an online store. Upon receiving a payment request, the application delivers a message to a broker. This message is handled by one or more applications with the aim of communicating with payment gateways, among other services. If there is a problem with the broker on the server, the messages are persisted in a queue called a dead-letter queue. Therefore, when the broker resource re-establishes its operation, unprocessed messages will re-enter the queue, ensuring that applications can process them. ASP.NET Core 9 applications can integrate with message brokers such as Azure Service Bus or RabbitMQ to handle asynchronous processing and inter-service communication, as in *Figure 11.22*:

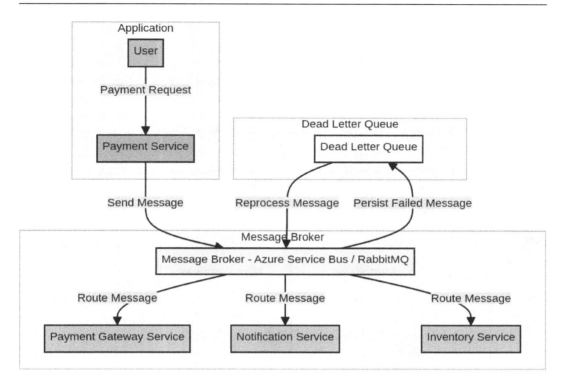

Figure 11.22 – Message broker with a dead-letter queue

---

**Dead-Letter queue**

A **dead-letter queue** (**DLQ**) is a specialized message queue used to store messages that cannot be processed due to some server or broker failure. Messages are kept isolated in the DLQ and retrieved for reprocessing after server problems are resolved. For more information, you can visit the Azure Service Bus DLQ documentation: `https://docs.microsoft.com/en-us/azure/service-bus-messaging/service-bus-dead-letter-queues`.

---

Understanding and applying Event-Driven architecture approaches is essential for creating cloud-native solutions, prepared to deal with different types of user demands.

Based on event-driven architecture principles, another crucial architectural paradigm for cloud-native development is microservices, further enhancing application modularity and scalability.

## Understanding microservices

Microservices are an architectural style that fully supports the development of cloud-native solutions and, in essence, applies the best practices mentioned in this chapter.

Microservices offer an approach that means an application has the following characteristics:

- It has a bounded implementation context
- It is autonomous and can therefore be deployed independently
- It is independent and scalable
- It does not depend on a specific language, so there can be different microservices with different technologies
- Your process runs independently and can benefit from different types of communication protocols, such as HTTP/HTTPS and gRPC and message queues
- In general, microservices manage their own data independently

*Figure 11.23* illustrates a comparison between microservices and monoliths:

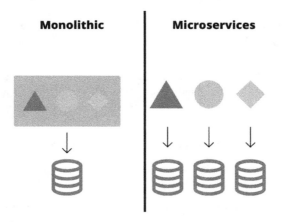

Figure 11.23 – Monolithic versus microservices

It is very important to keep in mind that microservices are not there to replace monolithic applications. Each approach has its respective advantages, disadvantages, and challenges. The choice of one approach over another will depend on the context and application requirements.

When analyzing *Figure 11.23*, we can see that in the monolithic approach, the application layer is responsible for managing all associated processes, represented by symbols, in addition to sharing access with all application states in the same database.

In the microservices approach, each service is contextualized in an independent application, managing the state in isolation, independently, but delivering the same business flow as in the monolithic approach.

There are several challenges associated with microservices, such as communication, transaction management, scalability, granularity, teams, distributed data, consistency, availability, reliability, and resilience.

Microservices can even be developed using a container strategy in conjunction with ASP.NET Core 9, which provides a powerful and performant platform, bringing several benefits to software engineers.

Furthermore, in addition to the development process, regardless of the architectural strategy used, at some point we must deliver solutions in a cloud environment. This process is very important and must cause as little impact as possible to users, which requires deployment strategies.

## Considering deployment strategies

Deployment strategies are essential in cloud-native development, enabling applications to be delivered with the least possible impact on users.

Cloud environments and other technologies support different deployment strategies. The following points mention the most common strategies:

- **Blue-green deployment**: Blue-green deployment is based on the use of two identical environments: blue (current production) and green (new version). New versions of an application are deployed in the green environment and, after carrying out validations, a swap is performed; that is, the traffic goes from blue to green. In Azure, this strategy can be implemented by configuring separate slots in Azure App Service. Through deployment slots, it is possible to carry out deployments in a secure manner, and if the new version has any errors, even after validation, you can simply run the swap again for the previous version to be made available. Azure App Service implements load balancing and directs user requests to avoid losses, as demonstrated in *Figure 11.24*:

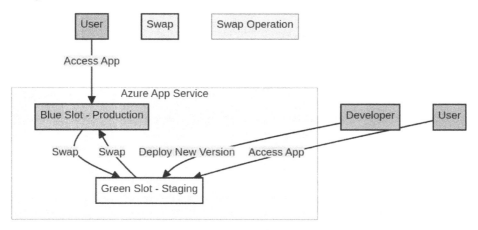

Figure 11.24 – Blue-green deployment with Azure App Service

- **Canary deployment**: Canary deployment is a variation of blue-green deployment that gradually introduces the new version to a small subset of users before rolling it out to the entire user base. Microsoft Azure provides traffic management tools, such as Azure Traffic Manager, to direct some traffic to the new version while monitoring its performance, as illustrated in *Figure 11.25*:

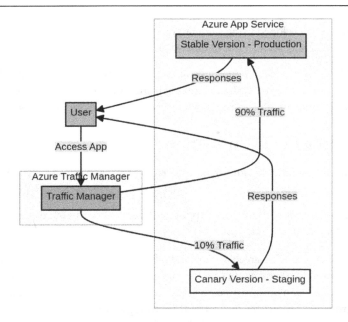

Figure 11.25 – Canary deployment with Azure Traffic Manager

The blue-green and canary deployment strategies significantly improve the reliability, flexibility, and security of the deployment process, minimizing impacts to users, in addition to allowing the restoration of the last stable environment in an agile manner.

The combination of these strategies, tools, and modern architectural models strengthens the mindset needed for cloud-native solutions.

ASP.NET Core 9 is a platform that is prepared for different contexts and challenges and offers powerful solutions in a cloud environment.

As a software engineer, it is important to consider the approaches and techniques mentioned in this book to take your solutions to a higher level.

## Summary

In this chapter, we discussed various resources, tools, strategies, and architectural approaches with the aim of developing a mindset focused on cloud-native solutions. We learned about the different layers of services offered by cloud environments, and we learned about CNCF and the CNCF landscape, which details excellent open source projects that implement cloud concepts and best practices. We also learned about the principles of the twelve-factor app, the CAF, and the WAF, and we discussed the principles of modern cloud architectures and value delivery strategies. The combination of all the content available in this chapter, together with the ASP.NET Core 9 platform, will enable any software engineer to go beyond code and deliver high-value solutions. It all starts with *Hello World*.

## Get This Book's PDF Version and Exclusive Extras

UNLOCK NOW

Scan the QR code (or go to `packtpub.com/unlock`). Search for this book by name, confirm the edition, and then follow the steps on the page.

*Note: Keep your invoice handly. Purchase made directly from packt don't require one.*

# 12
# Unlock Your Exclusive Benefits

Your copy of this book includes the following exclusive benefit:

- ☁ Next-gen Packt Reader
- 🗎 DRM-free PDF/ePub downloads

Follow the guide below to unlock them. The process takes only a few minutes and needs to be completed once.

## Unlock this Book's Free Benefits in 3 Easy Steps

### Step 1

Keep your purchase invoice ready for *Step 3*. If you have a physical copy, scan it using your phone and save it as a PDF, JPG, or PNG.

For more help on finding your invoice, visit `https://www.packtpub.com/unlock-benefits/help`.

> **Note**
>
> If you bought this book directly from Packt, no invoice is required. After *Step 2*, you can access your exclusive content right away.

## Step 2

Scan the QR code or go to packtpub.com/unlock.

On the page that opens (similar to *Figure 12.1* on desktop), search for this book by name and select the correct edition.

<packt>    🔍 Search...                                                    Subscription  🛒⁰  👤

Explore Products    Best Sellers    New Releases    Books    Videos    Audiobooks    Learning Hub    Newsletter Hub    Free Learning

**Discover and unlock your book's exclusive benefits**

Bought a Packt book? Your purchase may come with free bonus benefits designed to maximise your learning. Discover and unlock them here

Discover Benefits            Sign Up/In            Upload Invoice

Need Help?

✦ **1. Discover your book's exclusive benefits**                                    ⌃

🔍 Search by title or ISBN

CONTINUE TO STEP 2

👥 **2. Login or sign up for free**                                                 ⌄

☁ **3. Upload your invoice and unlock**                                            ⌄

Figure 12.1: Packt unlock landing page on desktop

## Step 3

After selecting your book, sign in to your Packt account or create one for free. Then upload your invoice (PDF, PNG, or JPG, up to 10 MB). Follow the on-screen instructions to finish the process.

## Need help?

If you get stuck and need help, visit
https://www.packtpub.com/unlock-benefits/help
for a detailed FAQ on how to find your invoices and more. This QR code will take you to the help page.

> **Note**
>
> If you are still facing issues, reach out to customercare@packt.com.

# Index

## A

**access token  172**
**Administrator  165**
**Angular  20, 180**
**APIs  76**
  documenting, with Swagger  77-81
  requesting, with access token  173, 174
  securing, with ASP.NET Core
    Identity  166-168
**application routes**
  securing  168-172
**application security**
  strengthening  176
**ASP.NET Core  4, 5**
**ASP.NET Core 9  4**
  benefits  4
  performance improvements  5, 16
  reference link, for migrations  159
  reference link, for performance
    improvements  5
**ASP.NET Core 9 OpenAPI**
  reference link  77
**ASP.NET Core 9 SDKs**
  installing, for Linux  11
  installing, for macOS  10
  installing, for Windows  8-10

**ASP.NET Core Identity  154**
  architecture  154
  data access layer  155
  database context, configuring  157, 158
  database, updating  158-160
  data source  155
  identity manager  154
  identity store  154
  integrating  155-157
  roles  155
  routes, adding  160, 161
  services, adding  160, 161
  user claims  155
  user logins  155
  users  155
  working with  154
**ASP.NET Core MVC project**
  patterns and conventions  39-42
  structure  38, 39
**ASP.NET Core SignalR application**
  hosting  109
**ASP.NET Core UI  20**
  rendering  20, 21
**asynchronous processing  139**
  reference link  139
**asynchronous programming  195**
  reference link  197

async keyword  196
attributes, model validation
    reference link  76
authentication  150-152, 218
authorization  150-152, 218
authorization middleware  174-176
await keyword  196
AWS Secrets Manager  180
Azure App Configuration  258
    ASP.NET Core 9 application,
        connecting to  269-271
    ASP.NET Core 9 MVC application,
        configuring to interact  260-268
    feature toggles, managing  271-275
    reference link  258
    setting up  258, 259
Azure App Configurator  133
Azure App Service  109, 287
    reference link  287
Azure Data Studio  116, 119
    reference link  116
Azure Key Vault  180
Azure Kubernetes Service (AKS)  332
Azure Monitor  347
Azure Tools extension  297

**B**

base image and initial configuration  303
behavior management  257
best practices, HTTP request  190
    asynchronous methods, using  191
    caching  192-195
    compression  192-195
    input sanitizing  190, 191
    input validating  190, 191
bind  64
    working with  72-74

Blazor  44
    component structure  46
    project structure  47, 48
Blazor Server  45
Blazor WebAssembly  44, 45
    reference link  44
blue-green deployment  357, 358
Brotli  195
build stage  303, 304
built-in middleware
    reference link  238
business as a service (BaaS)  56, 57

**C**

cache
    in controller class  200-205
Cache-Control header  192, 193
caching  192, 198
canary deployment  357, 358
capital expenditure (CapEx)  324
CD pipeline  310
    benefits  311
CI/CD pipeline
    creating  316-319
    running  319, 321
CI pipeline
    flow  309, 310
circuit breaker pattern  207
    closed state  209
    half-open  209
    implementing  208, 209
    objectives  210
    open state  209
claims  174
client  20, 92
client application
    preparing  98-101

**Cloud Adoption Framework (CAF)  326, 327**
govern  327
innovate  327
manage  327
migrate  326
plan  326
ready  326
reference link  327
strategy  326
**Cloud Native Computing Foundation (CNCF)  330, 331**
reference link  331
working with  331-333
**cloud-native mindset  328**
creating  324
**cloud-native tools**
working with  329, 330
**C# model**
interacting with  29-34
**code obfuscation  177**
**code review  310**
reference link  310
**command-line configuration provider  247**
**Command Line Interface (CLI)  8, 94**
**Command Query Responsibility Segregation (CQRS)  353**
**compression  192**
**configuration providers**
adding  246
command-line configuration provider  247
environment variable configuration provider  247
JSON configuration provider  247
memory configuration provider  247
reference link  248
working with  246
**connection strings  122, 128**
reference link  122

**containerd**
URL  301
**container image**
generating  305, 306
**container registry  300**
**Container Runtime Interface (CRI)  301**
**container runtimes  301**
containerd  301
CRI-O  301
Kata Containers  301
LXC  301
Podman  301
Rancher  301
runc  301
**containers  281, 298, 300**
benefits  299
versus virtual machines (VMs)  299
**continuous delivery (CD)  149**
**continuous deployment (CD)  310, 311**
**continuous integration and continuous deployment (CI/CD)  281**
**continuous integration and delivery (CI/CD)  257**
**continuous integration (CI)  149, 309**
**Controller  37**
**ControllerBase class**
reference link  71
utilities  70, 71
**controller-based API**
creating  67, 68
**Countdown  107**
**Create, Read, Update, Delete (CRUD) operations  58**
**CRI-O**
URL  301
**Cross-Origin Resource Sharing (CORS)  180, 218**
enabling  181, 182
reference link  182

**cross-site request forgery (CSRF) attacks  183**
  preventing  184
  reference link  184
**cross-site scripting (XSS) attacks  183, 190**
  reference link  183
**CSS  20**
**cultures, ASP.NET Core  9**
  reference link  32
**custom binds  74**
**custom configuration provider**
  creating  248-250
**custom middleware  224**
  implementing  224-226

# D

**Dapper**
  reference link  130
  working with  140-142
**Dapper SQL Builder  142**
  reference link  142
**Database Management System (DBMS)  116**
**Datadog  347**
**data persistence  116**
**data persistence models**
  comparing  126
**DbContext object  128**
**DbSet  128**
**dead-letter queue (DLQ)  354, 355**
  reference link  355
**Debian  116**
**DELETE method  57**
**dependency injection container (DIC)  246**
**dependency injection (DI)  251**
  reference link  117
**dependency injection (DI)**
    **design pattern  117**
**deployment strategies  357**
  blue-green deployment  357, 358

canary deployment  357, 358
**development environment**
  preparing  7
  testing  12-15
**development tool  7**
**DevOps culture  146, 308**
**DI container (DIC)  195, 227**
**distributed cache  198**
**Distributed Denial-of-Service**
    **(DDoS) attacks  238**
**Docker  109, 300, 331**
  installing  116
  installing, on Linux  116
  installing, on Mac  116
  installing, on Windows  116
  reference link  119
  tutorial for installations, references  116
**Docker CLI  300**
**Docker container**
  running  306-308
**Docker Engine  300**
**Dockerfile  300**
**Docker Hub  300**
**documentation**
  improving  81-86
  working with  76
**DOM (Document Object Model)  45**
**Dotfuscator Community**
  reference link  177
**dotnet CLI tool  22**
  reference link  25
  templates  23
**dotnet-ef tool  156**
**dotnet publish CLI tool**
  options  283, 284
**dynamic configurations  257**
  benefits  257
**dynamic settings**
  working with  257

**dynamic web-based applications  20**
  backend  20
  frontend  20

**E**

**EF Core  5, 129**
  reference link, for conventions  129
  working with  131-139
**EF Core database providers**
  reference link  132
**Elasticsearch  347**
**EntityFramework  157**
**EntityFrameworkCore  156**
**Entity Framework (EF)  127**
**environment variable configuration
    provider  247**
**event broker  352**
**event consumer  352**
**event-driven architectures  351, 352**
**event producer  352**
**event source  352**
**Explicit Dependencies Principle (EDP)  226**
**extension method  169**
  creating, for middleware
      registration  239-241

**F**

**factory-based middleware**
  working with  227-229
**Factory pattern  248**
**FeatureGate attribute  273**
**feature toggles  257**
  managing, with Azure App
      Configuration  271-275
  reference link  257
**Fedora  116**

**G**

**General Data Protection
    Regulation (GDPR)  146**
**GET method  57, 202**
**GitHub Actions  313**
  components  314
**GitHub Actions editor  317**
**GitHub-hosted runners**
  reference link  314
**GitHub repository**
  preparing  314, 315
**global error handling middleware  230-233**
**Grafana  332, 347**
**Gzip  195**

**H**

**HEAD method  57**
**Heroku  333**
  URL  333
**hexagonal architecture  337, 338**
  reference link  338
**horizontal scalability  343**
**HTML  20**
**HttpContext.User object  174, 175**
  reference link  175
**HTTP protocol  57**
**HTTP request**
  best practices  190-195
**HTTPS enforcement  180**
**HTTP status code 500  231**
**HTTP status codes  58, 59**
  references  58
**HTTP Strict Transport Security
    (HSTS) protocol  27**
**HTTP verbs  57**
  DELETE  57
  GET  57

HEAD  57
OPTIONS  57
PATCH  57
POST  57
PUT  57
**Hub  95**
creating  95, 96
**hybrid solutions**
working with  50-52
**Hypertext Transfer Protocol
Secure (HTTPS)  180**

**I**

**IConfiguration interface  244**
centralized management  245
configuration sources  244
environment-specific settings  245
examples  245, 246
flexibility  245
hierarchical configuration  244
Options pattern  244
reference link  246
strongly typed configuration  245
**IFeatureManagement interface  273**
**ILoggerFactory interface  211-214**
methods  213
**ILogger interface  211, 214**
convenience methods  211, 212
example  212
log methods  211
methods  213
scope method  212
**image  300**
**Index.cshtml page  98**
**Infrastructure as a Service (IaaS)  326**
**in-memory cache strategy  198**
**inversion of control (IoC)  117**

**J**

**JavaScript  20, 180**
frameworks  48-50
**JSON configuration provider  247**
**JWT**
reference link  173

**K**

**Kata Containers**
URL  301
**Kubernetes  109**

**L**

**labels**
reference link  267
**Language Integrated Query (LINQ)  140**
**LibMan  94**
**Linux**
ASP.NET Core 9 SDKs, installing for  11
Docker, installing on  116
**logging  211**
**logs  215, 347-349**
**Logstash  347**
**long polling  91**
**LTS(Long Term Support)  6**
**LXC**
URL  301

**M**

**macOS**
ASP.NET Core 9 SDKs, installing for  10
Docker, installing on  116
**Manager role  165**
**memory configuration provider  247**

message brokers  354
Micro ORM  123, 130
    versus ORM  130
microservices  355
    characteristics  356
    versus monoliths  356
Microsoft.AspNetCore.Identity.
        EntityFrameworkCore  156
Microsoft.AspNetCore.Identity library  157
Microsoft.AspNetCore.OpenAI package  77
Microsoft Container Registry (MCR)  303
Microsoft.Extensions.Logging
        namespace  211
middleware  176, 217
    benefits  222-224
    best practices  224
    global error handling  230-233
    HTTP context objects, obtaining  227
    rate-limiting  235-238
    request logging  233-235
middleware flow  220, 221
middleware order  221
    reference link  221
middleware pipeline  218, 219
middleware registration
    extension method, creating for  239-241
migrations  127
minimal API project
    creating  60-65
minimal APIs  59, 60
ML.NET  5
Model  37
ModelState  75, 76
Model-View-Controller (MVC)
        architectural pattern  14, 21, 37, 66
modern design architecture
    working with  351
monitoring  211

multi-stage build
    reference link  304

## N

.NET  6
.Net Aspire  5
.NET Foundation
    URL  6
.NET Framework  6
.Net MAUI  5
.NET roadmap  16
.NET Runtime  286
    reference link  286
Node Package Management (NPM)  94
NoSQL
    benefits  125
    versus SQL  123-126

## O

OAuth 2.0  152
    flow  152, 153
object orientation  127
object-oriented programming (OOP)  126
object-relational mapping (ORM)  123, 126
    benefits  129
    cons  129
    pros  129
    versus Micro ORM  130
    working  127, 128
Onion Architecture  337, 338
    reference link  338
OpenAPI Specification
    reference link  77
Open ID Connect (OIDC)  152
    OAuth 2.0, complementing  152

OpenTelemetry 332, 348
reference link 348
operating expenditure (OpEx) 324
OPTION requirement 57
Options pattern 134, 250-252
implementing 252-256
reference link 134

# P

PATCH method 57
pipeline 176
Platform as a Service (PaaS) 124, 287, 326
Podman
URL 301
Polly 207
reference link 207
Postman 169
POST method 57, 202
product controller 68-70
project templates 24
Prometheus 332, 347
publication package 282
publishing package
generating 283, 284
generating, for UrlShortener
application 284, 285
publishing process
significance 282
publish stage 304
PUT method 57

# R

Rancher
URL 301
rate-limiting middleware 235-238
reference link 238
Razor 22

Razor Pages 21
page model 34-36
using 92
working with 27-29
Razor Pages project 25
creating 22-24
Razor Pages project, structure
appsettings.json file 26
Pages folder 26
Program.cs file 26, 27
wwwroot folder 26
Razor syntax
interacting with 29-34
React 20, 180
Reader 165
real-time communication model 90
Redis Insight
configuring 205, 206
Relational Database Management
System (RDBMS) 123
relational databases 123
Remote DIctionary Server (Redis) 198
integrating, in application 199, 200
URL 198
render interactive mode 46
reference link 46
Representational State Transfer
(REST) 56, 57
request logging middleware 233-235
resilience mechanisms 207-210
retry pattern 207
implementing 208
objectives 210
role-based authorization 165, 166
roles 174
RPC (Remote Procedure Call) 91
runc
reference link 301

# S

scalability
  horizontal scalability 343
  vertical scalability 343
SDK(Software Development Kit) 7, 8
Secret Manager tool 178
secrets
  managing 177-180
security 146
server 92
server application
  preparing 97, 98
server-sent events 91
service lifetimes
  reference link 229
SignalR 45, 90
  components 91
  streaming 103
SignalR application
  hosting 109, 110
single-page application (SPA) 44, 94, 147
  components 147
Single Responsibility Principle (SRP) 270
  reference link 270
single sign-on (SSO) 153
SoC (Separation of concerns) 222
Software as a Service (SaaS) 149, 269, 326
Sonar Cloud
  URL 149
SonarQube
  URL 149
SQL client
  using 120-123
SQL database
  connecting to 116, 117
SQL injection attacks 148, 183
  preventing 183

SQL Server 155
  preparing 117-120
static code analysis 149
streaming 103
  implementing 104-108
  limitations 103, 104
Structured Query Language (SQL) 117
  versus NoSQL 123-126
STS(Standard Term Support) 6
Swagger 5, 68
  APIs, documenting 77-81
System.Text.Json API 16

# T

tag helper 43, 272
TaskManager application 99
  client and server communication
    flow 101-103
  client application, preparing 98-101
  server application, preparing 97, 98
  working with 92-94
TaskManager project
  hosting 105
thread blocking 191
thread pool exhaustion 191
token cancellation 139
  reference link 139
twelve-factor app methodology 333
  significance 350
  URL 268, 333
twelve-factor app principles
  admin process 349
  backing services 337, 338
  build, release, run 338-340
  code base 334, 335
  concurrency 343
  config 335, 336

dependencies 335
dev/prod parity 346-348
disposability 344-346
port binding 341, 342
processes 340, 341
**two-factor authentication (2FA) 154**

# U

**Ubuntu 116**
**Unit of Work design pattern 133**
reference link 133
**UrlShortener application**
Azure App Service, using as
    web host 288-292
Azure SQL Server, configuring 292-294
packing 302-304
publishing package, generating 284, 285
publishing, with Visual Studio Code 295-297

# V

**validations**
performing 75, 76
**vertical scalability 343**
**View 37**
in ASP.NET MVC 42-44
**virtual machines (VMs) 298, 299**
versus containers 299
**Visual Studio 7**
**Visual Studio Code 7, 11**
command 12
URL 11
UrlShortener application,
    publishing 295-297
**vulnerabilities**
preventing 182

# W

**web-based applications**
security principles 146-149
**WebSockets 91**
**Well-Architected Framework
    (WAF) 326, 327**
cost optimization 327
operational excellence 327
performance efficiency 327
reference link 328
reliability 327
security 327
**Windows**
ASP.NET Core 9 SDKs, installing for 8-10
Docker, installing on 116
**Winget 8**
**WorkingWithIdentity.csproj project 156**

# X

**XML comments 87**
reference link 87

# Y

**YAML Ain't Markup Language
    (YAML) file 313**
**YML/YAML file structure 313**

packtpub.com

Subscribe to our online digital library for full access to over 7,000 books and videos, as well as industry leading tools to help you plan your personal development and advance your career. For more information, please visit our website.

## Why subscribe?

- Spend less time learning and more time coding with practical eBooks and Videos from over 4,000 industry professionals
- Improve your learning with Skill Plans built especially for you
- Get a free eBook or video every month
- Fully searchable for easy access to vital information
- Copy and paste, print, and bookmark content

Did you know that Packt offers eBook versions of every book published, with PDF and ePub files available? You can upgrade to the eBook version at packtpub.com and as a print book customer, you are entitled to a discount on the eBook copy. Get in touch with us at customercare@packtpub.com for more details.

At www.packtpub.com, you can also read a collection of free technical articles, sign up for a range of free newsletters, and receive exclusive discounts and offers on Packt books and eBooks.

# Other Books You May Enjoy

If you enjoyed this book, you may be interested in these other books by Packt:

**Minimal APIs in ASP.NET 9 - Second Edition**

Nick Proud

ISBN: 978-1-80512-912-7

- Become proficient in minimal APIs within the .NET Core 9 framework
- Find out how to ensure scalability, performance, and maintainability
- Work with databases and ORMs, such as Entity Framework and Dapper
- Optimize minimal APIs, including asynchronous programming, caching strategies, and profiling tools
- Implement advanced features like dependency injection, request validation, data mapping, and routing techniques
- Create and configure minimal API projects effectively

**Blazor Web Development Cookbook**

Pawel Bazyluk

ISBN: 978-1-83546-078-8

- Build modular, reusable, maintainable code in component-based architecture
- Exchange data between a UI and external service while ensuring UI responsiveness
- Implement efficient user interactions and event handling
- Present data in a structured and user-friendly manner using grids
- Understand state management strategies crucial for complex applications
- Create user-friendly and robust data input forms with smart validations
- Explore routing capabilities and leverage navigation events
- Enhance forms with AI-powered features and implement your own AI chatbot

## Packt is searching for authors like you

If you're interested in becoming an author for Packt, please visit `authors.packtpub.com` and apply today. We have worked with thousands of developers and tech professionals, just like you, to help them share their insight with the global tech community. You can make a general application, apply for a specific hot topic that we are recruiting an author for, or submit your own idea.

Hi,

I am Albert S. Tanure, author of *ASP.NET Core 9 Essentials*. I really hope you enjoyed reading this book and found it useful for increasing your productivity and efficiency.

It would really help me (and other potential readers!) if you could leave a review on Amazon sharing your thoughts on this book.

Go to the link below or scan the QR code to leave your review:

`https://packt.link/r/183546906X`

Your review will help me to understand what's worked well in this book, and what could be improved upon for future editions, so it really is appreciated.

Best Wishes,

Albert S. Tanure